IDEOLOGY AND
LINGUISTIC THEORY

IDEOLOGY AND LINGUISTIC THEORY

Noam Chomsky and the
deep structure debates

Geoffrey J. Huck and John A. Goldsmith

History of Linguistic Thought

London and New York

First published 1995
by Routledge
11 New Fetter Lane, London EC4P 4EE

Simultaneously published in the USA and Canada
by Routledge
29 West 35th Street, New York, NY 10001

Reprinted 1996, 1997
First published in paperback 1996

© 1995 Geoffrey J. Huck and John A. Goldsmith

Typeset in Baskerville by
LaserScript Ltd, Mitcham, Surrey
Printed and bound in Great Britain by
Biddles Ltd, Guildford and King's Lynn

British Library Cataloguing in Publication Data
A catalogue record for this book is available from the British Library

Library of Congress Cataloguing in Publication Data
A catalogue record for this book is available from the Library of Congress

ISBN 0–415–11735–6 (hbk)
ISBN 0–415–15313–1 (pbk)

To our teachers

Bill J. Darden, James D. McCawley, and Jerrold M. Sadock
Noam Chomsky, Morris Halle, and John Robert Ross

To believe your own thought, to believe that what is true for you in your private heart is true for all men, – that is genius.

Ralph Waldo Emerson

CONTENTS

PREFACE

It has been customary in science to attempt to separate ideas from those who have had them. Increasingly, historians of science have argued that it is misleading to do so, that what are often thought of as personal or social factors play a nontrivial role in the conduct of scientific inquiry. If this is true in science generally it is surely true in linguistics, where for three decades and more the academic stage has been dominated by the imposing persona of Noam Chomsky. Chomsky's importance and influence in linguistic work worldwide during this period has been unmatched, and there are few who doubt that his views will continue to affect profoundly the direction of theoretical discussion in linguistics for years to come.

As significant as Chomsky's views have been for linguistics and the cognitive sciences, he is not the only intellectually respected figure who has been engaged in theory construction in these fields during his lifetime. And in fact Chomsky has made it clear that much of his work has been done in response to the work of those with whom he has found himself in disagreement – sometimes in vigorous disagreement. To consider his ideas apart from this context would be to miss a great deal of what has given them their distinctive flavor and contemporary appeal. This is not to suggest that conflict and controversy have played a suspicious role in the advancement of these ideas; to the contrary, we understand that scholarly argument forms a crucial part of scientific life and that the acquisition of knowledge depends vitally on the questioning of dogma. But it is certainly a measure of how deeply they have cut that Chomsky's critiques have received the attention they have; indeed, a number of the academic arguments in which he has been involved have become so concentrated and so fraught with controversy that they have managed to catch the notice even of those who might otherwise have had no interest in the scientific issues themselves. Among these, Chomsky's dispute with the Generative Semanticists in the late 1960s particularly stands out. This dispute was notable not simply because it became so bitter, but also because it involved a goodly proportion of the theoretical linguistics community at the time and represented what has clearly been the most serious organized challenge to Chomsky's views to date.

The four Generative Semanticists who were at the center of these disagreements with Chomsky were Paul Postal, George Lakoff, James McCawley, and John Robert Ross. Postal was a colleague of Chomsky's at the Massachusetts Institute of Technology in the early 1960s who moved to the City University of New York in 1965 and then to IBM in 1967. McCawley and Ross had been students of Chomsky's and Postal's at MIT; McCawley accepted a position at the University of Chicago in 1964, and Ross was appointed to the faculty at MIT in 1966. Lakoff completed his dissertation in 1965 at Indiana University, then becoming a researcher and instructor at Harvard.

In fact, Generative Semantics, as a coherent research program, did not last long. By the end of the 1970s, none of the original Generative Semanticists was still involved in that program at least under that standard, although Chomsky's competing program was steadily gaining adherents. To explain this turn of events, many have concluded that Generative Semantics ultimately failed in consequence of certain inherent inadequacies of *theory*: either the theories offered by Generative Semanticists were empirically falsified, or they were overly powerful, or they attempted too much. In each case it has been supposed that the failures were necessary failures, and that they followed from the theory-constructing behavior of the Generative Semanticists themselves.

But while the Generative Semanticists unquestionably faced theoretical obstacles of various sorts, there are also good reasons to believe that the demise of their program was not a consequence of theoretical weakness. Indeed, we will argue in what follows that it is not possible to find, internal to the idea of Generative Semantics as it was evidently originally understood by Lakoff, McCawley, Postal, and Ross, adequate grounds to explain its widespread abandonment in the 1970s. We will be concerned to evaluate the linguistic evidence on its own terms, paying particular attention to the theoretical assumptions that underlay the various critiques, and will conclude that one must turn to external explanations to account adequately for what transpired. But although external factors undoubtedly affected the way that the various proposals in the dispute were understood and received, we would also suggest that a focus on the relatively dramatic personal and social aspects of the interactions in which the participants were involved has tended to obscure the conceptual significance of the positions they took. In fact, those positions were considerably more compatible theoretically than one might suppose, given the animosities that developed as the issues were debated.

We will assume in this book at least passing familiarity with the goals and methods of modern generative linguistics, such as might be acquired from an introductory text. We should emphasize that we will not attempt a complete survey of linguistic work in the 1960s and 1970s, and the names of some of those who contributed importantly to linguistic theory during this period will unfortunately not appear here. To pay tribute to the diversity of views that we believe should be considered in any fuller historical study, and to make clear that the particular issues with which we are concerned form only part of the story, we include in an appendix transcripts of conversations with some of the participants. We hereby thank them for permission to reproduce this material.

We would also like to express our sincere appreciation to a large number of linguists who have offered us their thoughts, recollections, and opinions during the writing of this book, including Stephen Anderson, Thomas Bever, Bill Darden, Elan Dresher, Susan Fischer, Robert Freidin, H. A. Gleason, Lila Gleitman, Georgia Green, Robert A. Hall, Morris Halle, Eric Hamp, Randy Harris, Zellig Harris, Roger Higgins, Charles Hockett, Henry Hoenigswald, Ray Jackendoff, Susumu Kuno, Terence Langendoen, Judith Levi, David McNeill, Alexis Manaster-Ramer, Younghee Na, William O'Grady, Barbara Partee, Jessie Pinkham, Paul Postal, Peter Reich, John R. Ross, Nicolas Ruwet, Jerrold Sadock, Ivan Sag, Edwin Williams, Victor Yngve, and Arnold Zwicky. We are especially grateful to Noam Chomsky, George Lakoff, James McCawley, Frederick Newmeyer, and several anonymous reviewers for stimulating commentary on earlier drafts of various parts of the manuscript. It should hardly need to be added that none of the above necessarily agrees with our characterizations or conclusions.

We would also like to thank Karen Peterson for transcribing the interviews that appear in the Appendix and Claude Vandeloise for making it possible for portions of Chapter 2 to appear, in different form, in *Communications* 53 (1991).

A large part of the first three chapters of this book was written between 1987 and 1991 with the support of a grant to the second author from the American Council of Learned Societies. Chapter 4 is the sole responsibility of the first author.

Finally, it was impressed upon us early on in our research that there are at least as many distinct perspectives on the debates as there have been those who participated in or were affected by them. We do not anticipate that our account will be equally satisfying from each of these perspectives, and we are well aware that our own histories have not been irrelevant to the conclusions we have drawn. One of us was a student of McCawley's at the University of Chicago, where the other, having been a student of Chomsky's and Ross's at MIT, now teaches; indeed, we have professional relationships of various kinds with most of those whose work we discuss. We wish to acknowledge the deep respect and high regard we have for all of them. It is in fact this respect and regard that has motivated much of our concern for the issues we raise.

1

INTRODUCTION

Many linguists today assume that theirs is an empirical and deductive science, and that scientific progress in the domain of their research is possible. They believe that they, like their colleagues in the physical or biological sciences, are able to contribute measurably to the growth of knowledge by formulating and testing a sequence of empirically more successful and encompassing theories – each improved theory arising upon the falsification of a previous one.[1]

Consistent with this belief in the empirical and progressive character of theoretical linguistics is the received view of its recent history. Whatever the status of linguistic work prior to the emergence of the generative paradigm in the last half of this century, there is general agreement that today's generative theories are more successful in accounting for the facts than the generative theories of thirty or thirty-five years ago, and that one can point to instances in the intervening period when a particular theory has been falsified by comparison with a competing theory that was demonstrably superior to it.

While there may be no unanimity concerning which among the train of successful linguistic theories is in the forefront these days, just about everyone seems to agree that there was a significant theoretical failure during the last few decades of generative syntactic work. On just about everyone's account, the theory that failed was Generative Semantics. That Generative Semantics has become such an exemplary failure has, no doubt, something to do with its successes. It was a theory that for a time in the late 1960s attracted a large number of adherents, produced impressive results, and had a substantial and lasting impact on the course of future work in the field. The Generative Semantics movement also challenged, with a good deal of brio and flair, the alternative – known as Interpretive Semantics – that was then being developed by Noam Chomsky.

The oft-repeated story told about the great collapse of Generative Semantics when it came in the mid-1970s is fully compatible with the credo of progress referred to above: if the central claims of Generative Semantics

1

were empirically disconfirmed – or perhaps worse, if they led to a theory of grammar which was so vague as to be uninteresting – then the rapid dissolution of Generative Semantics might be explained as the result of its having been rationally rejected by the linguistics community in favor of ultimately more successful and interesting alternatives.

This standard story is by and large the one that is told in Newmeyer's (1980, 1986) historical survey and that appears, in various guises, in popular texts (van Riemsdijk and Williams 1986), monographs (Jackendoff 1983), and research articles (Katz and Bever 1976).[2] But there is a difficulty with this account that a number of historians, including Newmeyer, have noticed – a difficulty that is growing more and more difficult to ignore. It is this: significant chunks of what were evidently standard Generative Semantics analyses began to reappear in the syntax literature shortly after the movement's demise and are now often regarded as constituting preferred solutions to contemporary problems. Indeed, the picture of grammar presented in much contemporary work, including, for example, Chomsky's *Lectures on Government and Binding* (1981) and *Knowledge of Language: Its Nature, Origin, and Use* (1986b), is similar enough in certain crucial respects to that painted by Generative Semanticists in the late 1960s that one who accepts the standard story must be prepared to explain why criticisms of the latter do not also apply to the former.

It might be maintained that contemporary theorists have simply recovered usable parts of a discredited approach that did not work because of the way it was put together and because certain other hypotheses that it relied upon were shown to be wrong. Such a view would have its merits: Interpretivists from the very start were keenly interested in the questions the Generative Semantics program raised and openly incorporated its results when this could be done in terms they could accept. In effect, they and their descendants have wanted to show that the semantic enterprise was one that they could run better. But this also suggests that if there were problems with Generative Semantics, those problems were not necessarily systemic. The challenge would then be to determine which isolable propositions of Generative Semantics would have required replacement for the theory to have survived the empirical tests that were undertaken. But no critique of Generative Semantics has ever been attempted along such lines.[3]

Indeed, looking back now on the debates of the 1960s and 1970s, one cannot help but be impressed by their inconclusiveness in case after case, by the way in which fragments of information were routinely transformed into facts which one side thought constituted crucial evidence but which the other side felt were misconstrued or required more study. Since more study rarely confirmed original hypotheses in exactly the form in which they had been offered, and since many of the ensuing arguments in any case sputtered off in tangential directions or were simply not seen through to a point where consensus could be reached, it might be more natural to ask whether anything at all was learned in the debates, or whether they simply demonstrate that linguistic theories up to now have been not so much scientific theories as untestable collections of a priori beliefs.

In this book we reject the standard story of the rise and fall of Generative Semantics and propose a different approach to understanding its advocates' disputes with Interpretive Semanticists. In general, we agree that, at least within each of the programs, there were empirical issues that were rationally pursued. In fact, we share the credo alluded to in the opening paragraph of this chapter that work undertaken during the generative period has led to a significant increase in linguistic knowledge, even if disagreements about particular analyses persist.

Nevertheless, we will conclude that the debates about deep structure failed to settle a number of the larger issues, although settlement is often presumed in current research. We will show that in many of these cases no metatheoretical conclusions could rationally have been drawn from the evidence offered, which was insufficient in itself to decide in favor of one or the other of the theories. At the same time, we will observe that Generative Semanticists and Interpretive Semanticists, while starting from conceptually different positions concerning the organization of grammar, were led to approach some important issues in quite analogous ways. The two programs were in fact quite complementary, and the tensions between them not only bound each to the other, but also steered them jointly on to a more productive path than either of them individually might otherwise have taken.

In the following chapter we will review in some detail the chief arguments put forward by Interpretivists against the Generative Semantics program. We will first suggest a rough definition of empirical failure that we will use when we come to assess those arguments. Then we will briefly consider the development of both the Chomskyan program and the rival program launched by the Generative Semanticists in the intellectual contexts in which they arose. When we look at the Interpretivists' critique of Generative Semantics, we will do so primarily from the standpoint of the Generative Semanticists – which is to say that we will attempt to reconcile the criticisms with our reconstruction of what the Generative Semanticists were proposing. We will conclude that the arguments against Generative Semantics proposals were not strong, and that over a significant range of issues Generative Semantics approaches and Interpretive Semantics approaches were a good deal more congruent than their advocates on either side were at the time prepared to acknowledge.

Chapter 3 focuses on the rhetorical techniques used in the dispute. In particular, we will compare the logical content of some of the arguments with the force of the language in which those arguments were framed. In this way, we may better understand why each side found the other's approach so unpersuasive and, ultimately, so distasteful.

3

Chapter 4 considers why, if the Generative Semanticists did not accept Chomsky's arguments against their program, the movement fell apart as rapidly as it did in the 1970s. It will be suggested that Generative Semantics failed for reasons that did not have much to do with the quality of the results it had turned up.

We conclude in Chapter 5 with some thoughts about the meaning of the dispute about deep structure for contemporary linguistic work.

2

GAPS IN THE PARADIGM

Mediational and distributional themes in theoretical syntax

REMARKS ON DEVELOPMENT AND PROGRESS IN SCIENCE

There are well-known problems with a simple progressive view of scientific history according to which knowledge grows when improved theories replace those which have been falsified in confrontation with the facts. As Kuhn (1970) and Lakatos (1970) among others have made clear, serious questions must be addressed before it can be maintained that scientific theories can be falsified at all. Since a theory embraced by members of an active research community is an ever-changing constellation of propositions, and since anomalies can often be accommodated by minor adjustments to the theory, the effect of a counterexample to a theoretical prediction need not be considered fatal to the theory itself. Moreover, as Duhem (1954 [1905]) brought into stark focus, theoretical propositions usually work in combination, so that when a prediction fails it is not always clear which proposition of the many comprised by the theory is at fault. Hence, a research community may, with good reason, reserve its concern when challenged by what the skeptics may call "failed crucial experiments," relying on the belief – sometimes quite correct – that future work will straighten things out. But then, if counterexamples have no force, the assertion that science progresses as falsified theories are replaced by improved ones is called directly into question.

Problems of this sort have of course caused some historiographers to give up hope that a coherent argument can be made for progress in science. The more reasonable view in the eyes of many is that not every element of a theory need actually be empirically justifiable for that theory to have, overall, an empirical character. A variety of models has been proposed in the philosophical, sociological, and historical literature which attempts to salvage a progressive science by appealing to just such a precept.

We will not be concerned here with the question of whether linguistics fits one or another of these models, although we will in a general way (but

5

only in a general way) follow the scheme of Lakatos (1970). We take the position that linguistic research programs comprise a body of falsifiable propositions, but also that such programs have a sociological dimension as well. As to the former, we will assume that there are empirical propositions held by members of a research program which, if the facts warrant, the researchers are willing to revise or replace, and we will say that such propositions constitute the *auxiliary hypotheses* of the theory. But since predictions of a theory are generally based on a conjunction of propositions, when a prediction is falsified the choice of which particular proposition is to be discarded may remain in the hands of the researcher. When the researcher shows a consistent methodological policy of not letting certain propositions be damaged by disconfirmation, we conclude that he or she is treating those propositions as part of a protected *core* of the theory.

The propositions of the core in effect constitute strategies for theory construction.[1] Since they will not themselves be subjected to empirical test (although evidence in their favor may be occasionally collected and sometimes even vigorously sought), they may never be precisely formulated. But the coherence of the research program depends on general agreement by its members concerning the content of these propositions. And, to a significant extent, what these core propositions are is determined by what the members of the research program hold to be its ultimate goals. We will call any general statement which characterizes such a goal of a program an *orientation,* or an *orientational proposition* of the program. Like core propositions, program orientations are irrefutable in practice, but unlike those propositions, they express desiderata: "Our theory should ultimately explain . . . " or "The goal of our enterprise is to explain . . . " are forms such orientations commonly take.

The distinctions among auxiliary, core, and orientational propositions as drawn here are notional, but this is because the category of a proposition depends more on the context of its use than on its content. What one researcher may understand as a core proposition another may take to be an orientational proposition or an auxiliary hypothesis, and so on. Moreover, competing research programs can, and frequently do, share propositions at all levels, including orientations. However, when research programs have very different sets of orientations, their respective results may prove incommensurable.

In Lakatos's view, theories become successful, or are *progressive*, when continued adjustments of their auxiliary hypotheses lead to continued discovery of hitherto unexpected facts without the concomitant loss of empirical content to the theory. It follows from this that there might be any number of reasons why a research program would fail to generate new auxiliary hypotheses that are corroborated by the discovery of new facts. For example, it could be that crucial experiments keep turning up anomalies rather than corroboratory evidence; in such a case, if the program fails it would be reasonable to say that the theory has been empirically discon-firmed. But it may also be that the members of the research program have merely stopped doing constructive research, for lack of time, money, interest – or whatever.[2] Hence, it may logically be claimed that there can be empirical progress, even though not all failures are necessarily empirical failures.

Lakatos's particular strategy for evaluating progress has been criticized (see, e.g. Laudan 1977: 77 ff. and Suppe 1977: 664 ff.). Of course, anyone who wishes to argue that Generative Semantics was rationally rejected *on the basis of its empirical failures* must at least assume with Lakatos that the empirical contents of the theories of distinct research programs can be compared in some scientifically respectable fashion. Whether or not Lakatos's overall scheme should turn out to be defensible, we will suggest that it is not possible to locate clear empirical grounds in the arguments offered in the 1960s and 1970s on which a decision between Generative Semantics and Interpretive Semantics could be based. More generally, we see no reasonable measure of even the *conceptual* contributions of the two programs that would have selected one over the other, say, *circa* 1971. In subsequent chapters, we will suggest that linguists had at their disposal other, perhaps more salient grounds on which to make comparisons.

THE DEVELOPMENT OF A DISTRIBUTIONALIST ORIENTATION FOR LINGUISTIC THEORY

Before discussing the particular issues which separated Generative Seman-tics and Interpretive Semantics, however, it will be useful to review briefly the context in which these theories arose. It must first be recognized that there are two distinct orientations with roots that go deep into this century under which research programs in theoretical syntax, broadly conceived, have been organized. The first orientation has assumed that linguistic analysis should be undertaken in an attempt to discover and explain the relationship between sound and meaning, between outer form and inner form. We will call this orientation the *mediational* orientation to emphasize that language on this view is something that mediates between two very different types of phenomena.

The second orientation has taken it that linguists' central task is to ex-plain the patterning and distribution of the formal elements of language. An essential presumption of this orientation is that there *is* a formal structure to language and that it can be described and explained on its own terms. We will call this orientation the *distributional* orientation, empha-sizing the importance of distributional features of language study on this view. The distinction between the mediational and distributional orient-ations will play an important role in what follows.

To be sure, these two orientations are not necessarily or logically incompatible, and they could jointly define a single program. Indeed, most linguists in this century have at one time or another explicitly embraced both. For example, the mediational relation between sound and meaning is crucial in the work of Leonard Bloomfield, although some have errone-ously interpreted the antimentalism that Bloomfield espoused to indicate that he had no place for semantics in his conception of grammar. The importance of the sound–meaning connection for Bloomfield is perhaps nowhere clearer than in his definition in his book *Language* (1933: 160) of a constituent as "the common part of any (two or more) complex forms" which bear "partial phonetic-semantic resemblance[s]" to each other. Although Bloomfield sometimes spoke of "forms" (= "phonetic forms") as stretches of sound, he intended the technical term "complex form," on which his definition of constituency depended, to denote a sound–meaning combination. That is, a *linguistic form* for Bloomfield was "[a] phonetic form with its meaning" (1933: 166). Thus, *John* is a constituent of the complex forms *John ran* and *John fell*, since these two sentences contain stretches which are not only phonetically identical, but which also carry identical meanings (1933: 159). Indeed, Bloomfield (1943: 272) explicitly denied that a consideration of meaning could be excluded from linguistic analysis:

> In language, forms cannot be separated from their meanings. It would be uninteresting and perhaps not very profitable to study the mere sound of a language without any consideration of meaning.

At the same time, Bloomfield was wary of the indeterminacy of semantic concepts as compared with the better understood distributional properties of sounds. In *Language* (1933: 140), he called the statement of meanings "the weak point in language study" and suggested it will remain so "until human knowledge advances very far beyond its present state." He later contended that the difficulty in analyzing meanings is a consequence of the fact that "the things and happenings in the world are many and varied and also because different languages classify them in different ways" (1943: 274). Thus,

> It is easy to describe, classify, and arrange the forms of a language, but even if we commanded the entire range of present-day knowledge, we should still be unable to describe, classify, or arrange the meanings which are expressed by these forms.
>
> (1943: 273)

All of this suggested to Bloomfield that language analysis must start with forms and not with meanings (1943: 273). "Meanings," he stated flatly at one point, "cannot be defined in terms of our science and cannot enter into our definitions" (1931: 156).

It should be understood that this last statement did not directly contradict

Bloomfield's earlier assertions about the importance of meaning in linguistic analysis. From a mediational perspective, it is clear that he had no doubts about the place of meaning in the sound–meaning dyad: "If we had an accurate knowledge of every speaker's situation and of every hearer's response" – in short, if we had a scientific theory of meaning – then

> Linguistics, on this ideal plane, would consist of two main investigations: *phonetics*, in which we studied the speech-event without reference to meaning, investigating only the sound-producing movements of the speaker, the sound waves, and the action of the hearer's ear-drum, and *semantics* in which we studied the relation of these features to the features of meaning . . .
>
> (1933: 74)

In such an idealization, then, everything that we today consider to be part of grammar would be included for Bloomfield in semantics. However, since "our knowledge of the world in which we live is so imperfect," that research program must be postponed. In the meantime, we must "act as though science had progressed far enough to identify all the situations and responses that make up the meaning of speech forms" and (at least in the case of our own language) "trust to our everyday knowledge to tell us whether speech-forms are the same or different" (1933: 77). Hence, we are to rely on "the fundamental assumption of linguistics": we must assume that "*in every speech-community some utterances are alike as to form and meaning*" (1933: 78).

In distributional analysis, the linguist was to use the fundamental assumption to identify the linguistic forms of a language:

> Only by finding out which utterances are alike in meaning, and which ones are different, can the observer learn to recognize the phonemic distinctions.
>
> (1933: 93)

> In studying a language, we can single out the relevant features of sound only if we know something about the meaning . . . . An observer who first hears the Chippewa of Wisconsin or Michigan will note down such forms as [gi:zik, gi:sik, ki:zik, ki:sik], and he will not know whether he has recorded one, two, three, or four different words. Only when he learns that all four indifferently mean "sky" and when he finds similar variations for other unit meanings, will he realize that these variations are not significant.
>
> (1943: 272)

That is, there are two ways in which meaning might enter into an analysis. First, an analyst might assume with Bloomfield that linguistic forms are sound–meaning bundles and attempt to identify them by noting stretches

9

of sound which carry identical meanings. This can of course be accomplished without a theory of the structure of meaning beyond that which is necessary for a determination of synonymy (although "Since we cannot with certainty define meanings, we cannot always decide whether a given phonetic form in its various uses has always the same meaning or represents a set of homonyms" (1933: 145)). Second, an analyst might employ broader hypotheses about the structure of meaning in a particular analysis (such as, for example, that "nouns denote 'things'"). It was this latter that Bloomfield wished to rule out.

An undisciplined resort to meaning was easier to abjure in theory, however, than in practice. Among linguists in the 1940s and 1950s (as today) it was common "to use the meanings of utterance fractions as a general guide and short-cut to the identification of morphemes" (Trager and Smith 1951: 54). For example, given the Huichol forms *kʌye* "tree," *kʌyezi* "trees," *pʌkʌye* "It is a tree," and *pʌkʌyezi* "They are trees," the linguist[3] would be expected to isolate the morpheme *-zi* by noting the meaning difference between *kʌye* and *kʌyezi*. Any analysis which omitted a translation of the Huichol words and postulated morphemes, relying only on the native speaker's judgment that the words all have different meanings, would seem barren and unconvincing. Indeed, it is not just the fact that the four words have different meanings which permits the standard analysis, but rather the fact that their meanings are related in a certain way.[4]

On the other hand, certain Bloomfieldians, most notably Zellig Harris, Bernard Bloch, and George Trager, sought to purge the intrusion of meaning as fully as possible from the theoretical apparatus. Since Bloomfield himself had not entirely delimited the distributional role he envisioned for meaning, these Bloomfieldians took its elimination in that sphere as a worthwhile goal and at the same time assumed that, in doing so, they were parting company with their teacher (see, e.g. Bloch's statement (1948: 6) "our approach differs in some respects from Bloomfield's – chiefly in that Bloomfield invokes meaning as a fundamental criterion . . .").

Trager, who campaigned vigorously for the exclusion of meaning from distributional analysis, made explicit what was implicit in Bloomfield's approach: "microlinguistic analysis [i.e. phonology, morphology, and syntax] works with *difference of meaning* only: it asks, 'Are these two items the same or different?'" (Trager 1953, cited in Hymes and Fought 1981: 140). Thus, "the syntax of a language like English can be constructed objectively, without the intervention of translation meaning or any sort of meta-linguistic phenomena" (Trager and Smith 1951: 68).

But if Trager did not depart significantly from Bloomfield with respect to the place of meaning in grammar, Harris did. Harris's pronouncement in 1940 that "the structures of language can be described only in terms of the formal, not the semantic, differences of its units and their relations" (1940: 701) presaged the development of a distributional approach in which even difference of meaning has no place. In his *Methods in Structural Linguistics* (1951), Harris proposed a rigorous procedure for determining whether two stretches of sound in a corpus are descriptively equivalent:

> we ask two informants to say these [stretches] to each other several times, telling one informant which to say (identifying it by some translation or otherwise) and seeing if the other can guess which he said. If the hearer guesses right about fifty percent of the time then there is no regular descriptive difference between the utterances; if he guesses right near one hundred percent, there is.
>
> (1951: 32)

This procedure, which came to be known as the *pair test*, clearly does not depend on "difference of meaning," in Trager's sense; in fact it "precludes our asking the informant if two morphemes are 'the same'" (1951: 38). Harris underscores this distinction near the end of the book:

> In determining the morphemes of a particular language, linguists use, in addition to distributional criteria, also (in varying degrees) criteria of meaning difference. In exact descriptive linguistic work, however, such considerations of meaning can only be used heuristically, as a source of hints, and the determining criteria will always have to be stated in distributional terms . . . . The methods presented in the preceding chapters offer distributional investigations as alternatives to meaning considerations.
>
> (1951: 365)

It should be emphasized that the issue of the place of meaning in grammar was for Harris by no means simply a *methodological* one, as some (e.g. Newmeyer 1980: 31) have supposed. Harris assumed that the structure of meaning differs from the structure of form:

> It is true that language has a special relation to meaning, both in the sense of the classification of aspects of experience, and in the sense of communication. But the relation is not simple. For example, we can compare the structures of languages with the structure of the physical world . . . , or with what we know about the structure of human response (e.g., association, transference). In either case, it would be clear that the structure of one language or another does not conform in many respects to the structure of physical nature or human response – i.e., to the structure of objective experience from which we presumably draw our meanings . . . . If one wishes to speak of language as existing in some sense on two planes – of form and of meaning – we can at least say that the structures of the two are not identical, though they will be found similar in various respects.
>
> (1954: 780–1)

11

This perception, like Bloomfield's dictum that "Meanings . . . cannot enter into our definitions," obviously proceeded from an assumption about the nature of the object examined, rather than about the examining process itself. The crucial conclusion here, however, was that on the "plane of form," language has a discoverable structure which does not simply follow from its function or meaning – that is, that the systems of phonology, morphology, and syntax are autonomous and independent of the system of meaning. Joos (1950: 353) provided a simple simile:

> Linguists . . . have elevated their descriptive technique to the rank of a theory about the nature of language. They say, in effect, that the design of any language is essentially telegraphic – that the language has the structure of a telegraph code, using molecular signals made up of invariant atoms, and differing e.g. from the Morse code principally in two ways: the codes called "languages" have numerous layers of complexity instead of only two, and *in each layer there are severe limitations upon the combinations permitted.*
>
> (emphasis added)

The assumption that the forms of language are structured independently from the meanings of language (and are subject to "severe limitations" with respect to their combinability at each formal level) appeared to fit well with Bloomfield's desire to postpone the investigation of meaning "until human knowledge advances very far beyond its present state." That is, descriptive linguistics could (and should) be limited to questions of distribution – of "the freedom of occurrence of portions of an utterance relatively to each other" (Harris 1951: 5).

THE *LSLT* PROGRAM

It was, however, Harris's student, Noam Chomsky, who became the most celebrated advocate of the distributionalist approach. In a manuscript entitled "The logical structure of linguistic theory," which he completed in 1955–6, Chomsky (1975c: 63) attempted to defend the claim that "a linguistic theory constructed on a 'distributional' basis does delimit an interesting and significant area of linguistic behavior." In that manuscript, he distinguished *syntax*, which he defined as the study of linguistic form, from *semantics*, which he defined as the study of how syntax is actually put to use in a speech community. "Syntax and semantics are distinct fields of investigation," he noted in his preface (1975c: 57); "[t]he subject of investigation [of this book] will be syntactic structure, and we shall study it as an independent aspect of linguistic theory."

In support of the distributionalist orientation he accepted for linguistic theory, Chomsky also accepted as a core proposition the idea that distributions of linguistic elements are determined to some significant degree by the structural properties of the strings made up of those elements. Following this, he assumed that speakers of a language have various "intuitions about linguistic form" (1975c: 62), such as that some sentences are grammatical, are of the same type (say, declaratives), are ambiguous in certain ways, and so on; the point of a linguistic analysis would then be to give a general account of the structure of language "that will provide automatically" for such intuitions. "Our problem is to . . . bring to light the formal patterns underlying the sentences of a language, and to show how these observed regularities might account for particular decisions about which sequences are grammatical and how these are to be understood" (1975c: 62–3).

Chomsky's commitment to an independent syntax entailed that the structural properties of the strings in question not be defined in terms of semantically-based notions, and this provided his program with a second core proposition. In a paper delivered at a Georgetown University conference in 1955, Chomsky took the position that

> semantic notions are really quite irrelevant to the problem of describing formal structure, and . . . their irrelevance is disguised only by their unclarity and by the failure to formulate the purported dependence of linguistic analysis on meaning with sufficient care and precision.
>
> (Chomsky 1955: 141)

The idea that syntactic analysis could (in fact, must) be done without recourse to semantic terms, which has come to be known as the "autonomy hypothesis," has played a central role in all of Chomsky's work since his undergraduate days. It was also, as we have seen, a crucial component of the structuralist program of his teacher Zellig Harris.

Another of Chomsky's teachers who had a significant influence on him was the philosopher Nelson Goodman. Having taken several courses with Goodman at the University of Pennsylvania, Chomsky was struck by the similarity between Harris's perspective on language and Goodman's perspective on philosophical systems generally, what Goodman called "constructional systems."[5] The important feature of constructional systems in this regard is that there exist objective criteria for evaluating how simple or complex they are. Thus, if a theory of language were a constructional system, then that theory would be subject to the principles that govern such systems; that is, it could be evaluated according to criteria of simplicity and economy. Furthermore, as a constructional system, the theory of language should be formalizable; in fact, if language is to be evaluated as a constructional system, it must be formalized, because only in that way can its simplicity relative to other theories be measured. Viewing the theory of language in this restrictive way was of course consistent with the conclusion that it was a scientific theory. This conclusion was not original with Chomsky – indeed, it had been central to Bloomfield's work – but tying it

13

to Goodman's theory of systems gave him a solid philosophical foundation to rest it on.

The issue of formalizability bore upon a third principal core proposition of the early Chomskyan program, which was that structural differences among grammatical sentences of a language can be accounted for by a set of phrase structure rules and the transformations that apply to them. The idea of transformations Chomsky of course adapted from Harris,[6] but Chomsky's concern that linguistic theory be a constructional system undoubtedly influenced his selection of Post production systems, whose logical and mathematical properties had been studied in detail, as a model for the base rules of the grammar.

The sketch we have given here of the orientational and core propositions of Chomsky's program *circa* 1956 (summarized in (1)) hardly does justice to its depth and breadth, since the properties of the program that ultimately gave it its vast appeal resided mainly in its more technical auxiliary hypotheses. Whatever antecedents this program had in his predecessors' work, virtually everyone active in the American linguistics community in the late 1950s and early 1960s was at least aware that something very different and exciting was being put together by Chomsky along these lines, even if they were not fully at home with the new theory. But for those younger scholars who became involved with the Chomskyan program, the experience was, quite obviously, exhilarating. Chomsky's writings and lectures during this period so compellingly suggested the rich potential for his theory that the once vigorous structuralist program from which it had developed was made to appear for those scholars stale and flat by comparison.

(1) The *LSLT* program
    Orientation   Core
    1 Distributional 1 The distribution of linguistic elements is deter-
                         mined by structural properties of the gram-
                         matical strings made up of those elements.
                      2 The formal (phonological, syntactic) part of the
                         grammar is autonomous from the semantic part.
                      3 Structural differences among the grammatical
                         sentences of a language can be accounted for
                         by a set of phrase structure rules and the
                         transformations that apply to them.

TOWARDS A MEDIATIONALIST ORIENTATION

In the distributionalist vision of Chomsky's *LSLT* – and of his more widely-read *Syntactic Structures* (1957a) – the grammar was organized by means of a set of levels, as in Harris's work as well. However, in Chomsky's model, representations on the different levels were related by a set of rules that applied sequentially, in such a fashion that the representations on one level could be viewed as the input to such a set of rules, while the output of those rules could be viewed as the representation on the "next" level, in most cases (all cases, roughly, except the transformational level). The "top" level of the grammar was the level of *T-markers*, which recorded which *P-markers* (or *phrase markers*) were assigned to the sequences composing a sentence as well as which transformations had applied to them. The phrase structure level in turn contained rules from which the P-marker of a sequence was to be reconstructed. To sequences derived at this level, rules applied to derive sequences successively at the levels of categories, words, morphemes, and phonemes.

Chomsky called a sentence that had been derived through the application only of obligatory transformations a *kernel* sentence.[7] In addition to being either optional or obligatory, transformations were also classified as being either *singulary* or *generalized*. Recursion was accomplished by the generalized transformations, which could conjoin two or more phrase markers or embed one phrase marker in another; singulary transformations could only copy, adjoin, or delete elements within a single phrase marker. For example, the sentence *The boy who was talking was sent home by the proctor* might be derived by a generalized transformation that embedded the relative clause *who was talking* under the noun phrase *the boy* in the sentence *The proctor sent home the boy* and then by singulary transformations that passivized the resulting sentence, moving the direct object into subject position while putting the subject in a prepositional phrase.

Chomsky did not offer an explicit theory concerning the relationship between the representation of a sentence at the various grammatical levels and its meaning, although he was prepared to acknowledge that one must exist:

> Having determined the syntactic structure of the language, we can study the way in which this syntactic structure is put to use in the actual functioning of language. An investigation of the semantic function of level structure . . . might be a reasonable step towards a theory of the interconnections between syntax and semantics.
>
> (1957a: 102)

Indeed, one of the important conclusions that Chomsky had reached in the mid-1950s was that the meaning of a sequence depended to a significant degree on its grammatical analysis (1957a: 92). He had identified numerous cases of constructional homonymy, for example, where he claimed that an adequate syntax would be required to assign a particular string alternative structural analyses corresponding to its alternative readings. However, no systematic investigation of the theory of semantics was attempted at this point.

15

Some significant progress in overcoming the difficulty of dealing with semantics was felt to have been made in the work of Jerrold Katz and Jerry Fodor (1963), which attempted to place an upper bound on any semantic theory which was to be part of a linguistic description of a language. In Katz and Fodor's view, semantic rules – called *projection rules* – would apply to each distinct grammatical structure of a sentence to produce a semantic interpretation for the sentence. They set three criteria by which a theory of semantic interpretation might be evaluated: the interpretations "must mark each semantic ambiguity a speaker can detect; they must explain the source of the speaker's intuitions of anomaly when a sentence evokes them; [and] they must suitably relate sentences speakers know to be paraphrases of each other" (1963: 493).

It is worth pausing at this point to consider why Katz and Fodor felt it important to postulate a distinct *linguistic* level of semantic interpretation, since previous work in generative grammar had been at best vague about the relation of meaning to grammar. Katz and Fodor simply accepted that the primary goal of linguistic research was to provide an account of "a fluent speaker's . . . ability to produce and understand the sentences of his language, including indefinitely many that are wholly novel to him" (Katz and Fodor 1963: 481). But the "lower levels" of grammar (= phonology, morphology, and syntax), could in their view only go so far in contributing to such an account; hence, what was left over (i.e. that which was above the lower bound and below the upper bound) must properly belong, they argued, to linguistic semantics.

Katz and Fodor argued that several important kinds of phenomena fell between the two bounds. For example, they noted sentences that they claimed were paraphrases but which evidently could not be grammatically related, for example, *Two chairs are in the room* and *There are at least two things in the room and each is a chair.* Opposed to these, they also noted sentences that were understood to stand in a transformational relation but were clearly not paraphrases, for example, *The man hit the ball* and *The man did not hit the ball.* In neither case would the assumed analyses at the phrase structure and transformational levels provide a satisfactory account of the meaning differences or similarities holding between the sentence pairs.

The appeal of Katz and Fodor's hypothesis of a linguistic semantic level was manifest in the proliferation of empirical work on lexical selection and meaning, quantification, anaphora, and so forth, that followed in its wake, work which the hypothesis had clearly facilitated. But because Katz and Fodor's argument was not itself really empirical, it was open to criticism and reinterpretation from two sides. First, it could be argued that they had set their upper bound too high and that (at least some of) the phenomena with which they were concerned were not properly in the province of grammar, strictly defined. Second, it could be argued that they had assumed a lower bound that was too low and that the "lower levels" of phonology, morphology, and syntax actually extended farther upward than they had realized; in particular, while they had advocated a scheme in which some instances of ambiguity, synonymy and anomaly received treatment in the syntax and other kinds in the semantics, it could be argued that there had never been substantive justification for such a division. In fact, Chomsky was eventually to assemble both kinds of arguments against the idea of a linguistic semantic level in the Katz–Fodor tradition, although his initial reaction to their proposal in 1963 was to attempt to make use of it to the extent possible in his program.

No doubt one reason why Katz and Fodor's program seemed so attractive at the time was that by incorporating a level of semantic interpretation in the grammar which was determined by rule from syntactic structure, they had demonstrated that Chomsky's transformational theory could be legitimately considered a significant step toward a satisfactory mediational theory of language. The principal problem with the Katz–Fodor view from the mediational perspective, however, was the extreme indirection of the relationship between surface form and semantic interpretation. A semantic interpretation was to be arrived at by applying projection rules to each derivation of each of the kernels of the sentence as well as to the output of any generalized transformations or of any singular transformations that changed meaning. The semantic interpretation for a sentence was then a union of sets of readings for each of the constituents of the sentence.

Now, mere complexity in the relation between levels in a theory is not in itself a mark against it, as long as the theory as a whole is demonstrably simpler than its competitors. But the more complexity there is, the more difficult it becomes to state conditions on the relation that capture broad and significant generalizations. Nevertheless, the chief complaint lodged against the Katz–Fodor theory was that their postulated readings did not contain sufficient structural information to distinguish nonsynonymous strings made up from the same lexical items (Weinreich 1966, McCawley 1968a).

Two developments during 1963 and 1964 significantly reduced the complexity of the proposed relation between syntax and semantic interpretation in the *LSLT* theory. The first proceeded from Katz and his colleague Paul Postal's (1964) hypothesis that no singular transformations change meaning: if sustained, the hypothesis meant that the rules of semantic interpretation could be constrained to apply just to the inputs to singular transformations, and not to their outputs. The second derived from Charles Fillmore's (1963) proposal to the effect that all singular transformations applied to a sentence before it could be embedded into another sentence by any generalized transformation, and that singular transformations only applied to a sentence after all generalized transformations had applied to it. If the position in a matrix sentence into which another sentence is to be embedded by a generalized transformation is

17

always marked by a special symbol, as Katz and Postal (1964) had argued, then the interaction of the singulary and generalized transformations will be entirely predictable. Following this, in *Aspects of the Theory of Syntax* (1965), Chomsky proposed to eliminate generalized transformations altogether and to permit the phrase structure rules to introduce recursion.

From a mediational perspective, these moves were of considerable importance, since they entailed that there was a single level – *deep structure*, as Chomsky called it – which was both the output of the phrase structure rules, and the level to which the rules of semantic interpretation applied. As has been often observed, these moves also paved the way for a deepening of the concept of deep structure as a result of which the distance between that level and the level of semantic interpretation as it was understood was substantially reduced.

One question which the semantic investigations of Katz, Fodor, and Postal during this period did not satisfactorily resolve is precisely what kind of thing a semantic interpretation for a given sentence was to be. Katz and Postal (1964: 26) had accepted Katz and Fodor's (1963) three criteria for the evaluation of a semantic level, and added the requirement that in a satisfactory theory a semantic interpretation for a sentence must also indicate "such properties as whether or not the sentence is analytic, synthetic, or contradictory." But the latitude permitted by these criteria in the formation of a semantic theory was considerable. Furthermore, as Janet Fodor (1977: 68) has pointed out, although Katz and Postal apparently intended the output of their projection rules to be readings which would attach to the nodes of a deep structure, they never explicitly specified any conditions on the form that such a semantic interpretation would take.

THE GENERATIVE SEMANTICS REORIENTATION

The work of Katz, Fodor, Postal, and Fillmore contributed to the creation of a climate in which serious mediationally-oriented research could be undertaken within the generative paradigm. At least some of the younger generation of students at and around MIT in the early 1960s were only too happy to take up the challenge of developing the theory in this direction. As one of these former students – James McCawley – has written,

> *Aspects* brought semantics out of the closet. Here was finally a theory of grammar that not only incorporated semantics (albeit very programmatically) but indeed claimed that semantics was systematically related to syntax and made the construction of syntactic analyses a matter of much more than just accounting for the distribution of morphemes.
>
> (McCawley 1976a: 6)

Hence, for those who eventually became known as Generative Semanticists, "a grammar is a specification of what the relationship between semantic structures and surface structures is, and the claim that a distinction between syntactic rules and semantic rules must be drawn is a claim requiring justification" (McCawley 1976a: 10–11). The program of generative syntax had thus reached a point in its development where importantly different conceptions of the goals of the program could find justification in the theory as it stood.

By adopting a mediational orientation for their program, and by insisting that it be given at least as much priority as the distributional orientation, the Generative Semanticists were pressing for significant changes. And the changes that they were willing to accept included changes to the auxiliary hypotheses of the theory and to the core that shaped them. They did accept the first and the third of the core propositions of the *LSLT* program, but as regards the second concerning the autonomy of syntax, all of the Generative Semanticists were willing to give it up if necessary, that is, to take it as a refutable auxiliary hypothesis. It appears to us that it was this shift towards a mediationalist commitment, and the concomitant restructuring and reranking of the core propositions of Chomsky's research program, more than a disagreement over the content or validity of the testable hypotheses that were proposed, that the disputes of the 1960s and 1970s were primarily about. The issues that were actually debated, we suggest, were no more than proxies for these more fundamental and less technical disagreements.

GENERATIVE SEMANTICS'S POSITIVE PROPOSAL

In work undertaken early in 1967 and published in 1968, McCawley argued that semantic representations were labeled trees which resembled in certain respects constructions of standard logics, in that they took the predicate–argument organization of the clause to be basic and expressed quantificational scope and anaphor–antecedent relations directly (McCawley 1968b, 1968c). Since the idea that the semantic level of a grammar should have at least some of the properties of the logical calculus might seem obvious (and indeed McCawley was not the first to propose it[8]), it may be worth emphasizing that there were also some well-known objections to that idea:[9] what distinguished McCawley's approach was his highly persuasive demonstration that the assumption of such a level could nevertheless solve some significant linguistic problems and thus deserved serious consideration.

McCawley's proposal had a stimulating effect on those who were attempting to sort out the syntax–semantics interface: the level of semantic interpretation was at once made concrete and homogeneous, and since standard systems of symbolic logic had been developed in an attempt to deal with ambiguity, anomaly, synonymy, and so on, it was not hard to see how a level constructed from such logical materials might be highly rated according to the Katz–Fodor–Postal criteria. Most importantly, McCawley's

19

proposal, perhaps more than anything else, gave to the emerging mediational research program in generative grammar a shape and a plan: it provided those who were interested in undertaking mediational work in generative linguistics with the scholarly equivalent of marching orders.

McCawley's work should not, however, be viewed in isolation from that of his colleagues George Lakoff and John Robert Ross, with whom he had been in close consultation during this period and who were offering arguments that deep structure in the *Aspects* sense was not simply the input to the rules which determined the logical forms of the sentences of a language, but could be identified with those forms themselves. As Lakoff and Ross (1976 [1967]) attempted to show in a letter initially sent to Arnold Zwicky in March of 1967 and widely circulated thereafter, if deep structure were taken to be the level where grammatical relations and selectional restrictions are defined, and where lexical items are inserted, then new kinds of motivation would be needed for postulating such a level between semantic representation and surface structure. But if deep structures were semantic representations, then transformations, which had originally been posited to serve the distributionalist purpose of explaining patterns observed among surface structures, could now be understood as the principal mediationalist device in relating form to meaning. These proposals (summarized in (2)) about the composition of semantic representation and the relationship between surface and semantic levels of grammar showed how the theory's core and auxiliary hypotheses might be built up in such a way as to serve both mediationalist and distributionalist goals.[10]

(2) The Generative Semantics program, 1967

Orientation	Core
1 Mediational	1 The distribution of linguistic elements is determined by structural properties of the grammatical strings made up of those elements.
2 Distributional	2 Structural differences among the grammatical sentences of a language can be accounted for by a set of phrase structure rules and the transformations that apply to them.
	3 Syntactic and semantic representations are of the same formal nature, i.e. they are labeled trees.
	4 Semantic representations resemble the constructions of formal logic, with quantifier scope and anaphor–antecedent relations explicitly expressed.
	5 Syntactic and semantic representations are related via transformations.

The views of the Generative Semanticists concerning the roles of deep structure and transformations thus contrasted sharply with those of Chomsky in *Aspects* and in later work by him and the other Interpretive Semanticists. In the Chomskyan program, deep structure, and the transformational rules that related representations at that level with those at the level of surface structure, were indispensable in describing the distribution of the formal elements of language. But for the Generative Semanticists, transform-ational rules were indispensable for getting at meaning. As we will see below, these two different ways of conceiving of deep structure were not always distinguished, even when pernicious confusion was the result.

McCawley's sketch, although it did have ramifications for the way a gram-mar was to be constructed, left room for a wide variety of possibilities. For example, following some proposals in Lakoff's 1965 Indiana University dissertation (G. Lakoff 1970 [1965]), McCawley (1968c) suggested that lexical items may be inserted at various points in a derivation and that an individual item may correspond to a combination of semantic elements that have been manipulated by transformation. Accordingly, he proposed that an item like *kill* might be derived from the semantic elements under-lying the items in the phrase *cause to become not alive*; if so, then the fact that the one is a paraphrase of the other would be explained. Further support for such an approach was provided by Morgan (1969), who noted that the adverb *almost* in a sentence like *John almost killed Bill* can be ambiguously construed as (inter alia) modifying either the *cause* part of the meaning of *kill* or the *become not alive* part: for example, John could have shot at Bill but missed him or could have wounded him so severely that he almost died. This ambiguity would be accounted for if the adverb can appear in under-lying structure as a sister of either *cause* or *become*, with a subsequent lexical transformation substituting *kill* for the complex *cause to become not alive*.

THE PSYCHOLOGICAL REORIENTATION OF THE CHOMSKYAN PROGRAM

Bloomfield's acceptance of the distributional and mediational orientations for his program, discussed above, did not exhaust his views on the goals of linguistic research. For Bloomfield, a mediational linguistic theory was in effect a psychological theory as well. Indeed, he viewed the linguistic act as a behavioral response to environmental stimuli and conceived of it as being the linguist's ultimate task to construct an account of the relationship between them. Influenced by the physicalist psychologists of his era, and in particular by the behaviorist Albert Paul Weiss, Bloomfield imported from their work a conception of science into which linguistics might be integrated.

This is not to say that Bloomfield saw linguistic science as being part of or subordinated to a particular psychology; he noted in his "A set of

21

postulates for the science of language," for example, that "it is indifferent what system of psychology a linguist believes in" (1926: 71; see also Hymes and Fought 1981: 103 and Fries 1961: 203). But in Bloomfield's linguistics the speaker was never very far away from the center of things, and utterances were never taken as bearing no relation to those who uttered them.

Hockett had underscored the point – using terms that would not be out of place in a contemporary journal article – that a linguistic analysis is a theory of what speakers do and that children learning a language are just like "little linguists":

> The analysis of the linguistic scientist is to be of such a nature that the linguist can account . . . for utterances which are not in his corpus at a given time. That is, as a result of his examination he must be able to predict what other utterances the speakers of the language might produce . . .
>
>   The analytical process thus parallels what goes on in the nervous system of a language learner, particularly, perhaps, that of a child learning his first language . . . . The child's coining of an utterance he has not heard is, of course, a kind of prediction . . . . The parallel between this and the process of analysis performed by the linguist is close.
>
> (Hockett 1948: 279)

Beginning in the late 1950s, and then increasingly thereafter, Chomsky expressed in his published work considerable interest in the question of how a child can in fact acquire knowledge of his or her language. In a 1958 paper, Chomsky described the situation in terms which echoed Hockett's:

> The child who has learned a language has actually succeeded in developing something like a rather abstract theory to account for specific subject matter (observation of particular sentences); and the adult who recognizes and understands a sentence has succeeded in determining that this sentence is "predicted" (generated) by this theory, and in determining how it is generated . . .
>
> (Chomsky 1958: 433)

In his review in 1957 of Chomsky's *Syntactic Structures*, Chomsky's student Robert Lees had made a similar point:

> The mechanism which we must attribute to human beings to account for their speech behavior has all the characteristics of a sophisticated scientific theory. We cannot look into a human speaker's head to see just what kind of device he uses there with which to generate the sentences of his language, and so, in the manner of any physical scientist confronted with observations on the world, we can only construct a model which has all the desired properties, that is, which

also generates those sentences in the same way as the human speaker. If the model has been rendered maximally general, it should predict correctly the human speaker's future linguistic behavior. We may then attribute the structure of this model to the device in the human head, and say that we understand human speech behavior better than before.

(Lees 1957: 76)

As Chomsky was quick to realize, if it is assumed that a native speaker's knowledge includes formal knowledge independent of semantic and pragmatic knowledge, then the inductive problem facing a language learner attempting to learn a grammar from a finite input is considerable – especially if the grammar has the characteristics ascribed to it in Chomsky's *Logical Structure of Linguistic Theory.* As Lees put it:

If we are to account adequately for the indubitable fact that a child by the age of five or six has somehow reconstructed for himself the theory of his language, it would seem that our notions of human learning are due for some considerable sophistication.

(Lees 1957: 79)

Chomsky's solution to this problem was to propose that the autonomous syntactic system is not learned from scratch. He said in his 1958 paper:

. . . it seems to me that to account for the ability to learn a language, we must ascribe a rather complex "built-in" structure to the organism. That is, the [language acquisition device] will have complex properties beyond the ability to match, generalize, abstract, and categorize items in the simple ways that are usually considered to be available to the organism. In other words, the particular direction that language learning follows may turn out to be determined by genetically determined maturation of complex "information-processing" abilities, to an extent that has not, in the past, been considered at all likely.

(Chomsky 1958: 433)

This move was to stand on its head any possible critique of abstract grammar as being inconsistent with the learning theories of the day. That is, instead of taking learning theory as a bench-mark in relation to which linguistic theory must be calibrated, Chomsky's proposal capitalized on the idea that the linguist's grammar is a theory of what the speaker knows and demanded that learning theory accommodate itself to that.

Quite reasonably, Chomsky's suggestions during this period concerning "a rather complex" innate system were hesitant, considering how little was actually known about the ontogenesis of language. Beginning in the early 1960s, however, he shifted attention to the evident necessity for an inborn system of some sort. In his 1963 paper, "Formal properties of grammar," Chomsky wrote:

23

> For acquisition of language to be possible at all there *must* be some
> sort of initial delimitation of the class of possible systems to which
> observed samples may conceivably pertain; the organism *must, neces-*
> *sarily* be preset to search for and identify certain kinds of structural
> regularities. Universal features of grammar offer some suggestions
> regarding the form this initial delimitation might take.
>
> (Chomsky 1963: 330, emphasis added)

In fact, Chomsky went on to deny even the possibility of an alternative:
arguments against this view, he asserted, were they correct, would

> apply as well against any attempt to construct explanatory theories.
> They would, in other words, simply eliminate science as an intel-
> lectually significant enterprise.

This shift in the way that Chomsky spoke of what came to be known as "the
logical problem of language acquisition" accompanied a shift in his expression of the goals of linguistic theory. For example, in *Current Issues in
Linguistic Theory* (1964: 28) and, later, in *Aspects of the Theory of Syntax* (1965:
24–7), Chomsky focused on the different levels of success that might be
attained by a grammatical description associated with a particular linguistic
theory. At the level of *descriptive adequacy*, a grammar might achieve success
when it gives a correct account of the linguistic intuitions of the native
speaker. But success at the level of *explanatory adequacy* is said to be achieved
only when the associated linguistic theory provides a basis for selecting a
descriptively adequate grammar.[11] In this latter case, a linguistic theory
provides an explanation for the intuition of the native speaker if "data of
the observed kind will enable a speaker whose intrinsic capacities are as
represented in this general theory to construct for himself a grammar that
characterizes exactly this linguistic intuition." Chomsky left no doubt in
this and subsequent work that he felt that only a linguistic theory which
aspired to explanatory adequacy could lay claim to asking (much less
answering) fundamental scientific questions.

Chomsky has said that he was convinced from his days as a student of
Goodman's that there is no inductive learning (Chomsky 1975c: 33, 51),
and has also indicated that "the 'psychological analogue' to the methodological problem of constructing linguistic theory . . . lay in the immediate
background" of his thinking at the time he wrote *The Logical Structure of
Linguistic Theory* (Chomsky 1975c: 35). But whatever his implicit intent in
LSLT, the explicit concern there was with providing a formal basis for the
grammar. By 1963 or so that essentially distributional program orientation
had taken second place to the psychological orientation that had only been
alluded to in passing in his books and articles between 1955 and 1957.[12] If
the primary goal of linguistic research was now to be that of explaining how
a speaker has somehow acquired this knowledge of his or her language,

then the hypothesis that that knowledge is genetically determined "to an extent that has not, in the past, been considered at all likely" becomes far more interesting. Indeed, from this perspective, to show how a language can be learned at all, the linguist must be able to show how the learner can reduce the set of hypotheses available to a manageable number.

It needs to be emphasized that the logical force of this characterization of the induction problem facing the language learner depended on the prior assumption that the principles that determine the distribution of formal elements in language are, at least to some degree, autonomous from the principles that associate forms with meaning. To the extent that appeals to semantic principles (or any other principles – Freudian, astrological, or whatever) fail adequately to account for the facts of a particular language, then indeed there is a classical projection problem to be faced: how does the language learner establish a particular system of rules whose effects extend *correctly* past the data encountered so far?[13] On the other hand, to the extent that such facts are governed by other principles available to the learner – in particular by semantic principles – there is essentially no inductive problem to be solved.[14] Hence, the more the linguist sees autonomous principles affecting the distributions he or she is interested in, the more significant will the induction problem appear.

It also needs to be emphasized that the "innateness hypothesis" has never been merely an empirical (i.e. auxiliary) hypothesis of the Chomskyan program. Because it embodies more a methodological strategy than a proposition about what is innate, it has never been explicitly formulated, and can be falsified only in the trivial sense that a linguistic theory constructed according to the strategy is itself falsifiable. Similar remarks would apply to the autonomy hypothesis.[15] Although there are empirical issues that bear on the force and interpretation of these two hypotheses, failure to appreciate that neither of them was in fact intended to function as a testable, auxiliary proposition in the theory has resulted in much unproductive debate about their truth value.[16]

For their part, the Generative Semanticists never accepted the psychological reorientation of Chomskyan theory announced in *Aspects* and were, in fact, much more at home with the original, more transparent aims of the *LSLT* program as modified by the mediational work of Katz, Fodor, Postal, and Fillmore. If Generative Semantics was also a psychological theory, it was so (like Bloomfieldian theory) only because it was mediational. As regards innateness, the Generative Semanticists took the position that the only question of any contemporary significance concerning a linguistic theory was how well it predicted the mediational and distributional facts, that is, how well it predicted speakers' judgments concerning the acceptability and truth conditions of a given sentence in a particular context. Hence, they believed the linguist's immediate task was to get such facts straight and to discover the most elegant generalizations concerning them.

25

Since they felt not enough was then known about language to specify with any confidence which parts of it might be a consequence of autonomous principles, the induction problem was for Generative Semanticists a non-issue. How a neuroscientist might account for linguistic facts was no doubt an interesting question, but on their view it could not be meaningfully addressed as long as linguistic theories were as insecure as they then were.[17]

The Generative Semantics attitude toward autonomy was nevertheless sometimes confusing, if not contradictory. Since they argued that semantic interpretation rules and syntactic transformations could not be segregated, they rejected any interpretation of autonomy that entailed such a segregation. However, they were in general committed to discovering *structural* solutions to semantic problems – to demonstrating how meaning could be translated into a form that had all the characteristics of a syntactic level and that was related to superficial syntactic structure straightforwardly by formal rules. Generative Semanticists never attempted to determine the extent to which the terms of underlying structure could be defined without resort to semantic concepts, but in so far as they were concerned with the form of that level, nothing they said was really at odds with the technical view of autonomy, as Chomsky often pointed out. Moreover, at least McCawley and Ross regularly endorsed the idea of syntactic constraints on surface structure, and whether any or all of these might be found to be functionally or semantically motivated was an open question.

Where Generative Semanticists came to strongly differ with Interpretive Semanticists was over the usefulness of semantic and pragmatic explanations for distributional facts, and it was here that empirical issues were actually raised. The Generative Semanticists attempted a variety of analyses in which patterns of acceptable and unacceptable sentences were accounted for by reference to the denotations or entailments of those sentences or to the intentions of their speakers. The *Aspects* program of Chomsky (sum-

(3) The *Aspects* program

Orientation	Core
1 Psychological	1 The distribution of linguistic elements is determined by structural properties of the grammatical strings made up of those elements.
2 Distributional	
3 Mediational	
	2 The formal (phonological, syntactic) part of the grammar is autonomous from the semantic part.
	3 Structural differences among the grammatical sentences of a language can be accounted for by a set of phrase structure rules and the transformations that apply to them.
	4 The principles of Universal Grammar are innately specified.

marized in (3)) differed strikingly from this view by suggesting that such facts could be genetically determined. That is, the psychological and distributional orientations of the *Aspects* program were linked in a way that was simply not possible in the Generative Semantics program.

THE INTERPRETIVE RESPONSE TO GENERATIVE SEMANTICS

The Generative Semanticists believed and claimed that their theory improved on the *Aspects* theory. Between 1967 and 1970, Chomsky and others offered various arguments designed to demonstrate that the Generative Semantics program not only offered no improvement, but was thoroughly misconceived. We will examine a number of these arguments and show why we believe Generative Semanticists were justified in rejecting them. Indeed, developments in the theory of grammar in the interim have made it clear that such arguments do not serve to refute very similar propositions which are now in general currency.

We will focus particularly on Chomsky's arguments against Generative Semantics because these arguments have been most influential in explaining why that program failed, despite the paradox that this poses for contemporary theory. However, we do not mean to imply that we therefore believe that the Generative Semanticists were on any firmer ground when they attacked the Interpretive Semanticists, or that Chomsky's defense of Interpretivism was not well motivated (in general, it seems to us that they were not, and it was). Both sides raised issues that their opponents were obliged to deal with; but it was simply not enough to show, as each side attempted to, that there is some interpretation of the other's position under which the data cannot be accounted for: the crucial issue is whether that position was justified on the *intended* interpretation, or on alternative interpretations within reach. Of course, one may question whether the disputants in the Generative Semantics–Interpretive Semantics debates were engaging in a rational discussion, since there were differences between them in the way that they understood the terms that they commonly used which made the achievement of a common understanding difficult. For example, Chomsky had always insisted that the study of meaning is an essential task of linguistics (even if he regarded appeal to meaning as unjustified in syntactic analysis) and assumed that his program would provide the basis for such a study. From his point of view, semantics had never been, in McCawley's picturesque phrase, "in the closet"; but then on Chomsky's view, McCawley's efforts could do nothing to bring it out. And if, as Chomsky argued, the level of semantic representation is just another *syntactic* level – one perhaps more readily available for semantic interpretation – then McCawley's proposals offered merely a different form of syntax, one which Chomsky had in fact sketched as an option in the last chapter of *Aspects* (1965: 158–9).[18] The dialogues between the Generative Semanticists and the Interpretive Semanticists were rife with this sort of misconnection, although such differences do not satisfactorily explain (much less justify) the contentious dispute that ensued.

What was perceived to be Chomsky's first public response to Generative Semantics was a paper he wrote in 1967 and published in 1970.[19] In this paper, entitled "Remarks on nominalization," he attacked the hypothesis that what he called "derived nominals" (like *criticism* and *refusal*) were transformationally related to their verbal analogues (respectively, *criticize* and *refuse*), a hypothesis that played an important role in Lakoff's dissertation (1970 [1965]) and that seemed to be fully consistent with a Generative Semantics approach.[20] Chomsky's argument consisted of showing that (a) there were distributional irregularities that would not be accounted for if derived nominals could be freely produced by transformational rule (e.g. compare *John's eagerness to please* with **John's easiness to please*; (b) the meaning of a derived nominal is not a simple function of that of its verbal analogue (e.g. compare *marry* and *marriage* on the one hand with *revolve* and *revolution* on the other); and (c) derived nominals have the internal structure of noun phrases (e.g. *several of John's proofs of the theorem* evidently has the same structure as *several of John's portraits of the dean*), a structure which must exist independently. Chomsky claimed that this clustering of properties followed if derived nominals appeared in deep structure as noun phrases, but would be mysterious if they were transformationally derived from predicates.

There is no question that Chomsky demonstrated in "Remarks" that a transformational analysis of all nominalizations was not inevitable and that there were facts which seemed to be interestingly compatible with a lexical analysis along the lines he suggested. But had he shown that a theory which lacked a level of deep structure and according to which derived nominals were transformationally related to predicates in underlying structure could not *in principle* account for the data as elegantly? Certainly Interpretivists assumed that he had. However, from the Generative Semantics point of view Chomsky's arguments cut both ways.

Chomsky's claim concerning the unproductiveness of derived nominals can be summarized as follows. He first assumed that *eager* appears in the lexicon as either an adjective or a noun. When it is a noun (i.e. a derived nominal), it has the form *eagerness*. In either case, it is subcategorized to take optionally a sentential complement, which is why both *John is eager to please* and *John's eagerness to please* are permitted. To get this result, however, Chomsky also had to suppose that the transformation that deletes the implied subject of *please* in these examples (the same transformation that was assumed to be responsible for the deletion of *himself* in *John wants himself to be picked* to yield *John wants to be picked*[21]) operates in noun phrases as in predicates – an assumption that seems to be substantiated by the existence of independently existing noun phrases like *the Anglo-American strategy for defeating Germany*. But whereas *eager* is subcategorized to take a sentential complement, the subcategorization frame for *difficult* specifies that it is to be introduced in base structures with a sentential subject of which it is predicated. Here Chomsky crucially assumed that the transformations that apply to the structures underlying sentences like *To please John is difficult* to yield sentences like *John is difficult to please* do not apply within noun phrases; if they do not, then the nonoccurrence of **John's difficulty to please* is explained.

As McCawley (1975a: 15; see also Newmeyer 1971) later pointed out, however, it is not so much Chomsky's lexicalist hypothesis as the presumed domain of application of the transformational rules involved which have these implications. The question then is whether a transformational version, *mutatis mutandis*, would have more explanatory value than the lexicalist version. Chomsky concluded that no transformational version would fall out as naturally and hence that the transformational approach had been refuted. But he had not in fact shown this. And even if he had been able to demonstrate that the lexicalist version was less stipulative, that would hardly suffice to *refute* the transformational approach unless he could show that, *all things considered*, a lexicalist theory was inevitably more economical than a transformational one.

As to Chomsky's claim concerning the semantic idiosyncracy of derived nominals, it appears true that the semantic relationship they bear to their respective verbal analogues is not as straightforward as an unqualified transformational analysis of them would predict; but it appears equally true that that relationship is not random, as an unqualified lexical analysis of them would predict (see Newmeyer 1971: 791, 1980: 119, 1986: 110, McCawley 1975a: 18–19). The conclusion Chomsky drew that the idiosyncracy he observed strongly favors a lexical approach could only have been warranted if that approach brought with it a better hypothesis to explain the relationships that in fact obtain. No such hypothesis was offered, however.

Chomsky's third argument – that a lexical approach to derived nominals is supported by the fact that they have the internal structure of noun phrases – actually pointed to a larger problem for all transformational grammars: how are limitations on what surface structures are possible best expressed? The fact that adjectival modifiers can appear before derived nominals (*John's unmotivated criticism of the book*) but not before gerundive nominals (**John's unmotivated criticizing the book*) indicated differences in structure which the lexicalist approach appropriately captured. The natural (and essentially equivalent) solution from a Generative Semantics perspective would have been to assume a set of surface conditions to which the outputs of the transformational rules must ultimately conform (McCawley 1980, 1982, 1988).[22] However, the assumption that Generative Semanticists

29

made at the time of "Remarks" that allowed them to dismiss Chomsky's argument was that the sentential constituent that is subject to the nominalization transformation that yields derived nominals is the complement of a dummy noun in underlying structure and that together they constitute a noun phrase (see, e.g. E. Bach 1968, McCawley 1975a: 22). Generative Semanticists never satisfactorily worked out the details that would turn such an assumption into a persuasive solution, but there was evidence (e.g. the paraphrase relation between *John's refusal* and *the fact that John refused*, see Newmeyer 1980: 119, 1986: 110) that spoke in its favor.[23] Thus, as much as Chomsky had provided some good reasons in his paper for taking a lexicalist approach seriously, he had not succeeded in showing the Generative Semanticists (and/or those who might have been tempted to follow them) that the lexical approach necessarily improved on the transformational approach.

In fact, while "Remarks" had demonstrated that there were problems with the rather simplistic transformational accounts that he had considered, that paper had not so much solved those problems as pushed them under the rug. In a way that many saw as a step backward, Chomsky was now arguing that the kind of abstract analysis employed so compellingly in *The Sound Pattern of English* (Chomsky and Halle 1968) to explain the phonological and morphological regularities to be found in relationships between verbs and their corresponding derived nominals could not be extended to explain the syntactic and semantic regularities.[24]

Looking back now, it is difficult to see that the dispute over nominalizations proved anything about the truth value of the central propositions of the two research programs. In the first place, the proposals on both sides were so programmatic that it was not at all clear at the time that a reasonably coherent mechanism could be worked out by either. Subsequent work (e.g. Binnick 1970, Ross 1973, and Levi 1975 on the one hand, and Aronoff 1974, Siegel 1974, and Selkirk 1982 on the other) showed that both approaches were capable of interesting development, but did not resolve the matter. In the second place, whether lexical items are inserted all at once at the deepest underlying level, or may be inserted at more superficial levels is an issue that turned out to have few ramifications for the rest of the grammar. One might be an Interpretivist in respect of holding that there is a level of deep structure and at the same time seek to show that lexical relations of the sort at issue can be transformationally described; in fact, some recent work within the Interpretivist tradition has taken just this approach (e.g. Hale and Keyser 1987, M. Baker 1988, Lieber 1992).

While "Remarks" had not addressed the three core propositions (i.e. core propositions (3–5) in (2) above) that McCawley had proposed for the Generative Semantics program, it did set the stage for a more direct challenge. In correspondence with McCawley during 1967–8 and in his paper "Deep structure, surface structure, and semantic interpretation," written in 1968 and published in 1971, Chomsky argued that Generative Semantics as conceived by McCawley was "untenable" and "just plain wrong" and he offered what he characterized as a "definitive disproof" of it. Underscoring the standard objections to a logic-based semantics for grammar, Chomsky noted that "60 years of research appear to have shown that language can't be paraphrased" in first-order predicate calculus or some extensional logic.[25] More importantly, it is, he observed, well known that substitution – even substitution of synonyms – cannot be carried out in intensional contexts in such a way as to preserve truth conditions. For example,

> consider the context: (1) "everyone realizes that $4 =$ __." If we sub-
> stitute "four," (1) becomes true. If we substitute "the only natural
> number between three and the square root of twenty-five," (1) becomes
> false. Therefore, [the two alternatives] are not mutually deducible;
> they must have different meanings . . . . The fact is that referentially
> opaque contexts have the property that truth or falsity (hence,
> obviously, meaning) depends not only on intrinsic semantic content,
> but also on the form in which a belief or a concept is expressed,
> hence ultimately on surface structure. This observation seems to me
> to destroy the possibility of Generative Semantics.
>
> (p.c. to J. McCawley, 20 December 1967;
> see also Chomsky 1971: 197)

In a reply to Chomsky, written in January 1968, McCawley noted that although standard first order predicate logics may not suffice as the language of semantic interpretation, this did not mean that *no* predicate logics would. Thus, while Chomsky's objection did oblige McCawley to show how a working logical system might be developed that would avoid the usual criticisms (an obligation McCawley was not really able to repay for some years), McCawley did make clear that Chomsky had not demonstrated an insufficiency *in principle* of his theory.

With regard to Chomsky's "definitive disproof," McCawley wrote that it

> depends on the proposition that "four" and "the only natural number
> between three and the square root of twenty-five" have the same
> semantic representations, which I deny. The fact that a mathemati-
> cian can prove that those two expressions correspond to the same
> number is irrelevant here . . . .
>
> (p.c. to N. Chomsky, 18 January 1968;
> see also McCawley 1975a: 43–6)

Later on, McCawley argued (1975a: 45) that, even if deductive equivalents could be found that have different surface structures but the same semantic representation and which do not substitute for each other in intensional contexts, "it is not obvious that that would show any linguistic

31

theory to be inadequate," since what is important is how the predicate *realize* is interpreted: if it is taken to denote a relationship between an individual and a paired surface structure–semantic representation, then, as he noted, there would be no inconsistency in his position (see also G. Lakoff 1971: 282, Mufwene 1977).[26]

McCawley's response to Chomsky's objection in fact raised an important question: if deductive equivalents need not all have the same semantic representations, then which paraphrases should be transformationally related? Chomsky's position precluded the possibility of independent inferential rules of semantic equivalence apart from the system of rules that relate surface structures and semantic representations; he maintained (in Chomsky 1971: 197), for example, that "If the concept of 'semantic representation' ('reading') is to play any role at all in linguistic theory then [phrases like *John's uncle* and *the person who is the brother of John's mother or father or the husband of the sister of John's father or mother*] must have the same semantic representation." Moreover, it was generally assumed that Generative Semanticists were committed to exactly that position by the third Katz–Fodor criterion of adequacy for a semantic level ("[interpretations] must suitably relate sentences speakers know to be paraphrases of each other").[27] Supporting this assumption was the perception that they had elevated to an inviolable principle of theory construction the following methodological strategy suggested by Katz and Postal (1964: 157):

> given a sentence for which a syntactic derivation is needed, look for simple paraphrases of the sentence which are not paraphrases by virtue of synonymous expressions; on finding them, construct grammatical rules that relate the original sentence and its paraphrases in such a way that each of these sentences has the same set of underlying P-markers.

But, as McCawley (1970b) pointed out, the view that deductively equivalent sentences must have the same semantic representation was beset by serious problems (see also Shopen 1972). In the first place, distinct self-contradictory sentences have the same truth conditions but may clearly differ in meaning. For example, *Any girl who has five brothers is an only child* and *All triangles have two edges and five vertices* are both always false although, crucially, for different reasons. Similarly, a sentence like *Everyone loves everyone* may plausibly be given either of two mutually entailing representations, (a) *Every one$_x$, Every one$_y$ (loves x,y)* or (b) *Every one$_y$, Every one$_x$ (loves x,y)*; however, a counterexample to the (a) case would be someone who does not love everyone, while a counterexample to the (b) case would be someone whom not everyone loves. Even though the existence of one of these two persons entails the existence of the other, the fact that they are distinct suggests that there are aspects of the meaning of *Everyone loves everyone* that are not covered by its truth conditions. This may perhaps be made clearer when such a sentence is embedded in an intensional context: one could evidently realize that it is false that everyone here loves everyone without realizing that it is also false that everyone here is loved by everyone. McCawley therefore concluded that two supposedly different meanings should be considered the same only if substituting one for the other in a larger semantic representation preserves the truth value of the entire structure.[28] Hence, on this view, inferential rules would be required to relate distinct but deductively equivalent semantic representations at the semantic level. The consequences of these divergent approaches were largely unexplored at the time.[29]

In discussing this issue, Chomsky never made fully clear exactly what role he imagined for a level of semantic representation in linguistic theory. In *Syntactic Structures*, he had indicated his attraction to the so-called "use" theory of meaning, according to which the meaning of a sentence is determined by how it is used (1957a: 102). But he had also suggested he supported a referential account of meaning, in which "the notion of meaning of words can at least in part be reduced to that of reference of expressions containing these words" (Chomsky 1957a: 103). Precisely how a level of semantic representation would work in either of the theories was unaddressed. Subsequently, however, he argued against particularly broad realizations of such a level, as when he attacked the semantic project of Jerrold Katz:

> Why, then, raise a question about the possibility of a universal seman-
> tics, which would provide an exact representation of the full meaning
> of each lexical item, and the meaning of expressions in which these
> items appear? There are, I believe, good reasons for being skeptical
> about such a program . . . . It seems that other cognitive systems – in
> particular, our system of beliefs concerning things in the world and
> their behavior – play an essential part in our judgments of meaning
> and reference, in an extremely intricate manner, and it is not at all
> clear that much will remain if we try to separate the purely linguistic
> components of . . . "the meaning of [a] linguistic expression." I doubt
> that one can separate semantic representation from belief and knowl-
> edge about the world.
>
> (Chomsky 1979: 142)

Elsewhere, Chomsky indicated no commitment to the existence of a level of semantic representation of any sort. On this view, his theory was not designed to relate representations of outer form to representations of inner form, that is, meaning. The structure that he was concerned with was just that structure which there was little reason to think is a reflection of anything logical or semantic:

If I am correct in claiming that one achieves little or nothing by establishing a notion of "reading" or "logical form" in a universal semantic alphabet, then the argument strikes particularly at Generative Semanticists, for if they are saying anything at all, it is that these "readings" are so fundamental that in fact they are in some sense the "basis" of all syntax: i.e. they constitute S[emantic] R[epresentation] = P1, ... , where P1 is the initial phrase-marker of all derivations. I make no such exalted claim, and in fact have often suggested that I may be quite wrong to set up such a notion of SR (I've vacillated on this issue). But suppose it is wrong. . . . . then we go back to a theory exactly like that of *Syntactic Structures*. That is, we study the grammatical mechanisms, and an ancillary theory studies how they are put to use. Or take [the Extended Standard Theory (EST)]. If it is wrong to set up a notion of SR (readings, etc.), then nothing changes in EST except that what I've called rules of interpretation of the pairs (S[urface] S[tructure], D[eep] S[tructure]) will be principles that determine how these pairs are used in speech acts, or whatever. On the other hand, Generative Semantics (insofar as it is not merely a notational variant of EST) must be abandoned entirely.

(p.c. to John Searle, 19 June 1972)

Thus, Chomsky was arguing that his theory was preferable to Generative Semantics because it did not rely on particular claims about the nature of semantic representation and would therefore be invulnerable to critiques of any kind concerning that level. But he had also argued that his theory was to be preferred over Generative Semantics because it made a strong claim about the existence of deep structure:

the only substantive issue – a real one, to be sure – is whether deep structure exists, i.e., whether lexical and nonlexical transformations can be segregated into two categories with no intersection of ordering. If not, Generative Semantics . . . is correct; if so, it is wrong. Thus [Generative Semantics] simply accepts the weaker hypothesis, the less preferable on general grounds, in this case.

(p.c. to John Searle, 19 June 1972; see also Chomsky 1972a)

Of course the Generative Semanticists could have formulated a parallel counterdefense: they had made a strong claim regarding the level of semantic representation, hence their theory would be preferable on general methodological grounds. Their skepticism concerning another level of representation – deep structure – would then be a point in their favor, since no critiques of that level could affect their general position.

Notwithstanding the position he had taken on this issue, Chomsky had at other times assumed that the overarching theory of generative grammar was essentially a mediational one, one which included both a level of semantic representation and a level of surface structure. Indeed, the

34

assumption of the existence of a level of semantic representation led to what was perhaps Chomsky's best-known criticism of Generative Semantics – that it was unconstrained. For example, in *Language and Responsibility* (1979), he made the following observation (p. 150; see also Chomsky 1972a, Jackendoff 1972, Katz and Bever 1976):

> Where then does the expression "Generative Semantics" come from? . . . . What the theory asserted was that there exist representations of meaning, representations of form, and relations between the two. Furthermore, these relations between the two representations were virtually arbitrary; Lakoff . . . proposed arbitrary derivational constraints – arbitrary rules in effect. If all that is put forward as a theory is that there exist relations between some kind of representations of meaning and of form, then it is difficult to argue against that.

The "derivational constraints" that Chomsky alluded to in this passage refer to a distinct kind of rule that Generative Semanticists had originally appealed to in order to account for the fact that some passive sentences containing quantifiers evidently differ in meaning from their active counterparts. For example, Chomsky (1957a: 100) had noted that the sentences *Everyone in the room knows two languages* and *Two languages are known by everyone in the room* are for many people not synonymous: the first sentence might be true and the second false when one person in the room knows only French and German and another knows only Spanish and Italian. Such sentence pairs seem to be prima-facie counterexamples to the Katz–Postal hypothesis that transformations like passive do not change meaning. Katz and Postal (1964: 72) argued, however, that the two sentences did not in fact differ in meaning but were both similarly ambiguous. As Lakoff (1971: 238–40) observed, the Generative Semantics analysis naturally predicted such an ambiguity. That is, the Generative Semantics account of the active sentence with the meaning that everyone knows two languages but not necessarily the same two languages would be to assign it an underlying structure with the quantifier *every* taking scope over *two*, while the passive sentence with the meaning that everyone knows the same two languages would be assigned an underlying structure with *two* taking scope over *every*. A rule of Quantifier Lowering would then move the quantifiers into construction with the appropriate noun phrases. But if the passive transformation preserves meaning, then it should be able to apply to the former underlying structure as well to produce a passive version of the sentence with the same meaning as the active. However, Lakoff noted that for him, as for Chomsky, the active and passive sentences are not synonymous.

Lakoff's solution was to propose a new sort of rule, which he called a *global derivational constraint*, which would not simply specify, as ordinary transformations do, how one step in a derivation may differ from an

immediately preceding step, but rather would specify limitations on how
any ensuing steps in a derivation (including surface structure) may differ
from any earlier steps (including underlying structure). In the particular
case at hand, for example, he proposed a constraint on derivations that
would insist that if one quantifier commands another at underlying
structure,[30] then it must either command or precede the other at all more
superficial levels. Such a constraint would rule out the derivation of *Two
languages are known by everyone in the room* from an underlying structure in
which *everyone* has *two* in its scope.

Given global rules of the sort that Lakoff proposed, one could effectively
show how deductive equivalents may differ in meaning, as McCawley had
earlier argued. That is, two sentences may be mutually entailing only in
virtue of having mutually entailing but distinct semantic representations,
rather than in virtue of sharing the same semantic representations directly
derived from their surface structures. In the case of pairs of sentences like
Many men read few books and *Few books are read by many men*, which for most
people are not mutually entailing, the global rule would make the correct
prediction about which interpretation would go with which surface structure.
There is, of course, a sense in which such a global solution was a concession
to Chomsky's claim that surface structure plays a role in semantic interpretation. But there is also a sense in which looking at global rules that way
involves the same sort of serious confusion that led to claims that falsification of the Katz–Postal hypothesis entailed falsification of a Generative
Semantics theory. If constructions in a derivation are viewed as purely
syntactic objects that are themselves subject to semantic interpretation,
then a claim that transformations do or do not preserve meaning has
content. But if the rules (global or local) that determine the steps in a
derivation are conceived of as relating surface structure and semantic
representation, then it makes little sense to ask whether those rules are
meaning-preserving.[31]

Chomsky's concern about adding global rules to the grammar proceeded from the importance he attached to finding theoretical solutions
that serve to limit the choices available to the language learner. From his
perspective, any mechanism that complicated those choices was to be
avoided unless demanded by empirical necessity; the point of linguistic
research was to locate the most restrictive theory of Universal Grammar –
that is, of what is given (or innate) in humans – consistent with the facts, so
that learning would be simplified. But a learner whose innate equipment
includes global rules in addition to phrase structure rules and local transformations would generally face more choices than would one who does
not have to worry about the complications global rules might introduce.
Hence, Chomsky concluded that Interpretive Semantics was a better
theory *in principle* than Generative Semantics.

Of course, if Generative Semanticists had said nothing other than that global rules were required in addition to all the other mechanisms of the *Aspects* theory simply to describe the distributional facts, then as Baker and Brame (1972) had argued, the burden of proof would have been on them to demonstrate that the *Aspects* mechanisms themselves would not suffice. And if it should then have turned out that such a demonstration was not forthcoming, then Chomsky's claim would have been correct, the *Aspects* theory would have been a special case of the Generative Semantics program. But Generative Semanticists rejected this claim for a number of reasons.

First, it was incorrect to suggest that no restrictions in principle were imposed, or could be imposed, on the form and function of global rules. The global mechanisms proposed by Generative Semanticists were no less subject to constraint than were local mechanisms (transformations) (see Parret 1974: 177, 268). Moreover, since the Generative Semanticists denied the existence of a level of deep structure separate from the level of semantic representation, surface structure was predicted to mirror logical structure in ways that would never "filter through" on an *Aspects* model.[32] Generative Semantics shared with Chomskyan grammar a conception of simplicity according to which the fewer rules a language had, and the fewer specifications each rule had, the easier it was to learn, and the more "natural" the grammar was. Hence all other things equal, the more surface structure looked like semantic representation, the more natural it was from the point of view of Generative Semantics. Since on Chomsky's account relations between deep structure and semantic representation were arbitrary *ex hypothesi*, his critique was from the Generative Semantics perspective more relevant to his own theory, where such a convergence would be unexplained.

But however Generative Semanticists conceived of global rules operating in the grammar, the real issue was whether they were empirically justifiable. Chomsky's claim had rested on the assumption that Generative Semantics and Interpretive Semantics were empirically comparable, but that assumption would have been difficult to defend. If nothing else, Chomsky's suggestion that underlying structure (= semantic representation) in Generative Semantics could be conceptually identified with the output of the base rules of the syntax (= deep structure) in Interpretive Semantics constituted a considerable distortion. It was uncontroversial that an Interpretive theory would have to be supplemented by a theory of semantic interpretation; but if that theory assumed (as in Chomsky 1971 and Jackendoff 1972) a level of semantic representation related to surface syntactic structure via semantic interpretation rules, then, as McCawley (1975a: 79) observed, semantic interpretation rules *are* global rules and the Generative Semantics theory of such rules offered the only reasonably precise account at the time of their interaction. Any critique of global rules as increasing the power of the theory was then equivalently a critique of semantic interpretation rules, although such critiques generally focused on comparisons between the full Generative Semantics grammar and the Interpretive Semantics syntax.

For example, the "Modal Projection Rule" that Jackendoff (1972: 293) proposed in place of Lakoff's global rule in effect did just what that global rule did (as Jackendoff (1972: 336) himself recognized): it showed how the position in surface structure of a quantifier or a negative operator is to be related to its position at the level of semantic representation. He offered no restrictions on the operation of rules like the Modal Projection Rule that would distinguish them from global rules, although he did propose other restrictions that would limit the class of theories of *syntax* available for inclusion in a grammar.

Nevertheless, Jackendoff (1972: 336) claimed that his Interpretivist treatment employing the Modal Projection Rule was superior to the Generative Semantics treatment employing a global rule for three reasons. First, he contended that Lakoff's global rule was simply a filter on transformations, whereas on his approach, "the generalization follows as a direct result of the rules of interpretation, with no added machinery." Second, he offered empirical evidence that the theory of quantification he assumed Lakoff to have been using was inadequate. And third, he repeated Chomsky's argument that "the concept of derivational constraint is so general as to lead to an extremely unrestricted class of possible grammars, in conflict with our goal of constraining linguistic theory."

Much in Jackendoff's analysis was original and important, but none of his arguments supported the superiority of any research program over another. The first and third arguments only drew their force from comparing an Interpretive Semantics theory without semantic interpretation to a Generative Semantics theory with semantic interpretation. If the global rule was *ad hoc* "added machinery," then so equally was the Modal Projection Rule; and if global rules increased the power of the theory, then so did semantic interpretation rules like the Modal Projection Rule. Finally, although the second argument did provide an authentic empirical challenge to Generative Semantics, Jackendoff had not demonstrated that the core ideas of that theory were such that no acceptable solution would likely be consistent with them. In fact, this challenge could be answered within the Generative Semantics program in a straightforward way.[33]

Subsequent studies in the tradition of Jackendoff's work either have assumed something like the Modal Projection Rule (e.g. Reinhart 1976: 191, 1983: 188) or have reverted to Katz and Postal's original assumption that multiply quantified sentences are ambiguous (May 1977: 39, 1985: 14, Hornstein 1984: 20, Higginbotham 1985: 579).[34] In the latter case, some other explanation is required for the lack of ambiguity many people detect in such sentences in neutral contexts; for example, May (1985: 14) has suggested that preference of interpretation "is a matter that goes beyond grammar per se, taking into account various properties of discourse, shared knowledge of the interlocutors, plausibility of description, etc."[35]

More recently, McCawley (1988: 620–3; see also Kuno 1971 and Ioup 1975) has pointed out that a variety of factors can affect how easily scope ambiguities are perceived in multiply quantified sentences, which can be summarized as follows: (a) when one of the quantifiers in a multiply quantified sentence is negative (*no, few, not many*), it is extremely difficult or impossible to interpret the quantifiers as having "reversed scopes"; for example, in *Many men read few books*, *few* can only have narrow scope; (b) there is a tendency to assign a quantifier on the surface subject higher scope than a quantifier in the verb phrase, especially if the verb of the verb phrase exhibits agreement with the subject; (c) certain factors can override (b), for example, *each* seems to demand wide scope no matter where it is placed (*Two secretaries assist each executive* = for each executive, there are two secretaries who assist him or her). But however this is resolved, it would be quite incorrect to assert that the Interpretivist approach to scope ambiguities provided a satisfactory account of the data that involved a more restricted grammar than that proposed by the Generative Semanticists. Even if an extragrammatical theory were ultimately to be developed that successfully accounted for the data, it would be as congenial to a Generative Semantics approach as to an Interpretive Semantics approach, that is, it would simply reinforce the position originally taken by Katz and Postal and obviate the need for a global solution. In fact, there was a natural distinction from the Generative Semantics perspective to be made between global rules considered as direct relations between surface structure and semantic representation and global rules considered as filters on derivations. The latter, like other purely syntactic constraints, represented generalizations about distributions which begged explanation. Lakoff's generalization, as modified by the facts McCawley noted, has remained in this sense relatively robust.

Chomsky's argument against Generative Semantics on the basis of its tolerance of global rules, though vulnerable in the respect just discussed, was broadened to include a number of the other devices associated with the latter theory, most notably those called transderivational constraints (Gordon and Lakoff 1971, G. Lakoff 1971). Such constraints drew on information about one derivation to affect another, hence adding considerable power to the theory. But even with such devices, it is not at all clear that Generative Semantics would have been any less constrained than Interpretive Semantics if the latter had made precise proposals to handle the range of data that the Generative Semantics devices were designed to account for. And where restrictive solutions could be found, they were generally not *ipso facto* incompatible with a Generative Semantics perspective.

For example, the Interpretive Semanticists' critique of lexical decomposition

(Chomsky 1970, 1972a, J. A. Fodor 1970) was interpreted by them as being conclusive (see especially Chomsky 1972a: 150, 1975a: 106), but it left them with no formal mechanism for capturing certain regularities that the Generative Semanticists had observed. Thus, Chomsky's response to Morgan's (1969) observation that the sentence *I almost killed John* is ambiguous in a way that suggests adverbs can modify parts of the meaning of verbs was to "speculate that this is a universal characteristic of such verbs, and hence not to be described in a particular grammar" (Chomsky 1972a: 150). But since Interpretivists had no theory (nondecompositional or otherwise) of the "universal characteristics" of verbs like *kill* which would account for the ambiguity Morgan noticed, the rejection of the Generative Semantics explanation had the effect of reducing the domain of data for which reasonably well-articulated accounts might be given.[36]

It may well have been, as Sadock (1975) argued, that what could be done with abstract deep structures and global rules could equally well be done with less abstract structures and transderivational constraints, or, as Green (1974a) and Bever (1974) suggested, that what could be done with either could be done with a system that simply associates pragmatic interpretations with surface structures in some perhaps less formal way. But accounts employing one or another of these devices were the only relatively concrete accounts available at the time for a variety of facts, including those grouped under the rubrics of Main Clause Phenomena in subordinate clauses (Hooper and Thompson 1973, Green 1974a, 1976), syntactic amalgams (G. Lakoff 1974), whimperatives and queclaratives (Sadock 1970, 1971), and so on.

Nor is it the case that Interpretive Semanticists entirely avoided employing these devices themselves: for example, Chomsky (1970) admitted the possibility of something like transderivational constraints (under the name of "analogical rules") elsewhere in the grammar, as McCawley (1975a) pointed out, and J. A. Fodor's (1970: 438) nondecompositional solution to the fact that *do so* in *Floyd melted the glass although it surprised me that it would do so* can refer to an intransitive form of the verb *melt* not explicitly present in the surface structure of the sentence containing it was to propose a transderivational relationship with a structure in which that form of the verb is present. Fodor admitted that "how one goes about saying [this] in the framework of generative syntax is a problem I don't know how to solve," but in more recent years some Interpretively-oriented theorists have attempted to specify such regularities in the lexicon via transformations, much as the Generative Semanticists did (see Hale and Keyser 1987 and M. Baker 1988, for example).[37]

While the Interpretivist approach has of course been successful in focusing attention on restrictive syntactic solutions, it needs to be emphasized that Generative Semanticists were not committed to increasing the power of the grammar so much as they were interested in providing explicit accounts of the syntactic and semantic facts, wherever those accounts happened to lead. From a Generative Semantics perspective, a more restrictive solution was, all things equal,[38] better than a less restrictive one; but a less restrictive one was better than none at all.

THE AMBIVALENCE OF EMPIRICAL ISSUES

The Generative Semanticists had, by the mid-1970s, analyzed within the bounds of their theory a considerable variety of facts for which Interpretive Semanticists had no plausible account. Generative Semanticists were naturally inclined to consider this as evidence in favor of their approach as against Interpretivist approaches. The Interpretivists' response, as Newmeyer (1980: 168, 1986: 133) notes, was in general to disparage these facts as falling outside of the domain of grammar and thus as being of no importance to a grammatical description (see especially Katz and Bever 1976). For example, according to Bever (1974: 190), "Derivational and transderivational constraints are not grammatical formalisms. The acceptability facts they are invoked to describe are naturally predicted by the theory of speech perception or speech production or one of the other systems of linguistic skill and knowledge."

This methodology placed the defenders of Interpretive Semantics and its successors on the horns of an uncomfortable dilemma, one from which they have never succeeded in fully extracating themselves. What, after all, was the basis of the move to exclude any given set of recalcitrant data? If it were based on purely distributional grounds, then it was hardly a defensible position that a distributional analysis could clearly demarcate a class of phenomena that it could not then analyze. On the other hand, if the recalcitrant data could be identified and classified only once reference to meaning was invoked, then the distributionalist enterprise would be shown to have flawed underpinnings. Any other move would surely be subject to charges of circularity, so long as there were no independent methodological criteria for determining extragrammaticality.[39] As Langendoen (1976: 691) notes, the "narrow scope" view that there may be legitimate differences between the systematic distributions predicted by an optimal grammar and those actually observed reduces to an absurdity *unless* "the proponent of the narrow scope position is prepared to explain how such systematic differences arise."[40]

Consider, for example, Koster's (1978: 568) defense of Emonds's (1970, 1976) claim that Topicalization is possible only in "root" or main clauses.[41] Koster argued that the acceptability of a sentence like *The inspector explained that each part he had examined very carefully* (from Hooper and Thompson 1973: 474) does not stand as a counterexample to Emonds's claim because such sentences may be accounted for by extragrammatical principles (see also Emonds 1976: 35). But Koster produced no such principles for inspection, and without such principles his argument clearly could not be taken as supporting Emonds's analysis.

It is undoubtedly true, as Chomsky has sometimes pointed out (see, e.g. Chomsky 1977b: 4), that it is only in the light of a particular theory that any phenomenon can be interpreted. And Interpretivists had every reason to withhold judgment concerning Hooper and Thompson's examples. However, anyone who, in order to defend himself from counterexamples, invokes extragrammaticality without a theory of it is not in a secure position from which to attack a competing theory for purported empirical failures.

Moreover, it had been the Interpretivists' stance on extragrammaticality that had allowed them to maintain their criticism of Generative Semantics as being unconstrained at the same time as they themselves restricted the types of facts for which they were willing to offer an explanation. In his article, "The best theory" (1972), Postal had argued that, other things equal, Generative Semantics, with a single system of rules relating semantic representation and surface structure, should be considered a conceptual improvement over theories like Interpretive Semantics, which postulated two types of rules, transformations and semantic interpretation rules, for the same purpose. Chomsky (1972a) criticized this argument as follows:

> If enrichment of theoretical apparatus and elaboration of the conceptual structure will restrict the class of possible grammars and the class of sets of derivations generated by admissible grammars, then it will be a step forward (*assuming it to be consistent with the requirement of descriptive adequacy*). It is quite true that the burden of proof is on the person who makes some specific proposal to enrich and complicate the theoretical apparatus. One who takes the more 'conservative' stance, maintaining only that a grammar is a set of conditions on derivations, has no burden of proof to bear because he is saying virtually nothing.
>
> (Chomsky 1972a: 68, emphasis added)

Chomsky's focus during this period was on trying to develop a linguistic theory which offered a relatively small number of grammars consistent with a modest range of facts from a given language. Postal, along with the other Generative Semanticists, was concerned that linguists must work hard to develop linguistic theory so that it would be rich enough to provide even *one* grammar consistent with the facts we know of English. But these goals were complementary rather than contradictory. For both Chomsky and Postal, the ultimate purpose of doing linguistics was to make progress in the search for the most economical and compact theory of grammar that accounts for all the facts of all the languages.[42]

In the absence of an articulated theory of extragrammaticality, arguments like those of Katz and Bever, and Koster in fact threatened to detach Late

42

Interpretivism (see the summary in (4)) from the empirical base to which its predecessors had been anchored. As the residue of performance facts unaccounted for by the theory of competence was allowed to grow,[43] Late Interpretivism was increasingly vulnerable to the charge of having rejected the goal of explaining the kinds of distributional patterns found in introspective data that its predecessor distributionalist theories were concerned with. But if Late Interpretivism could no longer subscribe to the mediational and distributional orientations of the *Aspects* program, then it was in danger of becoming a theory without any concrete linguistic phenomena for it to be a theory of. It was perhaps the perception of this danger that led Late Interpretivists to try to recast the principal core propositions of the moribund Generative Semantics movement in terms that they could accept.

(4) The Late Interpretivist program
     Orientation   Core
     1 Psychological   1 Grammatical principles can be distinguished
                              from extragrammatical principles.
                          2 The distribution of linguistic elements is
                              determined by both grammatical principles
                              and extragrammatical principles.
                          3 The formal (phonological, syntactic) part of the
                              grammar is autonomous from the semantic
                              part.
                          4 Structural differences among the grammatical
                              sentences of a language can be accounted for
                              by a set of phrase structure rules and the
                              transformations that apply to them.
                          5 The principles of Universal Grammar are
                              innately specified.

THE CONVERGENCE OF MEDIATIONALISM AND DISTRIBUTIONALISM

Despite the evident differences between the Generative Semanticists and the Interpretive Semanticists over the interpretation of deep structure, there had always been potential for reconciliation. If, as George Lakoff put it, "the rules determining which sentences are grammatical and which ungrammatical are not distinct from the rules relating logical forms and surface forms" (G. Lakoff 1972: 551), then the distributionalist and mediationalist research programs should at least be compatible. This hypothesis – which we will refer to as the *Synthetic Conjecture* – admits of at least two interpretations. On the strong interpretation, a rule or principle serves the mediationalist goal if and only if it serves the distributionalist goal as well;

but if this is so, then the distributionalist and mediationalist programs should ultimately produce identical results. By contrast, on the weak interpretation – which Lakoff himself appeared to endorse at the time – there need only be some overlap between the results, and hence an autonomous syntactic component might still be retained, albeit one which did not account for all of the distributional facts of a language.[44] Of course, such an interpretation would also be consistent with the goal Chomsky had originally set for the *LSLT* program of providing a logical basis for grammar that would at the same time contribute to an account of how the sentences of a language are understood.

Ironically, the moves Interpretive Semanticists made in the late 1960s and early 1970s in reaction against the very idea of a Generative Semantics program prepared the way for them to adopt a stronger version of the Synthetic Conjecture and thus to accept some of the individual propositions for which Generative Semanticists had been arguing. As against the Generative Semanticist's reliance on the Katz–Postal hypothesis that transformations do not change meaning, Interpretivists had early on insisted that aspects of surface structure are necessary for the determination of semantic interpretation. The elaboration of this position resulted in a theory in which semantic interpretation was distributed over a derivation. However, the advent of the theory of traces (Chomsky 1973, 1975b, for example) permitted Interpretivists to say that semantic interpretation rules operated on surface structures only – that is, it straightforwardly gave them "a theory of semantic interpretation of surface structure" (Chomsky 1975b: 95). The important observation that led to this semantic theory was that the relation between the *wh*-word and its trace in the surface structure of a sentence like *The police know who the FBI discovered that Bill shot* closely resembles the relation between the quantifier meaning "for which person *x*" and the variable *x* it binds in a possible semantic interpretation of that sentence. Thus, to convert a surface structure enriched with traces to a "logical form" (or "LF"), "all that is required is the information that *who* is a quantifier binding [*x*] and meaning 'for which person [*x*]'" (Chomsky 1975b: 94). By taking this step, Chomsky noted, it became possible to "unify a considerable amount of quite fruitful research of the past few years" involving "scope of quantifiers and logical particles, anaphora, presupposition, and the like" (Chomsky 1975b: 116).

Chomsky has offered various conjectures regarding what the level at which LFs appear (itself also usually called "LF") represents: (i) in Chomsky (1975b: 95), LF was clearly meant to provide a "representation of meaning," though one that is circumscribed; (ii) Chomsky (1976) suggested that LF "incorporates whatever features of sentence structure (1) enter directly into semantic interpretation of sentences and (2) are strictly determined by properties of (sentence-)grammar." There he also allowed for the possibility that representations at LF may "suffice to determine role in inference, conditions of appropriate use, etc."; and (iii) in Chomsky (1977b: 71), LF had become "the level that expresses whatever aspects of semantic representation are determined by properties of sentence-grammar."[45]

Chomsky's acceptance of a level of LF in his theory of grammar not only served to answer the charges by Generative Semanticists that he had been insufficiently specific about what semantic representations were and how they were to be arrived at (see especially McCawley 1975a: 78), but it also demonstrated that the domain of data which Generative Semanticists had argued should be considered grammatical would not be entirely ignored in the evolving Interpretive theory. In fact, even though Chomsky has always attempted to put some distance between his conception of LF and standard logical notations, by the late 1970s that conception began to bear an unmistakable likeness to the semantic representations that McCawley had earlier argued for. In particular, representations at the level of LF (a) could be conceived of as labeled trees and (b) explicitly expressed predicate–argument, anaphor–antecedent, and quantifier scope relations, in accord with the third and fourth core propositions of the Generative Semantics program (see (2) above).

If the representations of LF were labeled trees which differed structurally from the representations of surface structure to which they were related primarily to the extent that an expression A in surface structure that was interpreted as having scope over another expression B was realized in LF as commanding B (Reinhart 1976, 1983, May 1977, 1983), then LFs might be derived from surface structures via simple movement, indeed, via transformation, as in Generative Semantics. Although Chomsky at this time explicitly expressed reservations concerning whether the semantic interpretation rules relating surface structure and LF were subject to the same restrictions as transformations relating deep structure and surface structure (Chomsky 1977b, 1981), there ended up being very little conceptual difference between the Generative Semantics rule of Quantifier Lowering (G. Lakoff 1971, McCawley 1973a) and, for example, Robert May's (1977, 1985) "Quantifier Rule," which had closely related syntactic and semantic effects.[46] Moreover, Chomsky's position in this regard reflected a significant shift away from a position earlier taken by Jackendoff (1972: 292) in which the scope of a quantifier at the level of semantic representation could not be uniquely determined from its structural position at any level.

This shift evidently accompanied a shift in the implications of the thesis of the autonomy of syntax. As shown in note 15, by 1975 Chomsky was willing to entertain the possibility that the hypothesis holds only conditionally and that meaning may enter into grammar through the lexicon. In one sense, it could be argued that this technical refinement embodied no essential change in the autonomy hypothesis, since phonology and syntax excluding the lexicon still required analysis in formal terms that would not be defined using the concepts of semantics. But in another sense, the weakening of the hypothesis reflected a considerable transformation of attitude toward semantic study, which, it was now being suggested, might bear upon syntactic study in importantly new ways. Moreover, the adoption of the level of LF and of rules relating that level to surface structure made it possible to define certain semantic notions like scope ambiguity structurally and therefore to expand significantly the domain of facts for which a structural account could be given.

Since Generative Semanticists themselves had in general subscribed to a methodological principle that sought formal definitions for semantic properties that played a role in grammar, the division between them and the Interpretivists on autonomy had been narrowed virtually to the point where they could be seen to be occupying the same ground. What remained for Interpretivists was to interpret autonomy as a statement of conviction about the value of research on traditional semantic issues in a program with chiefly distributionalist goals: according to this view, which we might call the *neoautonomist* view, studying relations between form and meaning may have a role in extending the explanatory domain of the theory (say, through the lexicon), but such study should not be expected to lead to any simplifications in the grammar. The opposing view, which Generative Semanticists clearly had held, was that studying distributions without paying attention to meaning, intention, and context could lead to spurious generalizations and would fail to illuminate the mechanisms that were driving the distributions.

Despite various contributions to it in the 1970s and thereafter, opposition to the neoautonomist position was effectively marginalized, in part as a consequence of the demise of the Generative Semantics program and in part as a consequence of the general acceptance of the Late Interpretivist approach to extragrammaticality. Nor was the defense assisted by the difficulty of determining exactly what motivates speakers. To take one example among many, Green (1974a, building on Hooper and Thompson 1973) attempted to demonstrate that the speaker's attitude toward what he or she says is significant in determining the distribution of outputs of the rule of Adjective Phrase Preposing (APP), another rule that, according to the scheme of Emonds (1976), would have to be classified as a "root" transformation and which would therefore be predicted to apply only in main clauses. Green pointed to the acceptability of sentences like *I think that very important to the Japanése is the amount of mercury being pumped into their bays*, which show that APP applies in some subordinate clauses. Her hypothesis was that APP serves the function of making a sentence more emphatic, and if *I think* is used parenthetically, then "the sentence is still a fairly strong statement about the Japanese, and it is appropriate to use the emphatic device of [APP]." She proceeded to note that if *think* is stressed instead of *Japanese*, acceptability declines significantly, since now the sentence becomes "a statement about the speaker's uncertainty regarding the embedded proposition." But if *I* is stressed and *think* destressed, accept-ability improves, since the sentence in this form "emphasizes the strength of [the speaker's] agreement with the content of the complement clause."

While Interpretivists were in fact concerned with Hooper and Thompson's original demonstration that some root transformations appear to apply in subordinate clauses (also demonstrated independently by Langendoen 1973), when they were not invoking extragrammaticality their responses were largely confined to arguments that the relevant transformations are not root transformations but are structure-preserving (Bowers 1976; see also Iwakura 1978 and Langendoen's (1979) response), or that even if the Hooper–Thompson data are correct there is different evidence that suggests something like the root constraint holds in other cases (Goldsmith 1978, 1981). But such arguments did not explain the alternation with stressed and unstressed *think*, which remains problematical for the root hypothesis.

Whereas between 1967 and about 1971 Interpretivists had been eager to reply to every new Generative Semantics charge, within a few years they had begun systematically to ignore new work in the Generative Semantics tradi-tion, just as Generative Semanticists had by and large ceased paying attention to developments in trace theory.[47] It should then not be surprising that Green's paper did not play any significant role in discussions of Emonds's structure-preserving constraint that followed publication of his book.[48] But some of the work that other Generative Semanticists – and McCawley in particular – were engaged in during this period bore directly on the Interpre-tivist arguments against Generative Semantics offered earlier in the decade.

For example, J. A. Fodor's famous argument (1970) against deriving *kill* from *cause to die* rested heavily on the observation that a sentence like *John killed Bill on Sunday by stabbing him on Saturday* is odd, but becomes accept-able if . . . *caused Bill to die* . . . is substituted for . . . *killed Bill* . . . (see also Katz 1970). Fodor concluded from this that the meaning of *kill* is not the same as the meaning of *cause to die* and therefore that the one should not be derived from an underlying representation of the other. McCawley (1978), however, suggested that the meaning difference could be directly accounted for by systematic pragmatic principles, in particular by Grice's (1975) maxim of manner. His claim was that while lexical causatives like *kill* are assumed to have meanings restricted to direct causation, paraphrastic causatives are neutral with regard to directness of causation.[49] Thus, if one uses a longer paraphrastic causative when a shorter lexical causative is also available, one implicates indirect causation even if that is not strictly speaking part of the meaning of that construction, else why would one expend the extra effort involved in using it? In support of this claim, McCawley cited evidence from Heringer (1976) which suggests that a paraphrastic causative can be used to convey direct causation just in case there is no lexical causative available for use in its place (cf. *Bill made Mary laugh/lose her balance*).

47

Much of the work of McCawley during the 1970s which culminated in his 1981 book on logic can be read as an extended reply to Interpretivist criticism (and in particular to the criticisms in Chomsky 1972b), but neither he nor his colleagues ever really engaged with a central issue raised by the neoautonomist critique: granting, as the Generative Semanticists generally did, that there must be room in the grammar for at least some autonomous syntactic rules and constraints, what principled basis is there for drawing the line, that is, for attributing some phenomenon to such rules and constraints, *except* by testing an empirical theory of them? In other words, once some autonomous syntactic principles are admitted, what *a priori* differences remain between a Generative Semantics perspective and an Interpretive Semantics perspective?

Although Generative Semanticists had in general attempted to be quite explicit about the relations between semantic representation and surface structure, they were considerably less specific (or, at any rate, considerably less in agreement) about the nature of any independent conditions on surface structure. Generative Semanticists of course denied that all of the facts that Interpretivists had arrayed required treatment in such a theory of independent surface conditions. But they did not deny that there were grounds on which a surface theory could be motivated (see, e.g. Ross 1967b, Postal 1971, McCawley 1982, 1988). Similarly, the Interpretivists denied that all of the facts that the Generative Semanticists had arrayed required treatment in their surface theory, while agreeing that semantic and pragmatic theories, or theories of performance, would be required to accommodate many of them. It is then not difficult to see why, as attempts were made to deal with expanded sets of data, the members of two research programs found each other's solutions worth exploiting. Indeed, to the extent that they shared assumptions about the elements of syntax (phrase markers, transformations, and so on) and that they agreed that a grammatical theory should have both mediationalist and distributionalist goals, these developments appear to have been quite natural.

The anomalous nature of surface structure – or, rather, the lack of a simple set of principles that would systematically determine the fit between surface structure and semantic representation – was always a problem for Generative Semanticists,[50] and the seriousness and centrality of this problem was reflected in the titles of the published versions of two theses that could be said with some justification to have marked the opening and the closing of the Generative Semantics era, George Lakoff's *Irregularity in Syntax* (1970 [1965]) and Georgia Green's *Semantics and Syntactic Regularity* (1974b [1971]). Whatever the names they went by – rule exceptions, output conditions, target structures, conspiracies, global derivational constraints, surface combinatorics – independent restrictions on surface structure were regularly invoked by Generative Semanticists in an attempt to deal with the residue of facts that were not explained by the rules designed to account for semantic phenomena, and in particular by the rules designed to relate synonymous expressions.

Lakoff's thesis had concerned itself with how irregularities should be handled in a grammar, that is, how exceptions to the linguist's generalizations should themselves be accounted for, if not simply by stipulation. For example, in English there is a general rule whereby a tense vowel becomes laxed before final *-ity*. This rule is responsible for the vowel alternations in *obscene/obscenity, vain/vanity, divine/divinity,* and so forth. But, as is also well known, the pair *obese/obesity* is an exception to this rule. Lakoff's project was to consider parallel cases in morphology and syntax and to provide a general account of them. His primary strategy was to extend the notion of "rule feature" from Chomsky and Halle (1968) to the syntax. In particular, he argued that a lexical item specified in the structural description of a syntactic rule (i.e. an item that could be said to "govern" that rule) could be marked so that structures in which it was embedded which otherwise met the structural description of the rule would be either required or permitted or forbidden (as the case may be) to undergo it. What was significant about this proposal was that it not only allowed the generalization to be retained in the unmarked cases, but also demonstrated how the marked exceptions might be generalized over as well.

However, if the set of governors for a particular rule could be seen to constitute a semantically coherent class, then there might be some hope of specifying a coherent set of semantic conditions on the application of the rule, rather than independently marking each governor as an exception. Developing this idea, Robin Lakoff (1968) proposed that the grammar incorporate lexical redundancy rules that would automatically mark verbs of certain semantic classes as rule governors of certain types; for example, "the semantic markers that define verbs of ordering will function syntactically in a redundancy rule specifying that, for this semantic class, one or more of the complementizer-changing rules must apply" (1968: 165). This proposal had the considerable virtue of making further generalization over exceptions possible. But it also gave rise to a second *kind* of exception – that is, those which were exceptions to the redundancy rules (cf. Kiparsky 1982).

Rule features of the sort that the Lakoffs had proposed to handle exceptions seemed a natural development in an *Aspects*-type theory. But by the time Green was writing her thesis three or four years later, Generative Semanticists had reached a number of conclusions about the structure of the semantic level that allowed for direct reference to features of representations at that level in the formulation of syntactic rules. Thus, Green felt she could approach the issue of exceptions "in a much more precise way than was previously possible":

This means that it is no longer necessary to define semantic classes as R. Lakoff did, in functional, operational terms, as classes of lexical items which share a set of semantic features which are relevant (i.e., function) in syntactic rules. Instead, one can define semantic classes in semantic and structural terms, referring directly to the structural position of the specific relevant semantic units in derived semantic constitutents.

(Green 1974b: 33)

Nevertheless, to the extent that there were still exceptions to rules, whether or not semantically restricted, Green was compelled to propose several mechanisms to deal with them. For example, Green conceived of the rule of "Negative Transportation," which was claimed to relate *These goodies aren't meant to be eaten until tonight* and *These goodies are meant not to be eaten until tonight*, as a governed rule that applied when the matrix verb was a verb of intention or opinion. But, as Green pointed out, there are certain verbs of intention like *hope* that clearly do not permit Negative Transportation – compare: *I don't hope Tom wins* and *I hope Tom doesn't win*, which do not share the same meaning. To account for such exceptions, Green hypothesized particular conditions on lexical insertion, which she (p. 53) conceived of more or less as the "mirror image" of rule features, that is, as lexical features that could restrict insertion on the basis of information about earlier stages in a derivation. But whereas the constraint on *hope* had to mention both semantic representation and surface structure, Green also appealed to the possibility of a second kind of restriction, – "output constraints" – on surface structure only, to rule out, for example, sentences like **You'll never know if you can write, unless you attempt*, while permitting *You'll never know if you can write, unless you try*. Like the *hope* constraint, output constraints were postulated as conditions on lexical insertion only. A third type of restriction that Green proposed (the most interesting for present purposes) was, however, considerably more general. For example, in her analysis of the dative alternation in English (e.g. pairs like *He gave John the ball* and *He gave the ball to John*), Green concluded that "there is not *a* dative-movement rule, but a 'conspiracy' of dative-movement rules of two kinds . . . . In the case of a dative-movement conspiracy, both of the output structures *V NP NP* and *V NP Prep NP* are target structures" (Green 1974b: 152–3). Green identified several classes of "dative-movement constructions" which she argued must be derived from different semantic sources. Moreover, she found certain cases (involving verbs like *teach*) where each member in an alternation pair had to be derived from a different semantic source, even though the rules that independently apply to structures underlying sentences containing them produce constructions that are indistinguishable at the surface level from dative-movement constructions containing *give, pass,* and so on.

The idea that there are target structures that the derivational constraints applying to semantic representations conspire to make surface structures conform to in fact offered a Generative Semantics equivalent of Emonds's theory of structure preservation, as McCawley (1988: 291) explicitly noted. Had this idea been seen to its logical conclusion, moreover, it might have resolved a number of problems that had grown out of the Katz–Postal methodological strategy of assuming that close paraphrases must be transformationally related. That is, if surface structures are conceived of as having independent status and not as merely the more or less accidental result of the application of transformations to deep structures, then there is really no question as to which of the members of an alternation is the more "basic." In this sense, Generative Semantics contained within it the seeds of a radically "lexicalist" theory much like that which Interpretivism was tending towards in the 1970s, in which standard transformational relations in their "Harrisian" sense were being replaced by implicational relations at either the lexical or semantic level. And indeed, some recent work that has developed out of the Generative Semantics tradition (see, e.g. Fillmore, Kay, and O'Connor 1988 and Goldberg 1992), has followed just that path.

COUNTEREXAMPLES IN GENERATIVE SEMANTICS

We discussed above the difficulties facing Interpretive Semanticists as a result of their approach to counterexamples. Although we have seen that Generative Semanticists rejected the critique of their theory offered by Interpretivists, it hardly needs to be emphasized that Generative Semantics was itself not immune to problems posed by disconfirmatory evidence. To a certain extent, the Generative Semantics attitude towards the discovery of new and interesting kinds of data actually encouraged the stockpiling of counterexamples. Moreover, the four principal Generative Semanticists clearly never felt quite the level of obligation to bring their work into conformity with each other's work that followers of Chomsky felt to bring their proposals into general conformity with his. This in turn meant that Generative Semantics was necessarily a less coherent theory than Interpretive Semantics was, and this lack of coherence, for a while at least, disguised the difficulties Generative Semanticists as a body were having coming up with a consistent set of explanations that had universal application.

From very early on, Generative Semanticists were quite forthcoming about their inability to account for all of the facts. The tone was set by Postal in some informal and unpublished notes that he circulated in the linguistics community in 1967:

> There are apparently endless numbers of fact types not incorporable within any known or imaginable framework . . . the class of facts not handled thus far are in nature quite different from those for which any linguistic framework has been constructed to deal.
>
> (Postal 1976 [1967]: 203–4)

This theme was picked up and variations on it were played in paper after paper published by Generative Semanticists. For example, consider the following brief excerpts from Generative Semantics papers published in the volumes of the Chicago Linguistic Society during the years from 1969 through 1971:

> I do not pretend that what follows contains definitive answers to all of the questions I am going to raise, but I hope that the raising of these questions will permit some insight into the nature and depth of the nagging doubts referred to above, so that we can get down to the serious business of looking for the answers which will lead to a definitive treatment.
>
> (Green 1969: 76)

> In conclusion, it is hardly necessary to point out the large number of stones which have been left unturned by this paper . . .
>
> (Heringer 1969: 94)

> Clearly I have raised many more questions than I have answered, and the answers I have offered will no doubt need extensive modification.
>
> (Morgan 1969: 176)

> The present paper is not a cogent study . . .
>
> (Binnick 1969: 295)

> Surely it is too early even to guess what sort of formal theory will be adequate for this task.
>
> (Green 1970: 279)

> In summing up this awesome display of cosmic mysteries, with scarcely a hint here and there of a likely denouement, we are reminded of the immortal words of Harry Reasoner . . . "We don't know whether these results are more surprising or less surprising that what we might have expected."
>
> (Horn 1970: 326)

> The remainder of this paper will be devoted to presenting data which not even the most powerful of existing models of reference can account for.
>
> (Morgan 1970: 380)

> Hence, what we have achieved is a partial understanding of the passive, with most of the mysteries yet to be unravelled.
>
> (R. Lakoff 1971: 160)

> I have no idea at present of how to characterize these extended environments of operation of the rule . . . All of these facts lead me to suggest the possibility, although I will not defend it here, that

sentences like (9), (52) and (53) come from more remote structures like (54), but there are numbers of immediate and obvious problems with such an analysis, so my suggestion should be taken as a question for future research rather than a serious proposal.

(Rogers 1971: 220)

There are, of course, many relevant horrendous problems to be solved.
(Schmerling 1971: 251)

Granted, the above excerpts are taken from the published versions of conference presentations; but they are not unrepresentative of the kinds of expressions of candor that Generative Semanticists frequently began or concluded their arguments with. It was, indeed, a point of honor with Generative Semanticists that they did not cook their data, that they neither ignored counterexamples nor pretended that there was none when they knew better. This is of course not to say that they felt their theories were more susceptible to counterexample than the Interpretivists' theories were – merely, perhaps, that they felt they were being the more honest about it:

like *all* trees drawn in discussions of syntax, our logical structures are fudges, the best we can do at present, but certainly subject to change. And like *all* rules of grammar mentioned in discussions of syntax, our proposed postulates are approximations at best. But they are sufficiently precise approximations to have a predictive value and to be refutable.
(Gordon and Lakoff 1971: 80, emphasis added)

It is true that some similarly cautious expressions were to be found in the Interpretivist literature, but when they did turn up there they usually also sat side by side with even stronger assertions of confidence in the general direction of the research undertaken. For example, Chomsky ended one paper of his during this period with the caveat that his assessments "must be quite tentative and imprecise at crucial points," but not before emphasizing his belief that the research he had been discussing "will prove to be of lasting impact and importance" (Chomsky 1972a [1969]: 199). In fact, Chomsky's papers are replete with judgments concerning the "naturalness" and "explanatory force" of the "important" and "very interesting" work supporting that research (see, e.g. Chomsky 1971 [1968]: 103, 106, 116), particularly as regards those issues on which he differed with the Generative Semanticists. It is then an interesting question whether the Generative Semantics program after all faced more significant empirical problems, or naturally produced less revealing solutions, than the Interpretivist program did. For reasons we have already discussed, there is no possibility of a straightforward answer to such a question, although we can of course attempt to evaluate the strength of the empirical criticisms of the program offered by critics of it. In this regard, it may be useful to consider in some detail one case that represented one of the most serious of the empirical challenges with which Generative Semanticists were confronted in the 1970s. In 1977, Richard Oehrle, who had received his Ph.D. from MIT the year before, published in *Language* a harsh critique of Green's *Semantics and Syntactic Regularity*, concluding that "in every case examined here, G[reen]'s analysis fails either on grounds of inaccuracy or on grounds of vagueness" (Oehrle 1977: 207). Green was recognized as a talented and capable Generative Semanticist, and her dissertation had produced some of the most detailed and extended empirical arguments for a Generative Semantics position. If a pattern of weakness had been discovered in those arguments, that would clearly say something of significance about the value of her program for other talented and capable researchers. Since that program had already been largely abandoned by the time Oehrle's review was published, Oehrle's critique was seen by many both in the Interpretivist camp and beyond it as explicitly confirming what they had already concluded must be the case.

It is important to separate the specific counterarguments Oehrle offered in his review from the general thrust of his attack. As to the specific counterarguments, some have interesting implications, but many also fail or seriously misconstrue Green's account. For example, Green, in Chapter 2 of her book, had undertaken a brief discussion of the sentence *This coat is warm* (from McCawley 1968b) on the interpretation that the coat makes its wearer feel warm. Green proposed a semantic representation for the sentence on that interpretation as something like ["this coat" CAUSE [NP FEEL [NP WARM]]], from which the surface structure would be derived by (among other things) a rule of Predicate Raising, which would create a constituent [CAUSE FEEL WARM] that could ultimately be replaced by the lexical item(s) (*be*) *warm*. Green (1974b: 42) noted that "The causative subject is not restricted to articles of clothing, as McCawley assumed, but to artifacts, materials, etc. which volitional agents intentionally use to produce or maintain body sensations." In his review, Oehrle criticized this proposal as follows:

> Regardless of whether [Green's proposed semantic representation] properly represents the interpretation at issue – which is rather doubtful – it is clear that no insight is offered into the problem of the ambiguity of *warm*: whether Predicate Raising does or does not apply is apparently an idiosyncratic fact, and every theory must take note of this fact in its lexical treatment of *warm*, whether it be listed as a single entry in the lexicon or as several. Furthermore, if this structure were correct, sentences like *This soup is warm* should be ambiguous, contrary to fact. In view of these and other difficulties, G[reen]'s proposal has no advantages over other proposals which are equally, or even more plausible.

> (Oehrle 1977: 199)

The reader who had read Green's book would notice that the only empirical fact that Oehrle offered among his several charges was from a domain that Green had in fact addressed. His other criticisms involved unfavorable but unsubstantiated comparison with an unidentified second theory. Oehrle's doubts were perhaps justified,[51] but there is no way to know, in the absence of an explicit comparative accounting, precisely what they imply for Green's approach, and that the reader is not given.

A little later in his review, Oehrle (1977: 200) offered the more interesting argument that Green's treatment of exceptions was necessarily less successful in capturing generalizations than the "standard" redundancy rule treatments that he had endorsed, because Green would require a large number of constraints to rule out cases where a lexical item sensitive to a particular rule appears in a family of constructions related by other rules. This was because lexical insertion was understood on Green's account to take place after the application of governed rules. Assuming that the verb *transfer* occurs only in NP V NP Prep NP constructions, and never in NP V NP NP constructions, but also that it falls into the semantic class of verbs that can appear in both types of structures, Oehrle concluded that Green would require separate output constraints to predict the nonoccurrence of **NP was transferred NP by NP*, **What did NP transfer NP?*, **NP, I wouldn't think of transferring NP*, and so on. Thus, on Oehrle's understanding, Green's analysis "fails to express properly certain dependencies which are an automatic consequence of more standard theories" (Oehrle 1977: 200).

It is true that the *transfer* facts potentially represented a problem for a Generative Semantics analysis in general and Green's analysis in particular, but only on some assumptions which were not universally accepted. First, if *transfer* could be shown not to fall into a class of verbs that can appear in prepositionless structures (however derived) on semantic or other grounds, then Oehrle's criticism obviously would not go through. Green did not propose an analysis of *transfer*, although she did briefly raise and reject the possibility that all such exceptions could be handled by phonological constraints (Green 1974b: 77–9). Nevertheless, in other work Oehrle himself (1976: 123–5; see also Pinker 1989: 45–7, 118–23, Levin 1993: 48) argued that a fairly strong case can be made that verbs of Latinate origin generally are excluded from the prepositionless structure for essentially morphological reasons. Second, Oehrle assumed that Green would have been forced to resort to a set of output constraints to restrict the insertion of *transfer*, but, as noted in the previous section, Green had also proposed constraints on lexical insertion that were permitted access to information about the derivational histories of the structures involved. Given the availability of such constraints, the redundancy rule account favored by Oehrle was no more parsimonious than Green's transformational account. Moreover, Green had offered at least one argument that favored her approach over the approach Oehrle was to take:

treating *hope* as an exception in the traditional sense requires not one, but several rules which raise negatives (a *never*-raising rule, a *not*-raising rule, *not ever-*, *no- . . . ever*, and *no*-raising rules, and probably a host of others as well) since *hope* would be an exception to some but not all of these rules.

(Green 1974b: 53)

In general, although Oehrle followed Green in assuming that the insertion of the lexical item *transfer* on a Generative Semantics account must necessarily follow the cyclic rules of Dative-movement, Passive, *Wh*-movement, and Topicalization, whether a case could be made for such an ordering was an empirical issue that was not resolved by either.

At one point in her book (1976: 33–4), Green had considered seven verbs she had classified as "verbs of communication": *deny, say, shout, write, inform, teach,* and *tell.* She had observed that this class is not syntactically homogenous, since the first four verbs take the preposition *to* before an indirect object followed by a sentential complement (*A said to B that the air was polluted*), while the latter three take no preposition (*A told B that the air was polluted*). Noting that saying and telling "both involve linguistic communication," Green then had asked: "How can we define markedness for the rule which determines whether or not a preposition precedes a pre-complement indirect object?" Green's solution had been to assign the two sets of verbs to different semantic subclasses: verbs of the second group, but not the first, denote acts of communication in which the indirect object is "affected by the communication, changed somehow, in a way that the subject intended – although not necessarily in all the ways that the subject might have desired" (Green 1974b: 34).

In his review, Oehrle criticized this account as follows:

the whole passage suffers from the fact that the premise is false: *inform, teach,* and *tell* do not necessarily involve linguistic communication, so there is no reason to consider them as members of a single class with the other verbs listed. This can be readily seen from the fact that these three verbs can occur with inanimate subjects (e.g., *The results of the experiment informed us that our theory was wrong*), whereas the other verbs on the list cannot. Admittedly, there is a distinction to be drawn concerning the way in which the 'indirect object' is affected (if at all), but this is not so easy to describe: thus it is not contradictory to say *I told Mary that Harry had left, but I guess she didn't hear me*; and if this sentence is true, it is difficult to see how Mary could possibly have been affected at all . . . Thus the argument again fails, and no conclusions can be drawn.

(Oehrle 1977: 205)

This criticism is worth examining closely, because in it Oehrle was evidently drawn to a conclusion very much like that which Green had reached, only a bit weaker: constructions containing *inform, teach,* and *tell* differ syntactically from those containing *deny, say,* and *shout,* and this difference correlates with a semantic difference concerning "the way in which the 'indirect object' is affected (if at all)," but one which is "not so easy to describe." However, the way he voiced his concerns suggested more significant discrepancies between his position and Green's than there apparently were. For example, with respect to his discussion of the *inform* case, what ultimately matters is not the terminology used to label the class but the susceptibility of the class to semantic analysis, and on this score Oehrle admitted to seeing Green's point. Green's account did not depend in any way on a characterization of that class as "linguistic" (Green herself regularly referred to the members of that class simply as "verbs of communication"), nor did such a characterization play any substantive role in distinguishing Oehrle's account from hers. It might have seemed that Oehrle's central point – that sentences like the one involving *tell* falsified her claim that the indirect object is "affected by the communication" – was more potentially damaging for Green. But this ultimately reduces to the empirical question of what the correct semantic representations for these sentences are. Oehrle's sentence suggests that the correct form in some cases should refer to *expectation* of reception or of uptake on the addressee's part ("the message is such that the hearer is supposed to come to know it" (Pinker 1989: 214; also Goldsmith 1980)), but the subtlety needed in the analysis does not affect Green's argument that "the syntactic property of permitting a preposition before the indirect object is correlated in a nearly one-to-one fashion with a certain aspect of meaning" (Green 1974b: 34–5).

Further on in his review, Oehrle noted that Green, having offered some criteria for setting up semantic representations, "refrains from actually stating rules which will operate on these representations" (Oehrle 1977: 206). This flaw was hardly unique to Green's account. The fact that Green was not able to provide a rigorous specification of the relation between form and meaning in each case she examined did suggest the difficulties inherent in the enterprise. But Oehrle's conclusion ("all we have is a taxonomy") did not follow: Green's analysis of the dative alternation, like most analyses of the time offered by both Generative Semanticists and Interpretive Semanticists (and, indeed, like the similar analysis of the dative alternation offered by Oehrle in his very rich and original thesis), suggested a framework within which specific rule-writing could be attempted, while not depending on the validity of any particular rule.[52] What is more, Green's account did make a variety of predictions that Oehrle claimed were not always borne out. For example, Green had assumed that an entailment of a sentence like *Max handed Doris a cigarette* is that as a consequence of the action indicated by the main verb Doris came to have a cigarette. But Oehrle countered that sentences like *Max handed*

Doris a cigarette, but she wouldn't take it seemed to him not contradictory. For our part, we don't find his sentence quite so acceptable as, say, *Max attempted to hand Doris a cigarette, but she wouldn't take it*, but even granting that there are dialects where it is pristine, few consequences of any significance follow for Green's approach. That is, the particular semantic structures crucial to her analysis evidently remain exactly as before whether or not a predicate of expectation appears as a higher node, just as in the discussion of *tell*, above.

The primary burden of Oehrle's review, and of his thesis, was to demonstrate that Green's syntactic account of dative alternations was less attractive than a lexical account. But everything we have looked at in Oehrle's argument that poses as a crucial case turns out to hinge on assumptions that Green probably would not accept or data for which there are alternative explanations or interpretations. In fact, what is most striking to a contemporary reader of these materials is how much Oehrle's analyses resemble Green's both in spirit and in technical detail.[53]

But granting Oehrle all of his specific arguments in both his review and his thesis, the *most* that he could be taken to have shown is that a lexicalist treatment of lexical insertion in the spirit of the Lakoffs had advantages over Green's transformational treatment in the cases he examined. A number of Green's central conclusions were accepted by Oehrle, including, crucially, her conclusion that the syntactic behavior of these constructions is importantly (but not entirely) determined by their semantic properties. Where Green had to stipulate to handle exceptions, Oehrle by and large had to stipulate too; where Green assumed that distributions were semantically controlled, Oehrle pretty much did too, and nearly twenty years of research since has not significantly changed our understanding of the balance between those two aspects of the construction. In addition, from a contemporary vantage point, they both similarly failed to give priority to an issue that now seems urgent: how are children able to acquire knowledge of the exceptions that do not appear to be semantically determined (C.L. Baker 1979)? Perhaps not surprisingly, contemporary answers to that question (Goldberg 1992, Pinker 1989) build on a foundation that owes at least as much to Green as to Oehrle.

3

RHETORICAL STRATEGIES AND LINGUISTIC ARGUMENTATION
Three case studies

The historical approach followed in the previous chapter has assumed that there are valid arguments and invalid arguments and that the distinction between them can reliably be drawn. But if so, why were the participants in the deep structure debates in such strenuous disagreement? Unquestionably, the Interpretive Semanticists believed they had shown that the Generative Semantics program was misguided and bound to fail, because the foundational propositions on which it rested led to unwanted conclusions. Just as firmly, the Generative Semanticists believed that the Interpretive Semanticists' arguments in this regard were mistaken and were designed simply to obscure the poverty of their own program. At one point in their correspondence, McCawley wrote to Chomsky that "the likelihood of either of us convincing the other of anything is about zero, particularly the matter of what can be said about the form of semantic structure" (p.c. to Noam Chomsky, 12 April 1973). Chomsky responded that "everything you say . . . is clearly wrong, ... The predictions come out . . . exactly contrary to what you say. This is so plain and obvious that I am, frankly, startled that you don't see it" (p.c. to James McCawley, 24 May 1973).

In asking his colleagues to devote some study to the rhetoric of their field – the processes by which they attempt to persuade one another – the economist Donald McCloskey lists the following benefit: "Economists," he says, "should become more self-conscious about their rhetoric, because they will then better know why they agree or disagree, and will find it less easy to dismiss contrary arguments on merely methodological grounds" (McCloskey 1983: 482). In fact, as McCloskey argues, economists do not in practice follow strict laws of scientific inquiry when laying down their analyses and would scarcely be able to get anywhere if they did.

The concept of rhetoric to which McCloskey subscribes derives most proximately from Booth 1974, where the term denotes neither the study of mere verbal trickery nor abstract methods designed to prove what is true, but rather the art of discovering good reasons, finding what really warrants assent, because any reasonable person ought to be persuaded . . . . . [It is] the careful weighing of more-or-less good reasons to arrive at more-or-less probable or plausible conclusions – none too secure but better than would be arrived at by chance or unthinking impulse.

(cited in McCloskey 1983: 482)

McCloskey's call for a broader study of rhetoric might, if heard in linguistics, have positive benefits here as well. Moreover, a rhetorical approach may shed some light on why the deep structure debates became as emotional as they did for many of the participants, and why those participants continue to harbor animosities.

We will not attempt in this chapter even a prolegomena to a rhetoric of linguistics, the scope of which would far exceed that of this book. Instead, we will only briefly and rather superficially examine some documents that played a role in the deep structure debates in order to offer some suggestions as to the kind of issues a rhetorical analysis might illuminate. We should emphasize what McCloskey (1983: 499) emphasizes, that the purpose should "not be to make the author look foolish or to uncover fallacies for punishment by ridicule" (since "fallacy-mongering is evidence of a legislative attitude towards method"), but to "see beyond the received view." Of course, seeing beyond the received view is what good science is supposed to be about in any case; where the rhetorical approach specifically aspires to contribute is in showing how and why it is that the way in which an argument is put affects its reception.

At the Texas "Universals in Linguistic Theory" conference in April 1967, McCawley read a paper entitled "How to find semantic universals in the event that there are any," published ultimately as McCawley 1968b under the different title "The role of semantics in a grammar." A crucial Postscript, added to the paper in May 1967, contained an argument that "the same transformation which produces the sentence *John and Harry love Mary and Alice respectively* is involved in the derivation of *John and Harry love their respective wives*" (McCawley 1968b: 163). The semantic representations of each of the sentences "can be represented as involving a universal quantifier, and the result of the *respectively* transformation is something in which a reflex of the set over which quantification ranges appears in place of occurrences of the variable which was bound by that quantifier" (p. 164). As an example, McCawley proposed that the semantic representation of the second sentence above is "something like . . . For all x in the set {John, Harry}, x loves x's wife." The *respectively* transformation would replace the first occurrence of the bound variable with *John and Harry* and the second with a proform that ends up as *their*. Similarly, an underlying structure of the form *That man loves Mary and that man loves Alice* would yield in surface form either *That man loves Mary and Alice* or *Those men love Mary and Alice respectively*, depending on whether the two underlying occurrences of *that man* have the same index or different indices. Since the *respectively* transformation then would have not only the properties of a rule of semantic interpretation (a "projection rule" in the sense of Katz and Postal 1964 and Chomsky 1965) but also would subsume "much of what has been regarded as a syntactic transformation of conjunction reduction" (p. 166), "the syntactic and semantic components of the earlier theory will have to be replaced by a single system of rules which convert semantic representation through various intermediate stages into surface syntactic representation" (p. 167).

McCawley realized that his rather facile proposal that semantic representations were the same kind of formal object as syntactic representations required some defending, at least to deflect the ready objection that while it was obvious that the leaves of a syntactic tree must be linearly ordered it was not so clear that the leaves of a semantic tree should be so ordered. For the purposes of this paper, McCawley assumed that semantic representations would be ordered[1] and then specified that two sentences would be considered identical in meaning "if their semantic representations are equivalent even if not identical" (p. 168). If so, then the synonymous sentences *I spent the evening drinking and singing songs* and *I spent the evening singing songs and drinking* "might be assigned semantic representations which differed in the order of two conjoined propositions but which would be equivalent by virtue of the principle $p \& q = q \& p$" (p. 168).

McCawley explicitly identified his argument about *respectively* with an earlier argument famously launched some years before by Morris Halle against an autonomous level of phonemics – and ultimately against the entire Bloomfieldian tradition in which the phonemic level had played a crucial role (Halle 1959). Halle's argument was that there are unified phonological phenomena which cannot receive a unified treatment in a theory with a phonemic level. For example, in Russian, voicing is distinctive for all obstruents except /c/, /č/, and /x/, which are voiceless unless followed by a voiced obstruent, in which case they are voiced as well. However, at the end of a word, all obstruents are voiceless unless followed by a voiced obstruent, in which case they are voiced as well. Halle pointed out, then, that in a phonemic theory of Russian, /c/, /č/, and /x/ in word-final position before a voiced obstruent would have to be treated differently from the other voiceless obstruents (e.g. /k/) in the same position: the voiced version of /c/ is a nondistinctive variant (an "allophone") of /c/, but the voiced version of /k/ is the separate phoneme /g/. The criterion in phonemic theory that guaranteed this distinction was called the "biuniqueness" condition, which required that every sequence of phonetic sounds correspond to a unique sequence of phonemes (and vice versa). Thus, the linguist committed to a phonemic level would be forced to posit two different rules – an allophonic one and a morphological one – in two different parts of the grammar to account for what is on the face of it a single process.[2]

McCawley asserted that the *respectively* facts constituted a similar problem for a theory which posited an autonomous level of deep structure ("I claim to have exhibited just such a phenomenon . . . namely, the *respectively* transformation" (McCawley 1968b: 166)). Since Halle's argument had been considered fatal to the Bloomfieldian program by Chomskyans, it was no small matter for McCawley to use it against the Chomskyan program itself. So there could be no mistaking the seriousness of his charge, McCawley emphasized near the end of the paper that "*respectively* cannot be treated as a unitary phenomenon in a grammar with a level of deep structure and . . . that conception of grammar must thus be rejected in favor of the alternative suggested above, which was proposed in Lakoff and Ross [1976]."

There are then at least two planes on which McCawley's argument would have been read. On one plane, McCawley was offering a standard linguistic argument, one based on a set of facts and an interpretation of them that he claimed were consistent with the Generative Semantics theory of grammar he had briefly sketched and inconsistent with the deep structure analysis of the *Aspects* theory as he understood it. Such an argument can be debated and the facts disputed, confirmed, or augmented in the usual way. On a more social or political plane, however, McCawley was challenging the Chomskyan research program for which these facts were claimed to be problematical, in much the same way that Chomsky earlier had challenged the Bloomfieldian program. McCawley's choice of the word *rejected* (rather than the more moderate *modified,* say) and his reference to an alliance with the aims of Lakoff and Ross 1976 announced that he had chosen to side *against* Chomsky and his specific theory of deep structure and to do what he could to overturn them "in favor of the alternative" he was promoting. He could not show that no other alternatives (including any that might salvage a level of deep structure) could possibly be brought to bear on these facts.[3] But he could and did express his opinion concerning the likelihood that the *Aspects* theory would deliver a satisfactory solution to the problem he had identified.

The distinction between these two planes of argument may perhaps be made more clear by comparing some work that McCawley did on the theory of "selectional restriction" in 1966 with that undertaken independently at about the same time by Chomsky's student Ray Jackendoff. In the *Aspects* theory, nouns had been assigned formal (syntactic) features such as ±Abstract, ±Animate, ±Human, ±Male, and so on, by the phrase structure rules of the base, and the anomaly of a sentence like *Colorless green ideas sleep furiously* was to be captured at deep structure by, *inter alia,* a restriction that prevented inanimate subjects from selecting (i.e. cooccurring with) verbs like *sleep.* McCawley and Jackendoff surveyed similar sets of facts (e.g. acceptable sentences like *It's crazy to talk of colorless green ideas sleeping furiously*) and arrived at essentially the same conclusion: satisfaction or violation of a selectional restriction is not a matter of syntax but of semantics and real-world knowledge. Jackendoff's later published account (Jackendoff 1972) appeared in the context of an extended argument in support of the Interpretive theory of Chomsky 1971 as against the Generative Semantics theory of McCawley 1968b and G. Lakoff 1971. He emphasized that his account was in fact consistent with Chomsky's *Syntactic Structures* in its treatment of selectional restriction, even if it departed from *Aspects*, and pointedly noted that certain arguments that Lakoff had given (in G. Lakoff 1968a) for a Generative Semantics approach to instrumental adverbs "hold only if one accepts the position of *Aspects* [on selectional restriction], which Lakoff has since given up in favor of" the *Syntactic Structures* position (Jackendoff 1972: 18).

McCawley's development of much the same empirical position has a very different tone. At the beginning of the paper in which it was eventually offered (McCawley 1968d), McCawley (p. 36) announced that he would "discuss certain inadequacies of the position" taken by Chomsky in *Aspects*. Later on (p. 55), he noted that "[m]ost of the discussion of selectional restrictions which has appeared in print is misleading," going on in particular to mention the *Aspects* treatment. Whereas Jackendoff's assertion of a connection to the theory of *Syntactic Structures* suggested that he was choosing between alternatives Chomsky had offered, McCawley could be much more easily read as criticizing Chomsky directly:

> despite Chomsky's assertion that "*every* syntactic feature of the Subject and Object imposes a corresponding classification on the verb" (*Aspects*, p. 97), no clear case has been adduced of a selectional restriction which involves a non-semantic feature.
>
> (McCawley 1968a: 56)

In the spring of 1966, McCawley, then less than two years out of MIT, sent Chomsky a draft of his paper about the base component. Chomsky responded to McCawley in a letter dated 10 June 1966, that, although he had found certain things to object to, he thought McCawley's paper was "very interesting . . . . . By and large, I agree with most of what you say, and think it should be said . . . . " McCawley also sent a copy of his paper to Lakoff and Ross, who used its conclusion that selectional restriction is a semantic phenomenon as evidence against a level of deep structure in their celebrated letter to Arnold Zwicky (Lakoff and Ross 1976 [1967]). McCawley (1976a: 159) has pointed out that Lakoff and Ross's letter "greatly influenced" the Postscript section of his "Role" paper.

McCawley sent Chomsky a copy of the manuscript of "The role of semantics in a grammar" not long after completing it in the late spring of 1967. Chomsky replied to McCawley in a twelve-page, single-spaced personal letter dated 20 December 1967; while Chomsky had a year and a half earlier been generally encouraging in his response to the base component paper, his reaction this time was considerably more negative:

I realize that it is easier to criticize than to accomplish, and the problems dealt with in your recent papers are real enough – I don't pretend to have answers to them. Still, I think the case you make is awfully weak, and doesn't convince me at all, frankly. I think that as you formulate your alternative to a Katz–Postal–Aspects type system, it is untenable. In fact, I think one can give as close to a definitive disproof of the possibility of a generative semantics in your sense as is possible, given the level of vagueness (to which I don't object, the nature of the problems being what it is). Besides, there are so many individual points where the argument is weak or, I think, just plain wrong, that I don't see how the conclusions have much credence.

(p.c. to McCawley, 20 December 1967)

Chomsky's letter to McCawley of course did not close the matter as far as the latter was concerned. McCawley replied in a personal letter to Chomsky dated 17 January 1968, that "your comments do not force me into any significant recantations." Taking each of Chomsky's points in turn, McCawley showed why he felt they failed to hit their mark. We will follow here just their dialogue concerning McCawley's Postscript to the "Role" paper; below and on the left are four of Chomsky's comments, and below and on the right are McCawley's responses:

Chomsky to McCawley, 20 December 1967	*McCawley to Chomsky, 17 January 1968*
A You suggest here that you are proposing an alternative to the Aspects-type theory [KPA] . . . It would, I think, be far more accurate to say that you are proposing a version of this theory with more abstract deep structures . . . the notion "identity of meaning" can be regarded as an equivalence relation defined on deep structures . . . The equivalence relation in KPA is the one defined by projection rules; the equivalence relation in your system is not further specified, but I would assume . . . that you think of it as involving only "logical operations"	There are a number of differences between my somewhat vague proposals and the KPA proposals . . . , notably the nature of the "equivalence relation" and the criteria for calling something a deep structure (for KPA) or a semantic representation (for me). However, I agree with you to the extent that I believe that if KPA were pushed to its logical extreme, you would end up with "deep structures" such that different deep structures could be said to have the same meaning only in cases where, e.g. they have conjuncts in different orders or one has a universal quantifier over a set defined by enumeration where the other has the conjunction of the propositions for each item in the enumeration, ...

64

STRATEGIES AND ARGUMENTATION

Chomsky to McCawley, 20 December 1967	*McCawley to Chomsky, 17 January 1968*
B It might be thought that your approach is fundamentally different because the deep structures are represented in "logic" and the operations that map them into equivalence classes are, perhaps, "logical operations." But there is a fatal ambiguity in your use of the term "logic." If you mean first-order predicate calculus, or some extensional logic, say, then you should at least mention the nontrivial fact that 60 years of research appear to have shown that language can't be paraphrased in such a system . . . Or, if you mean some sort of "modal logic," then which one?	You're right that I didn't specify what I meant by "logic" . . . What I had in mind was a system of formulas built up from symbols of types "individual, set, predicate" and perhaps some others according to formation rules essentially identical to those of extensional logics but allowing formulas of this type to appear as the arguments of predicates (i.e. the various modal operators are predications about sentences; the logic is "modal" to the extent of allowing one to say things about sentences but not in the sense of allowing extra "truth values").
C In fact, your remark (rather off-hand) that "logical formulas" can be expressed in phrase markers seems to me rather odd. Of course, we can define a coding procedure, etc., but that is not the point. I don't see any way (or any indication in your paper) of how the simple matter of quantification, with cross-referencing by variables, quantifiers ranging over structures of varying scope, etc., can be handled in terms of phrase-markers of which only grammatical transformations apply. (Obviously, if you want to extend the latter notion, then again your proposal is empty until the extension is specified.) Evidently it won't do to have quantifiers as "higher verbs," if one wants to preserve the structure of quantification theory. In fact, I have to say that I really don't know at all what you are talking about when you make these remarks about "logic" in the framework of phrase-markers and transformations.	The "coding procedure" which I had in mind is an isomorphism. The scope of a quantifier in my proposal is the sentence which appears as a nominal adjunct to it (i.e., is its "subject"); see p. 16 of "Where do noun phrases come from?" [McCawley 1970c] for an example. Unless you find some inadequacy in the representation proposed there (where I specifically treated an example of the same quantifiers having different scopes in the readings of a sentence), I see no problem.

Chomsky to McCawley, 20 December 1967   *McCawley to Chomsky, 17 January 1968*

D I think there is a near-definitive disproof of any conception that might be worked out within the general range of ideas that you hint at. It is a well-known fact that in referentially opaque contexts one cannot (by definition) carry out substitution salva veritatem, even substitution of synonyms. For example, consider the context: (1) "everyone realizes that 4 = —" If we substitute "four," (1) becomes true. If we substitute "the only natural number between three and the square root of twenty-five," (1) becomes false. Therefore, (1) and (2) are not mutually deducible; they must have different meanings . . . The fact is that referentially opaque contents have the property that truth or falsity (hence, obviously, meaning) depends not only on intrinsic semantic content, but also on the form in which a belief or a concept is expressed, hence ultimately on surface structure. This observation seems to me to destroy the possibility of generative semantics . . . .

Your interpretation of (1) and (2) depends on the proposition that "four" and "the only natural number between three and the square root of twenty-five" have the same semantic representation, which I deny. The fact that a mathematician can prove that those two expressions correspond to the same number is irrelevant here, since the proof depends on postulates which are essentially factual in nature . . . I am not convinced of your statement that "no matter how tight the relation" between two propositions you can't validly substitute one for the other in a referentially opaque context; for example, could you imagine it ever being correct to say "Arthur realizes that John and Harry are similar but he doesn't realize that Harry and John are similar"?

The issues that Chomsky raised in his letter were entirely legitimate. It is true that McCawley had been vague about what kind of logic would serve as a model for his level of semantic representation, nor had he shown in the paper how he would deal with the problem that referentially opaque contexts posed. McCawley's evident goal in his response was to show that, although he had not provided a fully worked-out analysis in his paper, he could sketch how he would go about constructing one. Each side, however, wanted to draw more ambitious conclusions from these arguments. Where McCawley had devised in his paper reasons to "reject" Chomsky's program, Chomsky now was offering arguments to "destroy" McCawley's. Chomsky says he does not know at all what McCawley is talking about; McCawley says he sees no problem and is unconvinced by Chomsky's reasoning.

Chomsky refined his arguments and prepared them for publication in an article written in 1968 and published in 1971 as "Deep structure, surface structure, and semantic interpretation," largely ignoring McCawley's counterarguments. In the article, Chomsky repeated the "definitive disproof" with changed examples – this time either (a) *John's uncle* or (b) *the person who is the brother of John's mother or father or the husband of the sister of John's father or mother* or (c) *the person who is the son of one of John's grandparents but is not his father, or the husband of a daughter of one of John's grandparents* is to be inserted in the context *Bill realized that the bank robber was* ___. Although McCawley had protested against Chomsky's previous argument that he (McCawley) would not assign the various alternatives the same semantic representation, Chomsky did not allow for that possibility here: "If the concept 'semantic representation' ('reading') is to play any role at all in linguistic theory," he said (Chomsky 1971: 197), "then these three expressions must have the same semantic representation." He then argued, as before, that the three sentences formed by embedding the expressions must all have different semantic representations, again "if the concept 'semantic representation' (or 'reading') is to play any serious role in linguistic theory." He asserted that this conclusion should be obvious:

> people can *perfectly well* have contradictory beliefs, can *correctly* be said to fail to realize that *p* even though (in another sense) they know that *p* . . . . Notice that *there is nothing in the least paradoxical* about these observations. It is the function of such words as "realize," "be aware of," etc. to deal with such situations as those just described, *which are perfectly common and quite intelligible.*
>
> (Chomsky 1971: 197, emphasis added)

To bolster his position, Chomsky added a footnote citing Mates (1950) and Scheffler (1955), but also admitted that "There has been considerable discussion of these matters, but nothing, so far as I know, to affect the point at issue here" (Chomsky 1971: 197).

But despite Chomsky's strong words, we have seen that there were two premises in his argument whose solidity had not in fact been demonstrated. McCawley *had* found grounds to reject the first premise (that synonymous expressions must have the same representation) and to accept only a qualified version of the second (that if *p* and *q* are synonymous but not identical, a statement like "Everyone knows that *p* = *q*" must be false). Nevertheless, Chomsky was led to conclude that:

> As far as I can see, an argument of this sort can be advanced against any variety of semantically based grammar (what is sometimes called "Generative Semantics") that has been discussed, or even vaguely alluded to in the linguistic literature. One has to put this tentatively, because many of the proposals are rather vague. However, at least this

much is clear. Any approach to semantically based grammar will have to take account of this problem.

(Chomsky 1971: 198)

The last sentence seems cautious and unobjectionable, although McCawley had in fact expressed his opinion on the matter directly in their correspondence. The first two sentences, by contrast, are a good deal more contentious: Generative Semantics in any variety has been refuted, and if not, it is only because its proposals are too vague to be tested.

In his 20 December letter, Chomsky had not dealt with McCawley's *respectively* argument in any thoroughgoing way. But in his "Deep structure" paper, Chomsky attempted to show that the argument was "based on an equivocation" and "shows nothing about the level of deep structure" (Chomsky 1971: 193). Chomsky's position was that McCawley's *respectively* transformation constituted not a single process, but rather combined four distinct rules: (a) a rule (call it I) relating semantic representations with quantifiers to the syntactic structures underlying sentences like *John loves John's wife and Harry loves Harry's wife*; (b) a rule (call it R) forming sentences like *John and Harry love their respective wives* from structures like *John loves John's wife and Harry loves Harry's wife*; (c) a rule (call it R') that forms noun phrases with *respective* from sentences with *respectively*; and (d) a noun phrase collapsing rule (call it C) which would take *That man(x) and that man(y) love Mary and Alice respectively* into *Those men love Mary and Alice respectively*. Chomsky noted that these four rules could be straightforwardly accommodated in an Interpretivist theory: I is a semantic interpretation rule relating semantic representations and deep structures, and R, R', and C are local transformations involved in the derivation of surface structure from deep structure. McCawley's equivocation, on this view, lay in his use of the term "*respectively* transformation":

> in the analysis [McCawley] proposes . . . , the "*respectively* transformation" carries out four totally different operations; hence it does not express a "unitary phenomenon." If, on the other hand, we use the term "*respectively* transformation" to denote R . . . , then it does express a "unitary phenomenon," but it no longer relates semantic to syntactic representation in one case and syntactic to syntactic representation in the other . . . Therefore, McCawley's analysis, right or wrong, is simply a realization of the [*Aspects*] theory, once equivocations of terminology are removed.

(Chomsky 1971: 193)

Chomsky presented this argument in lectures in the fall of 1968. One of those in the audience later showed McCawley his notes from these lectures, prompting McCawley to write Chomsky on 10 December 1968, a brief letter complaining that "I never said that your examples . . . were related in the way that you attributed to me." Specifically, McCawley objected that, as he understood and meant to convey it, the *respectively* transformation (call this T) takes the semantic representation "For all x in {John, Harry}, x loves x's wife" into the surface structure associated with *John and Harry love their respective wives* not through the intermediate stage underlying *John loves John's wife and Harry loves Harry's wife*, but directly. As McCawley was to write Chomsky in another letter a month later after he had seen the draft of Chomsky's "Deep structure" paper, he felt Chomsky's argument:

> misrepresents my argument about *respectively* (although on rereading my paper . . . , I recognize that I am partially to blame since I did a lousy job of separating the straw men that I was knocking down from the final analysis that I proposed); the derivations that you attribute to me are a mixture of pieces of my analysis and pieces of analyses that I took up and rejected while leading up to the eventual analysis. . . . .
> My point was that all sentences with *respectively* or *respective* derive from a semantic representation having a universal quantifier that binds two or more occurrences of its variable, and I did in fact propose a single rule that would cover all the cases that I mentioned. The point on which you can legitimately criticize me is not equivocation about the term "*respectively* transformation," (since two of the three "*respectively* transformations" that you mention don't figure in my eventual analysis) but on whether my analysis works . . . .
>
> (p.c. to Chomsky, 8 January 1969)

Chomsky responded to McCawley on 12 February 1969, that "I simply don't see the 'eventual analysis' that you mention. . . . What I see are just the 'bits and pieces' that I tried to pull together, but no rejection of them." In particular, he said he didn't see "any single rule" that does what McCawley had said it should do. As to whether the analysis itself works, "I wasn't concerned with the problem of 'respective(ly)' but rather with the logic of your argument: specifically, with your claim that you had presented a Halle-type argument against deep structure." He thus decided to "leave things as they are, which is the best reconstruction that I seem able to make from the paper" (p.c. to McCawley, 12 Febuary 1968).

Thus, although McCawley had argued that Chomsky was distorting his intentions, Chomsky refused to consider the alternative that McCawley had said he had intended to convey: "[T]o be frank," Chomsky concluded, "I don't feel that I misrepresented what appears in the paper – at least to the best of my ability to reconstruct the argument, which I find very loose."[4]

McCawley acknowledged in his published critique of Chomsky's "Deep structure" (McCawley 1975a: 39) that his argument about *respectively* had been "badly bungled," though "not incorrigibly so" (see, e.g. McCawley 1972, 1973b), and not for the reasons that Chomsky had listed. He reiterated his original point that an *Aspects* theory in which the transformational rule R was needed to derive *John and Harry love Mary and Alice respectively* and the semantic interpretation rule T to derive *Those men love their respective wives* would miss a significant generalization that McCawley's theory, with its single rule T, would capture. McCawley's assumptions about *Aspects* were not unreasonable, since he had shown that a derivation involving rules I, R, R', and C could not be sustained for sentences like *Those men love their respective wives.*[5]

Chomsky never directly addressed this facet of McCawley's argument, which clearly constituted a serious problem for an Interpretive approach. Nevertheless, for McCawley's argument to have had the force of Halle's, he would have had to have demonstrated that there was a principle of Interpretive theory that *required* postulation of both rule T and rule R. But as McCawley admitted, *Aspects* "has few implications as to what can be the deep structure of any particular sentence" (McCawley 1975a: 40), and it was not clear that an Interpretivist could not simply base-generate all the relevant sentences. Thus, the question of the relevance of the issue to a decision between Generative Semantics and Interpretive Semantics remained logically unresolved.

Another argument against an Interpretive theory of deep structure that also sought to identify itself with Halle's critique of the phonemic level was offered by George Lakoff in an article published in 1972 (Lakoff 1972). This was as clear a statement as could be found of the commitment Generative Semanticists had to a theory whose primary goal is the decoding of the surface facts of a language – a decoding that of necessity yields a very different kind of representation from surface structure, rather than just an annotation of it. It was only natural that Lakoff should call upon the Hallean argument in support of such a view of grammar, since Halle and Chomsky's phonological theory was the exemplar *par excellence* of a theory that posited underlying representations radically distinct from surface (phonetic) forms. Lakoff wanted to draw attention to this analogy: semantic representation was to an abstract phonological representation as surface syntactic structure was to phonetic representation. But if so, was not an intermediate level of deep structure as otiose in syntax as a phonemic level was in phonology? Halle's point had been that voicing assimilation in Russian was unquestionably a rule of the language, but its theoretical status (as a morphophonemic rule or a rule of allophony) in phonemic theory depended in an uninteresting fashion on essentially irrelevant properties of the segment it applied to in any given case. Lakoff's point was that there were uniform grammatical processes that were, for the Interpretivist, motivated in some cases by semantic considerations and in other cases by distributional considerations, the former justifying a semantic interpretation rule relating surface structure and semantic representation and the latter motivating a transformation relating deep structure to surface structure.

Lakoff's argument proceeded as follows. He claimed that the rule of Adverb Preposing, which relates sentences like *Sam smoked pot last night* and *Last night, Sam smoked pot*, must be assumed to be a syntactic rule, because it is evidently involved in distinguishing grammatical sentences from ungrammatical sentences. More specifically, the rule is conditioned to move an adverb out of a lower clause into a higher clause only in certain cases. For example, long-distance movement of an adverb out of an embedded clause is possible when the verb of the higher clause is *think*, but not when it is *realize*; thus, *Last night, I think that Sam smoked pot* is grammatical, but **Last night, I realize that Sam smoked pot* is not. However, even when a verb does not in general permit long-distance extraction of an adverb from an embedded clause, the result of performing such an extraction may turn out to be grammatical anyway: *Last night, I realized that Sam smoked pot* is grammatical, although in this case the adverb modifies *realized* rather than *smoked*. Lakoff's conclusion is that:

> Here we have a case where the violation of a rule of grammar does not guarantee that the sentence generated will be ungrammatical. The violation only guarantees that the sentence will be ungrammatical relative to a given reading. A sentence will be fully ungrammatical only if it is ungrammatical relative to all readings. This suggests that the role of rules of grammar is not simply to separate out the grammatical from the ungrammatical sentences of English, but also to pair surface forms of sentences with their corresponding meanings, or logical forms. Thus, rules like A[dverb] P[reposing] appear to have two functions: to generate the grammatical sentences, filtering out the ungrammatical sentences, while at the same time relating the surface forms of sentences to their corresponding logical forms, while blocking any incorrect assignments of logical form to surface form . . . . The only way [this conclusion] could be avoided would be to assume that there were two rules which did the same job as A[dverb] P[reposing] and had exactly the same constraints and that one was a rule of grammar and the other a rule relating surface forms to logical forms. This would necessarily involve stating the same rule twice, and thus missing a significant generalization.
>
> (Lakoff 1972: 548–53)

Lakoff went on to say that "the theory of Generative Semantics is the only theory of grammar that has been proposed that is consistent" with the conclusion that rules have this dual function. As McCawley had done earlier, Lakoff made direct reference to Halle's attack on Bloomfieldian phonemics: "If one agrees that classical phonemics has been shown to be wrong on the basis of such arguments, one must accept" the conclusion that Interpretive theory is "not just inelegant, but empirically incorrect". Moreover, "by refusing to accept such arguments, one is deciding a priori, by fiat, that there is no relation between grammar and logic" (G. Lakoff 1972: 553–4).

In a reply published in 1975, Chomsky summarily rejected Lakoff's argument and the assumptions on which it was based. If semantic interpretation proceeds off deep structure or off a surface structure annotated with "traces" in such a way that deep structure relationships can be reconstructed, then the restriction on Adverb Preposing needs to be stated only once:

> The rule of A[dverb] P[reposing], constrained as Lakoff suggests, . . . will generate *Last night, I mentioned that Sam smoked pot* only from *I mentioned last night that Sam smoked pot.* The structures assigned to the various sentences considered are exactly those that give the right semantic interpretations. There is only one rule of A[dverb] P[reposing], a syntactic rule. The underlying forms determine the meaning, by whatever principles apply independently to the examples with no preposing. The argument does not bear at all on . . . the autonomy thesis, or on any position developed in *Syntactic structures.*
>
> (Chomsky 1975a: 54)

To appreciate the distance between Chomsky's position and Lakoff's it is necessary to understand that no less than four distinct theories of grammar were at issue in this exchange and that they were being compared as regards the predictions they each made concerning two distinct data sets. The first theory was the *Aspects* theory, in which semantic interpretation rules were held to apply only at the level of deep structure to yield semantic representations. Generative Semantics was the second theory, which of course identified deep structures with semantic representations. The third theory was the Extended Standard Theory of Chomsky 1970, 1971 and Jackendoff 1972, in which semantic interpretation rules applied not only to deep structures, but also to surface structures and to various other stages in the derivation. The fourth theory was the Trace Theory of Chomsky 1975b, in which Semantic Interpretation Rules applied only to annotated surface structures. As to the data sets, the first – which we will call Set A – comprised the sentences with temporal adverbs Lakoff had discussed; as Lakoff had shown, semantic interpretation of these sentences depended on the position of the adverb in underlying structure. Set B contained sentences involving "subject oriented" adverbs like *carelessly* and *intentionally* whose interpretation Jackendoff 1972: 82–7 had demonstrated depended on their position at surface structure.

The theory against which Lakoff had been arguing in his paper was the Extended Standard Theory, which was the theory Chomsky and Jackendoff were on record as defending at the time Lakoff was writing. On that theory, if Set A adverbs were interpreted according to their surface position, then Lakoff was correct: the restriction limiting Adverb Preposing to the clause except in certain specified cases would have to be stated twice, once as a condition on that transformation and once as a condition on the semantic interpretation rule relating surface structure and semantic representation. On the other hand, if Set A adverbs in the Extended Standard Theory were to be interpreted according to their deep structure position, then the theory could not claim a uniform interpretation of adverbs at any one level, since Set B adverbs presumably had to be interpreted at the surface. Lakoff appeared to assume that this fact would favor the Generative Semantics approach, although he did not formally demonstrate that it would.

Chomsky's reply to Lakoff considered only Set A adverbs and assumed a theory in which such adverbs were interpreted either (as in the *Aspects* theory) at the level of deep structure or (as in Trace Theory) at the level of annotated surface structure. His terse dismissal obscured the fact that the *Aspects* theory was not adequate for Set B adverbs and that Trace Theory had not been on the table at the time of Lakoff's article. More significantly, Chomsky did not really address the question of whether an Interpretive approach of any kind to both Set A and Set B adverbs could be shown to be as economical as the Generative Semantics approach, thus avoiding the central substantive issue that separated the two positions.[6] Nevertheless, the rhetorical effect of Chomsky's comments was to make Lakoff's confident assertions look somewhat foolish, although perhaps Lakoff's only mistake had been to underestimate the resources Interpretivists had available. This was a mistake that was repeated on both sides with considerable regularity.

While matters were raised in the two cases we have just examined that called out for further work that was not forthcoming, sometimes the insults – imagined and real – that each side endured during the debates spurred intensive and productive research. One particularly interesting example of this involved an article Paul Postal wrote in 1969 entitled "On the surface verb 'remind'," published in *Linguistic Inquiry*'s inaugural issue in 1970, in which he argued that the English sentence *Pete reminded Max of his father* is transformationally derived from the same complex source that underlies *Max struck Pete as resembling his father*. Crucial to this account were four hypothesized rules: (a) "Complement Subject Raising," which would move the underlying subject *Pete* of the embedded clause enclosed in brackets in *Max struck [Pete as resembling his father]* into a structural position where it could serve as direct object of the predicate realized as *struck*; (b) "Psych Movement," which would switch the subject and object noun phrases; (c) "Predicate Raising," which would form a complex predicate from the elements underlying *struck* and *resembling*; and (d) a lexical insertion rule that would insert *remind* for the complex predicate. All four rules had been argued for elsewhere in the Generative Semantics literature (Postal 1971, G. Lakoff 1969, McCawley 1968c).

73

Chomsky briefly considered Postal's analysis in his paper "Some empirical issues in the theory of transformational grammar" (Chomsky 1972a: 152), offering evidence that it would be inadequate to account for other sentences he felt were formally analogous to those containing *remind*. In an aside, he mentioned that Subject Raising and Psych Movement furthermore seemed to him "at best dubious rules," although he gave no reasons for that conclusion. As we will see, this characterization set in motion activity that resulted in considerable entrenchment on both sides of the issue.

In a letter he wrote to Chomsky on 23 April 1970, commenting on a draft of the "Empirical issues" paper, John Ross recommended that the aside about the dubiousness of the two rules (evidently worded more strongly in the draft) be dropped.

> [I]f you want to reject Psych Movement (or Flip), then take up the thirty pages of discussion that Postal gives in Ch. 6 of *Crossover* [Postal 1971]. To merely state, without going into cases, that the rule is "without syntactic motivation" is an unnecessary slap in the face for Postal. Similarly, you should either discuss, point-by-point, all the prior discussion (by Rosenbaum, Lakoff (in "Deep and surface grammar" [G. Lakoff 1968a]), [and] Postal (in *Crossover*)) of Subject Raising, if you find it highly dubious.
>
> (p.c. to Chomsky 23 April 1970)

Chomsky replied to Ross in an undated letter that he felt Ross was being "oversensitive."

> I went through the crossover arguments in class in Jan., 1969, and showed, to my satisfaction at least, that they give no argument for Psych Movement (or Flip) . . . I am simply stating my opinion that these rules have no serious motivation, and then say I won't pursue it, because it doesn't matter to the argument. However, if you feel that this is unfair, I'll qualify it even more. Same with respect to Subject Raising.
>
> (p.c. to Ross, no date)

Chomsky then suggested that Ross compare his "rather qualified" comments about the rules with "dozens of others that I could easily show you," including a footnote in Postal's paper "Anaphoric islands" (Postal 1969: 233), in which Postal had referred without further elaboration to an Interpretivist discussion of pronominalization by one of Chomsky's students as "particularly unfortunate"; a passage in a review by Georgia Green (1970b) which read, "As developed since 1966, [grammatical theory] may be considered an explicit framework for investigating the properties of natural languages"; and George Lakoff's paper "On Generative Semantics," which mimicked in a number of passages the style of Chomsky's

"Deep structure" paper. These things had clearly offended Chomsky; he added that, after reading the papers in the proceedings of fifth annual meeting of the Chicago Linguistic Society (1969), "I was thinking quite seriously about quitting the field" (p.c. to Ross, no date).

Postal acknowledged in a letter to Chomsky written on 19 November 1970, that the arguments he had assembled in support of Subject Raising had all been directed against an alternative which supposed, for example, that the noun phrase *Arthur* in the sentence *Max believes [Arthur to be a vampire]* was never in a clause indicated by the brackets, and that none of these arguments had in fact contemplated the possibility – which Chomsky was evidently now embracing – that that noun phrase not only was once in such a clause but also remains there throughout the derivation. But Postal pointed out that any proposal to take such a possibility seriously would face obvious problems. For example, reflexive marking and reciprocal marking are assumed to be clause-bounded; but if so, then on the hypothesis Chomsky was apparently championing acceptable sentences like *Max believes [himself to be a werewolf]* and *Harriet and Joan consider [each other to be honest]* should not be generated. "Just to keep matters straight for the public," he said, he was circulating a list of further objections to the position he assumed Chomsky was taking, and enclosed a copy of that as well. Finally, he asked Chomsky to reveal "just what motivates your wish to abandon a uniform rule of [Subject] Raising . . . Even my not inactive imagination is at a loss here. The Raising analysis seems to be among the best supported pieces of English grammar."

Chomsky replied to Postal on 20 January 1971, that the reason "why I want to drop [Subject] Raising into object position is that it seems to me an unmotivated rule." He noted that he had given some class lectures "about a more general approach to a whole variety of questions," in which two categories of sentence, tensed and nontensed, were set up. The principle governing extraction and insertion would then be that tensed sentences "are immune to either," except from the complementizer position. ("Thus just in case there is a rule that moves something into the complementizer position [of a tensed sentence] on one cycle, it can be extracted on the next cycle.") This would account for, *inter alia*, the possibility of reflexivization or passivization operating on the subjects of infinitival complement clauses, but not on the subjects of finite complement clauses. Finally, he added that:

> what so arouses your ire is a side remark (unsupported, as my text makes clear) that I regard some rule as dubious. Even if that were erroneous, your response would be astonishing. In fact, even if I had given a wrong argument, made a factual error, or whatever, such a response would be astonishing – it is doubly so when what is involved is a statement that I regard a proposal as dubious. You act as though

it is a kind of lèse-majesté to mention that one regards something you believe as dubious, or to criticize it. This kind of reaction makes discussion impossible, too unpleasant to be worth pursuing.

(p.c. to Postal, 20 January 1971)

Postal replied to Chomsky on 1 April 1971 that, "while there is unquestion-ably something right to a distinction between 'tensed' and 'non-tensed' especially infinitival clauses," he could "find little merit" in Chomsky's specific proposal. For one thing, that proposal would seem to undermine "one of the key arguments for the lexicalist position" that Chomsky had adopted in Chomsky 1970, namely that the contrast between *Bill's belief that Mary is dead* and **Bill's belief of Mary to be dead* is a function of the failure of Subject Raising to apply in nominals. And as to the claim that material is extractable from a tensed sentence only if it has previously moved into complementizer position, that would seem to be contradicted by the existence of sentences like *Who did Joan say that Mary kissed?*, where *who* has been extracted from an embedded tensed clause in which the complementizer position is already filled by *that*. More generally, he concluded that:

we are so far apart and so lacking common assumptions and judg-ment that the time has possibly come when discussion is largely fruitless beyond picking up occasional counterexamples to proposals, which opposing-hostile thought generates with great facility. Frankly, I find it increasingly hard to see the kind of work you do and sponsor as part of a common field of interest.

(p.c. to Chomsky, 1 April 1971)

The positions taken informally in this correspondence were subsequently refined and developed by Chomsky in his article "Conditions on transform-ations" (Chomsky 1973) and later works (Chomsky 1975b, 1977b) and by Postal in his 447-page monograph *On Raising* (Postal 1974b). The issues that separated them became increasingly technical and complex, and will not be rehearsed here. However, it is worth pointing out that even now, more than twenty years after Postal and Chomsky originally staked out their respective positions, there is no consensus on the matter.[7] In some respects, "Raised" subjects behave as if they are matrix direct objects, and in others they behave as if they are still embedded subjects, and there is enough conflicting evidence to give encouragement on both sides. Still, the fact that fundamental disagreements of this kind remain concerning a sentence like *Bill wanted Mary to win* underscores the great difficulty of constructing compelling analyses of the surface forms of even the appar-ently simple constructions.

The three cases we have examined in this chapter illustrate the difficulties facing anyone who sets out to argue against another's research program.

Real issues were in fact raised in these exchanges, but were obscured as each side proved unwilling to engage with the other on exactly the other's terms. Positions shifted; assumptions were missed or ignored; agreement could not even be reached about what the data to be explained were. Not surprisingly, then, while they encouraged allies, the strong statements used in the arguments only fed the disregard each side felt for the other. Moreover, the participants could not help but see in their opponents' polemical efforts at least some evidence of ill will. Not being able to understand the rational basis for the arguments used against them, they were naturally tempted to locate the source of the dispute in personality traits of their antagonists.

4

WHAT HAPPENED TO
GENERATIVE SEMANTICS?

While the strong critiques launched between 1968 and 1975 by Interpretive Semanticists against Generative Semantics positions involving prelexical syntax, global and transderivational constraints, and performative verbs did not exactly go unanswered, and despite repeated attempts by Lakoff, McCawley, Postal, and Ross to demonstrate the superiority of the Generative Semantics approach, by the mid-1970s it was clear that Generative Semantics was no longer the vital, cooperative research program it had been a few years before. Even if the Generative Semanticists for the most part rejected the Interpretivists' empirical and conceptual attacks, they were turning up in their own research empirical and conceptual problems for their theory that resisted easy solution. For example, critical papers written in the late 1960s or early 1970s by Stephen Anderson (1971), Jerry Morgan (1973a, 1973b), and Jerrold Sadock (1975), all of whom had previously made important contributions to Generative Semantic theory, raised serious questions both about the empirical basis for the hypothesis that the illocutionary force and presuppositions of a sentence are represented in underlying structure and about the coherence of the set of assumptions in which such hypotheses were usually included. More broadly, these challenges indicted the idea that all of what was widely assumed to go into the meaning of a sentence could or should be represented in underlying structure as part of the initial phrase marker in a derivation. The great initial appeal and promise of Generative Semantics had been that it would eventually permit a precise, structurally-driven specification of the route from form to meaning. But if abstract performatives and presuppositions were not part of underlying structure and had to be accommodated in some nonstructural fashion, the whole program was seemingly called into question.

There may perhaps have been those who saw such challenges as damning, or at least as providing sufficient grounds for abandoning the theory in favor of Interpretive Semantics. But, if so, it would be difficult to make a case that the fate of Generative Semantics rested in their hands. In the first place, neither Anderson nor Morgan nor Sadock can really have been read as arguing *in support of* any alternative to Generative Semantics; in particular, none was advocating a turn to Interpretivist theory, nor did it appear that the problems they identified for Generative Semantics had more natural solutions there. In the second place, Interpretive Semantics suffered perhaps more ambitious challenges through the years to no lasting ill effect: it is worth remembering that McCawley, Ross, and Perlmutter were themselves once students of Chomsky, and a sizeable number of other students of his (including Barbara Hall Partee, Arnold Zwicky, Joan Bresnan, Michael Brame, Nomi Erteschik-Shir, Thomas Wasow, Anthony Kroch, and Ivan Sag) have gone on to develop or work in competitor theories outside the Interpretivist tradition. In fact, the papers by Anderson, Morgan, and Sadock set the stage for what might well have been a deeper discussion of the role that semantic representation plays in grammar. As McCawley (1985) and Davison (1983) were later to show, the arguments against the performative hypothesis, at least, were not definitive. Nor did those arguments really bear upon on the viability of the core propositions of the theory. In particular, there was no reason to conclude from even a negative answer to the empirical question of whether performatives appear in underlying structure that no theory of semantic representation systematically related to surface structure was then possible.[1]

There were three questions in particular that required answer, from the Generative Semantics standpoint: (a) which *categories* of meaning play a role in determining the distribution of linguistic elements? (b) Of these, which are conventional (i.e. which are involved in the calculation of the literal meaning of a sentence from its constituent parts)? (c) What semantic justification is there for a level of semantic representation (especially if that level itself needs interpreting)? Prior to McCawley 1981, Generative Semanticists writing within the Generative Semantics framework had been able to report much progress only on the first of these (see, e.g. G. Lakoff 1972, McCawley 1972), and even then, serious problems remained. In fact, some of the most penetrating studies of these issues within generative grammar were being undertaken in the 1970s by those working in the Interpretivist tradition (Jackendoff 1972, Katz 1972, Wilson 1974, J. Fodor, J.A. Fodor, and Garrett 1975, Kempson 1975, Jackendoff 1976, Katz 1977a, 1977b, J.A. Fodor 1979, Chomsky 1980). However, the solutions that turned up in these studies generally did not decide between the Generative Semantics and the Interpretive Semantics approaches to grammar, and a Generative Semantics perspective on them surely would have been of interest.

Far more problematical for Generative Semantics was the fact that Lakoff, Postal, and Ross during the mid-1970s found themselves giving up on some of the central propositions not only of their theory, but of generative grammar generally. Concerned that acceptability judgments did not divide up data as neatly as the theory predicted, Ross investigated the possibility that categories were not discrete, largely deferring the question of how such a conclusion might be accommodated in the theory. Meanwhile, although Postal continued to seek out high-level generalizations, he severely narrowed the range of facts about which he was willing to talk, thus explicitly limiting the goals of the subtheory he was devising; in short order, he came to assert that grammatical relations (like "subject" and "direct object") had to be primitive in the theory and to deny that transformations had any role to play in syntax. For his part, Lakoff took the even more radical route of reexamining the logical foundations on which Generativist conceptions of semantics were assumed to rest, ultimately rejecting most of them on the basis of facts he argued could be accommodated only in a very different kind of theory. In fact, of the original Generative Semanticists, only McCawley ever really attempted in these later years to develop solutions to the anomalies that had been accruing in a way that was relatively consistent with the Generative Semantics program as initially conceived (see McCawley 1981, 1988).

As was pointed out in Chapter 2, the existence of counterexample is generally insufficient in itself to cause rejection of a theory; moreover, Generative Semantics, as we have seen, was probably no worse off than Interpretive Semantics as far as disconfirmatory evidence went. It is thus worth speculating why Lakoff, Postal, and Ross were no longer interested in defending Generative Semantics after the early 1970s.

One thing one cannot but be aware of when scanning the reference sections of Chomsky's works during the 1970s – especially during the critical period in the middle 1970s – is the large number of citations to his students. In Chomsky's six major theoretical publications between 1973 and 1977 (Chomsky 1973, 1975a, 1975b, 1976, 1977a, and Chomsky and Lasnik 1977), he refers to the work of no fewer than forty-eight linguists who had graduated or who would ultimately graduate from the linguistics program at MIT. Often in these publications, Chomsky relied on arguments suggested by these students in advancing his case. It can reasonably be inferred, therefore, that the role played in the development of the Interpretivist research program by MIT graduate students has not been inconsequential. This conclusion is further reinforced by remarks that Morris Halle – who cofounded the graduate program with Chomsky at MIT in the early 1960s – has made regarding his view of the responsibilities of MIT students (Halle 1987):

> The central experience of students in our program has always been their exposure to ongoing research . . . Specifically we made the research conducted by faculty, visitors and students the core of the teaching program. Students are exposed to the problems that others

in the group are working on, and they discover what role they can (and/or would like to) play in this work, how they can utilize in this work the knowledge and the skills that they already possess and what other knowledge and skills they must acquire to be effective. This approach . . . implies that each member of a research group can and should contribute materially to the results that are obtained and that these contributions need not be delayed until the person has completed a prescribed course of study.[2]

In fact, MIT's success in attracting bright students and rapidly turning them into productive members of the research program there is unparalleled among linguistics departments.

According to the MIT graduate school catalogue for 1973, the linguistics faculty in MIT's Department of Foreign Literatures and Linguistics that year consisted of Noam Chomsky, Kenneth Hale, Morris Halle, James Harris, Paul Kiparsky, David Perlmutter, and John Robert Ross. Also associated in one way or another with the linguistics program were Jerry Fodor, Merrill Garrett, Jerrold Katz, and Wayne O'Neil. Considering this list, and similar lists from preceding and ensuing years, we may identify several conditions, independently of Chomsky's own special status, on which the department's success had evidently rested during the 1970s. First, relative to other linguistics departments at the time, and despite the differences between Chomsky and Ross, the department at MIT was on the whole in fact quite homogeneous as regards theoretical orientation; most of the regular faculty had been Chomsky's students and all of the combined regular and associated faculty were at least participants in the same general research program deriving from Chomsky's work (i.e. that of generative grammar as broadly specified in Chomsky's *LSLT* (1975c)). Second, that program was unequivocally the focus of research in the department, which was roughly organized to advance it. And third, the faculty, as Halle suggests, not only made a concerted effort to recruit graduate students into the research program, but more importantly expected that its students would sooner or later contribute substantively to it.

There were four Generative Semanticists in the late 1960s and early 1970s who had more or less equal standing in the Generative Semantics research program (Lakoff, McCawley, Postal, and Ross), and all were working at different institutions for most of this time. As Newmeyer (1980: 172, 1986: 137) points out, of these, only McCawley at the University of Chicago was really in a position to build "a stable base and following" during the rise of Generative Semantics, since Ross was under Chomsky's shadow at MIT, Postal had no students at IBM, and Lakoff was moving from Harvard to Michigan to Palo Alto to Berkeley in the crucial years from 1969 through 1972. It is true that, at one point in 1969–70, when George and Robin

Lakoff were both teaching at the University of Michigan and McCawley was also in residence there as a visitor, Generative Semantics seemed to be on the verge of establishing a secure home in Ann Arbor. But by the fall of 1971 that possibility had evaporated, as the Lakoffs had departed for the Center for Advanced Study in the Behavioral Sciences in California and McCawley was back in Chicago, having carried a considerable part of the fortunes of Generative Semantics with him.[3]

It was of course at the University of Chicago where the Chicago Linguistic Society (CLS) had taken root, whose annual meetings provided Generative Semanticists with their most successful national forum. Moreover, McCawley's students at Chicago in the late 1960s – and in particular Robert Binnick, Bill Darden, Alice Davison, Georgia Green, and Jerry Morgan – together formed one of the earliest and most productive cohorts of committed second-generation Generative Semanticists. Given McCawley's stature in the Generative Semantics program and his ability to attract a following, it might have been expected that Chicago students in the 1970s would continue to do for Generative Semantics what MIT students were (now in increasing numbers) doing for Interpretive Semantics.

But they did not. With a few notable exceptions, after the Binnick cohort, Chicago students did not produce work that advanced the Generative Semantics program. And it seems to us that this fact is necessary to an understanding of the failure of Generative Semantics as a social institution. When doubts were raised about Interpretivist explanations, those in the Interpretivist community might reasonably expect one of its members to have something cogent to say on the matter, because there was a relatively coherent research program and a relatively cohesive research group working on the problems, a group regularly enlarged by a continuing supply of MIT graduate students whose fresh ideas and arguments could be counted on to move the program forward. After 1972 or perhaps earlier, no such help for Generative Semantics could be counted on from Chicago students (or students from anywhere else, for that matter). For example, in stark contrast to the forty-eight MIT students and graduates cited by Chomsky in his publications between 1973 and 1977, McCawley only found it appropriate to mention, in his fifteen major papers during the same period, the work of a total of five of their Chicago counterparts.[4]

We will focus on Chicago because it was perhaps the most obvious location for sustained resistance to the attacks coming from MIT to develop, and the reasons for its failure to develop there are therefore of some interest. Generative Semantics, for better or for worse, had defined itself in opposition to the Chomskyan program and had made a serious contest out of the disagreement. Its adherents had proclaimed it not only a viable alternative to Interpretive Semantics, but a provable improvement on it. So if Generative Semantics could not be seen to prevail somehow over Interpretive Semantics, it would fail on the basis of its own criteria for success. Meanwhile, Interpretive Semantics was intent on demonstrating its superiority to Generative Semantics and was building a populous and very active program that had that as an important goal. In the absence of Interpretive Semantics, a loosely knit Generative Semantics community might perhaps have survived for some time, even flourished. But the challenge posed by the MIT program in the 1970s was so severe that it could have been met only if Generative Semanticists had been able to put together some kind of well-organized opposition to which new recruits might have been attracted as rapidly and effectively as they were there. Moreover, there were forces that were pulling Generative Semanticists apart that might have been countered if a central training school for young Generative Semanticists had been established that had a demonstrably coherent and productive curriculum.

The University of Chicago Announcements for October 1972 lists thirty active members of its Department of Linguistics, including Howard Aronson (Chair), Kali Bahl, Miguel Civil, Bill Darden, Peter Dembowski, Gerard Diffloth, Gösta Franzen, Paul Friedrich, Ignace Gelb, Zbigniew Golab, Gene Gragg, Hans Guterbock, Eric Hamp, Kostas Kazazis, Carolyn Killean, James McCawley, Noriko Akatsuka McCawley, Raven McDavid, David McNeill, Norman McQuown, Anthony Naro, A. K. Ramanujan, Erica Reiner, Sheldon Sachs, Jerrold Sadock, Michael Silverstein, Dale Terbeek, Joseph Williams, Victor Yngve, and Norman Zide. The strength of the department had always been its broad and deep languages program, and courses in Akkadian, Albanian, Assyrian, Bulgarian, Cambodian, Chinook, Comparative Algonkian, Czech, Georgian, Greek, Irish, Mayan, Romanian, Sanskrit, Tamil, Thai, Urdu, and Welsh, among a number of others, were regularly offered. Many of the Chicago students had come to the University because of its special resources with respect to these languages, and in any case all students were expected to avail themselves of such resources in one way or another.

If MIT's linguistics faculty was relatively homogeneous theoretically, Chicago's was radically heterodox; of the thirty Chicago faculty in 1972, only four could fairly be described as advocates of some form of transformational grammar, and Prague School and American and European structuralist approaches were strongly represented. To the extent that the members of the department could be said to have had a common calling, it was devotion to painstaking inspection of the less familiar languages. In the face of this departmental diversity, McCawley's message to his students was essentially that there were important and interesting facts about language to be discovered in a variety of places and that theory construction depended importantly on the discovery of such facts. Evidently in reaction against what he saw as a deficiency in the deductive strategy prevalent among Chomskyan linguists (a reaction inspired perhaps in part by his embarrassment over some "sweeping and rash generalizations" he himself had earlier made – see McCawley 1979: viii), McCawley by the mid-1970s was not encouraging work by his students whose principal goal was simply technical improvement in the way some theory (including Generative Semantics) accounted for an already known set of data: what was prized was the discovery of new and unexpected facts and careful generalizations concerning them which *any* theory would have to accommodate.[5]

The papers of Binnick, Green, and Morgan from the late 1960s suggest that it must have been extremely stimulating for them as students to have been involved in laying the foundations for a new theory of grammar (see especially Benwick, le Fay, and Knight 1976 [1968]). But by 1970 or so, doing theoretical work in Generative Semantics had become a good deal more challenging, and the rewards at Chicago for students entering in those years were in any case largely reserved for more empirically-oriented pursuits.[6] This may explain why, in the CLS volumes in the important years from 1970 through 1972, there were more than twice as many contributions from Chicago students that did *not* address issues relevant to Generative Semantics as those that did.

The fact that their leadership was divided virtually from the start among four independent individuals at four different institutions meant that Generative Semanticists were never able to speak with a single voice. When Morgan (1973a) noted that conflicts among the various assumptions commonly adopted by Generative Semanticists were giving rise to "a growing feeling of confusion" and asserted that "[i]t is time to clear up some fundamental questions," we would suggest that what he was calling for in this case was not more research but rather some reasonable decisions by someone in charge. But in fact none of the four original Generative Semanticists was in a position to set the direction for the program as a whole. And while Chomsky was sharpening the focus of Interpretive theory, the Generative Semanticists were developing a more and more varied set of approaches to an ever widening range of data. As time went on, the interests of Lakoff, McCawley, Postal, and Ross – along with those who had joined them – inevitably diverged. When Postal started working on Relational Grammar, for example, there was some initial uncertainty as to whether his results might still belong to Generative Semantics. By 1974 or 1975, what was part of the theory and what was not had become even more difficult to determine, as studies in semantics and pragmatics began to take on a life of their own.

Even intramurally at Chicago, McCawley evidently had no deep interest either in setting a Generative Semantics agenda or in involving his students in his own personal research program. The work such students ended up doing was rarely inconsistent with that program and occasionally drew on its insights, but was not often crucial to it either. For example, of the twenty-six dissertations defended in the Department of Linguistics at Chicago in the years from 1972 through 1975, only four (Davison 1972, Morgan 1973b, LeGrand 1975, and Levi 1975) took up significant problems for Generative Semantics that attended McCawley's work. Thereafter, it is difficult to identify any Chicago dissertations that deal directly with what had originally been the central concerns of Generative Semantics, although of course McCawley himself continued to work in his version of it.

As for Sadock, who had been brought to Chicago in 1969 to make the intellectual climate there more hospitable for McCawley and his program, he found himself in the early 1970s increasingly unconvinced by the (*ad hoc*, he thought) mechanisms Generative Semanticists were routinely proposing to connect semantic representations and surface structures. Although he remained committed to the mediational orientation and core propositions of Generative Semantics, there were fewer and fewer of its auxiliary hypotheses in which he felt he could believe. In particular, the fact that Generative Semantics often allowed various different explanations for the same set of facts (Sadock 1974a, 1975) was evidence for him of a disturbing looseness in the theory. His alienation from the program became obvious when, instead of attempting to locate solutions to these problems within the program, he retreated in his work to issues of pragmatics that were at best tangential to them.

Whereas articles by Lakoff, McCawley, Postal, and Ross were widely and routinely cited in the developing Generative Semantics literature, it is potentially of some relevance that the contributions of others like Sadock who had allied themselves with the Generative Semantics movement were mentioned there far less frequently. Considered simply from the point of view of a crude cost-benefit model, if academic rewards are distributed at least to some significant degree in the form of citations, there cannot have been much incentive for Sadock and others to continue working along the lines they had. Indeed, despite the fact that the challenges facing the Generative Semantics program had always been reasonably clear, what it could offer those who wished to attempt to address those challenges was becoming much less so. By 1972 perhaps, it was no longer obvious what would constitute a signal contribution to Generative Semantics, since its focus had become so diffused. But if so, then the value of actually doing Generative Semantics in terms of real professional rewards would have declined significantly relative to doing Interpretive Semantics, where program objectives were more sharply defined.

To appreciate the magnitude of this problem for Generative Semantics, consider the quantity of citations to the work of Chicago students and graduates per article in the annual volumes of the Chicago Linguistic Society between 1970 and 1976 (see Figure 1). During this period, the absolute number of papers written by Chicago students which were intended to make a theoretical contribution to Generative Semantics of course increased, but the impact they had as registered in the bibliographies of syntax and semantics articles in these volumes not only did not increase, but actually declined. Although there might be several explanations for this decrease, since no other single group within Generative Semantics had emerged during the period whose influence was increasing relative to that of the Chicago group, it seems reasonable to suppose that it was to some significant extent determined by the increasing fragmentation of the framework.

By 1969, it had to have been clear within the Generative Semantics community that Interpretivism was not only not going to disappear, but was, if anything, well on the way towards gaining a firm upper hand, especially at MIT. If Generative Semanticists had been initially surprised at the force of Chomsky's resistance to their theoretical moves, they must

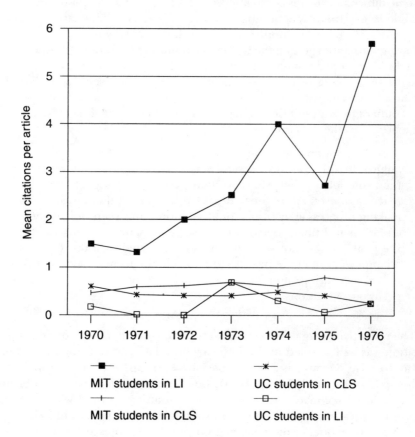

Figure 1 Bibliographical references to the work of University of Chicago and MIT students and graduates in articles on topics in syntax and semantics published in *Proceedings of the Chicago Linguistic Society* and in *Linguistic Inquiry* for the years 1970–1976

have found the way the controversy was playing out a couple of years later even more frustrating and unpleasant. When opportunities arose to disengage from the dispute, many of the Generative Semanticists took them, ultimately prompting their opponents to withdraw as well.

There were in fact two models for disengagement that were available in the 1970s to both Generative Semanticists and Interpretive Semanticists interested in semantic issues. The first was based upon the work of the philosopher H. Paul Grice. Grice, in his William James Lectures delivered at Harvard University in 1967 (see Grice 1975, 1978), had argued that standard formal logics can be made to survive objections concerning their ability to capture ordinary inferences by supplementing them with a compact set of conversational principles. The principles that Grice offered were informally presented and were justified intuitively – generally by anecdote – rather than by rigorous, formal proof. But they showed how some difficult problems at the intersection of logical and linguistic semantics could be overcome by appealing to "pragmatic" aspects of human rationality.

The force of this demonstration was felt particularly by those who were having difficulties getting the formal machinery of Generative Semantics to make the proper semantic predictions. These problems were especially acute in the area of presupposition, the subject of Jerry Morgan's 1973 Chicago dissertation. Morgan had tried to provide a Generative Semantics account of presupposition, but had not met with particular success; indeed, he began his thesis as follows:

> This dissertation can be most accurately described as a report of a failure. It is the result of several years' work toward the goal of the final solution to the presupposition problem. This goal was never reached or even approximated, and at times I felt that I was actually making progress away from a final solution. After years of frustration and despair, I finally decided to preserve my sanity by assuming that the problem was not with me but with my analytical tools, and to attempt to go it alone by stepping outside the formal aspects of the theory I was using, attempting to travel purely on the low-octane fuel of my own intuitions.
>
> (Morgan 1973b: i)

The route that Morgan followed towards a pragmatic account of presupposition was well traveled in the 1970s by both Generative Semanticists and Interpretive Semanticists (see especially Kartunnen 1974, Wilson 1974, Kempson 1975, and Gazdar 1979). But the idea that semantic problems might have pragmatic and nonstructural solutions proved widely adaptable in other areas as well (see, for example, the papers in Cole 1978).

A second model of disengagement from the disputes about deep structure, more appealing to those who wished to retain a formal approach, was provided by the work of the logician Richard Montague (especially

Montague 1973 [1970]). Montague offered a rigorous semantic theory, but explicitly restricted its domain to a relatively small "fragment" of English. Montague's program thus avoided a variety of problems that had engaged linguistic semanticists, and in particular Generative Semanticists, while giving promise of a very respectable theory of semantics that clearly would have linguistic applications. At the same time, it was well understood that one could pursue very specific semantic issues in such a scheme without having also to worry about *all* of the distributional complexities of surface structure.

A third alternative was of course to pursue issues that did not have an obvious immediate connection to the dispute between the Generative Semanticists and the Interpretive Semanticists, or that sought solutions to problems that transcended the dispute: Jackendoff, Lakoff, Postal, and Ross each in different ways followed this course.

5

CONCLUSION

By the late 1970s the situation in theoretical syntax – at least from the perspective of those uncommitted to one or another of the numerous research programs that had sprung up in the wake of Generative Semantics's demise – appeared thoroughly confused. As Edith Moravcsik (1980: 1) remarked at a conference held at the University of Wisconsin–Milwaukee in March of 1979, "The present scene . . . seems to consist of a number of syntacticians all following different approaches most of which have not been shown to be superior to, or even distinct from, the others." In response to this fragmentation, the organizers of the Milwaukee conference asked representatives of fourteen different theories to describe them "according to a set of uniform parameters" in order to "probe into the nature and significance of the differences that obtain among them" (Moravcsik 1980: xiii). Ross, who gave a talk on some aspects of Lakoff's work, urged the audience to take to heart an aphorism attributed to George Miller: "In order to understand what another person is saying, you must assume it's true and try to imagine what it could be true of" (Ross 1979: 1). But the general impression left by the presentations was captured by Robert Stockwell in his post-conference assessment: " . . . it turns out to be too dark to tell for sure who is in the same bed, or what they are doing there" (Stockwell 1980: 353).

Even so, it was by then clear that the theoretical standard – the theory against which all other theories would have to measure themselves – was Chomsky's. If there were any doubt that developments in the Interpretive tradition had come to dominate theoretical syntax, those doubts were blown away by the publication, in 1981, of Chomsky's *Lectures on Government and Binding*, a book which many felt announced a revolution as far-reaching for linguistics as *Syntactic Structures* had twenty-four years before. Meanwhile, the judgment of the four original Generative Semanticists was called increasingly into question, as the charge that they had advocated a false theory came to be more and more frequently repeated.

91

We began this book in an effort to resolve a paradox: if the theory of Generative Semantics had been falsified, why are its central claims by and large still accepted? After reviewing some of the better-known arguments for and against those claims, we concluded that, whatever the problems Generative Semanticists had had in maintaining a socially successful theory of language to compete with the theory that Chomsky was devising, empirical disconfirmation of their core propositions was not the primary factor in the demise of their program. At least, they themselves did not accept Chomsky's arguments against Generative Semantics and usually constructed rebuttals that in retrospect seem to us reasonably well grounded. Some say that Interpretivism prevailed because Chomsky was the more serious theoretician, his proposals the more subtle and complex, his solutions the more articulated and intellectually challenging. Perhaps so, although it is not clear how one might go about substantiating such a hypothesis, or what it might mean as regards the scientific status of anybody's theory. And if we pursue this question, we seem bound to get caught up in an issue in which Chomsky's structuralist predecessors had earlier found themselves entangled (see Joos 1957: 80): can the linguists' theories really aspire to say something about reality, or will they never be more than just pretty arrangements of an ultimately arbitrary selection of tokens? One reason why this issue has not been completely laid to rest (at least in the domain of syntax) is continuing doubt about the validity of the data from which such linguistic theories up to now have been constructed. If every solution can be challenged on the grounds that the data are defective, then it is difficult to defend the position that concrete results have been achieved.

If linguistics is a science and science is about making falsifiable predictions, then we should be able to compare linguistic theories in respect of their predictive power. There were four reasons, however, why none of the comparisons of Generative Semantics and Interpretive Semantics that were actually undertaken was very meaningful: (a) neither side had sufficiently developed theories to which crucial tests could be systematically applied which would clearly favor one set of core hypotheses over another; (b) the two programs differed significantly from one another in both orientation and theoretical coverage, so that even where tests of specific predictions were possible, they did not necessarily generalize; (c) in both programs, an extremely wide range of auxiliary propositions was compatible with the core, and individual propositions could be so readily added or dropped that counterexamples had little force; and (d) the two programs could not always be distinguished by reference to some subset of the propositions advocated by their members, since they began by holding a number of propositions in common, and over time exchanged others that had been independently developed.[1]

Moreover, how accurate a program's predictions are over a wide range of facts is not necessarily a fair measure of its appeal and obviously says little about its promise. The actual empirical coverage of *Syntactic Structures* was small, but it nevertheless showed how a few problems of apparent difficulty for a structuralist approach might receive simple solutions on a transformational one.[2]

This is of course not to say that the criteria by which people actually picked sides during the 1960s and 1970s could not have been motivated by defensible considerations. But we can conclude at least that such criteria could not have been scientific, in the standard sense.[3] For a similar reason, we regard contemporary claims that the Generative Semantics *program* was falsified as essentially ideological in character and scientifically unjustifiable.

What ended up looming so large in the deep structure debates were their ideological implications. It may not have been that Lakoff, McCawley, Postal, and Ross, either individually or in concert, had originally set out to overturn the Chomskyan research program. But soon enough the interaction evolved into an us-versus-them contest that both sides evidently concluded could have but one winner. The legacy of that is that today we characterize the debates in just those us-versus-them, winner-or-loser terms, although such a perspective very much distorts the science that was actually done.

Furthermore, even though the end of the deep structure debates hardly marked the end of the productive careers of those who had participated in them – even though Lakoff, McCawley, Postal, and Ross each went on, as Chomsky did, to do what may well prove to be their most enduring and important work after the discussions that we have considered had terminated – there is no doubt a temptation to see the debates as a watershed, to believe that one of the two paths must have been the superior (if not the right) one. We have argued that there is no reasonable basis for such a belief. And if anything, as these individuals have moved in their own separate directions, there has remained less and less in the way of a common ground against which their contributions can be measured. So, as much as we might wish to draw firm lessons from this history about the large issues debated by the Generative Semanticists and the Interpretive Semanticists, we see no legitimate way of doing so. Nevertheless, we certainly grant that the period of the late 1960s through the mid-1970s was marked by real progress in the understanding of particular linguistic processes. Not only were many new and relevant facts discovered, but important approaches to, or ways of dealing with, those facts were proposed. Sometimes the approaches were simply unintegrated generalizations over the facts, and sometimes the approaches appeared to have more deeply theoretical implications, though many of the most influential of them, such as Lakoff's global account of scope ambiguities and McCawley's analysis of *kill* and *cause to become not alive*, proved to be easily exportable.

In the end, it seems to us that the most significant of the differences between the Generative Semanticists and the Interpretive Semanticists lay in the methodological values they each held. For Chomsky, as we noted above, no datum had status until it had been explained by theory:

> In the study of language as in any other nontrivial inquiry, the phenomena are often dazzling in their apparent complexity and variety. Our glimmerings of understanding can only be expected to illuminate some narrow range. If we hope to proceed beyond taxonomy, it is necessary to select and discard, to concentrate on facts that seem to have some bearing on such explanatory principles as we can devise, ignoring much else in the hope that it will ultimately be explained by deeper theories or perhaps on quite different grounds.
>
> (Chomsky 1977b: 21)

By contrast, Generative Semanticists thought that the construction of "deeper theories" could only proceed if the theorist were prepared to take seriously the insights about data, as yet not satisfactorily explained by the theory, that were accruing at the frontiers of research:

> I think the greatest value of any theory is in the extent to which it makes phenomena accessible to an investigator: the extent to which it helps him to notice things that he would otherwise have overlooked, raises questions which otherwise would not have occurred to him, and suggests previously unfamiliar places in which to look for answers to those questions.
>
> (McCawley 1988: x)

With respect to data that their theory did not readily explain, the Generative Semanticists advocated a "bottom-up" approach: the methodological strategy was to attempt to construct the highest-level generalizations possible regardless of the ramifications for the overall theory. Interpretivists regularly attempted to denigrate this strategy as scientifically unsound and/or reflective of an unhealthy interest in taxonomy over explanation (see Chomsky's remarks above). But the Interpretivists' strategy (which, as Chomsky had also suggested, was to ignore the phenomena that did not fit) was scientifically on no firmer ground. In fact, nothing at all of scientific import was at stake in this issue, which simply reduced to a question of where to look for insights leading to deeper theories. No one really doubted that the best theory would be the one that most economically predicted all the facts. But Generative Semanticists were far less convinced than Interpretive Semanticists that that theory, once discovered, would look sufficiently like the current theory that there was any point to worrying about how restrictive the latter was; the principal issue in their eyes was how to expand the power of the theory to account for a wide variety of facts not currently within its range. This was, however, a matter of value, about which it is hard to see that there could have been any legitimate disputing.

In the years since the deep structure debates ended, the attention of the field has been rightly commanded by a wealth of important research results in syntax and semantics achieved by a new generation of researchers working on a variety of new problems in new domains. But it would be a mistake to dismiss the issues confronted during the Generative Semantics–Interpretive Semantics period as irrelevant to contemporary concerns. As we have seen, crucial questions about the relationship between syntax and semantics remain unanswered, and in no way has the tension between mediational and distributional approaches in linguistics been resolved. As we have also seen, conclusions reached during the debates have in fact played a significant role in the flowering of current theory.

It is perhaps to be expected that any dispute that generated the heat that this one did would not soon or easily be forgotten by those who were involved in it. One brief glance around will confirm that the field of syntax today remains uncomfortably divided into camps that feel they have little to learn from each other. To whatever extent this regime of separateness owes its perpetuation to the bitterness left by the debates, then to that extent might a judicious and dispassionate reexamination of the issues help us to chart a more productive course for research in the years to come.

APPENDIX

Conversations with Ray Jackendoff, George Lakoff, John Robert Ross, and Paul Postal

In 1986 and 1987, we recorded on tape conversations we had with four of the participants in the deep structure debates – Ray Jackendoff, George Lakoff, Paul Postal, and John Robert Ross. These conversations were subsequently transcribed, and although we originally had not intended to publish the transcriptions, we became eventually convinced, as the main text of this book was being written, that some version of them should be included here.

In the fall of 1992, therefore, we offered the interviewees an opportunity to review Chapters 1 through 5 of our text as it then existed and to revise and expand their interviews for publication in this Appendix if they desired. In consequence, one of the interviews (Lakoff's) was almost entirely rewritten; notes and references were added by the interviewees to two others (Postal's and Jackendoff's); and one (Ross's) remained comparatively unchanged from its earlier version. Lightly edited versions of these conversations are reproduced here.

RAY JACKENDOFF
in conversation with John Goldsmith

Ray Jackendoff received his Ph.D. from MIT in 1969. His 1972 book, *Semantic Interpretation in Generative Grammar*, did more than anything else to show that a rigorous and productive account of semantical issues could be given within an Interpretivist framework. In 1977, he published an important study, following suggestions by Harris and Chomsky, entitled *X-bar Syntax*, which attempted to provide an empirical basis for a restricted theory of the base component of a grammar (the term *X-bar* referring to the hierarchical system in which syntactic phrases participate). In subsequent work, he has investigated issues of language in relation to cognition. An important hypothesis in this work is that there is a level at which the linguistic component interfaces with other cognitive components. He is currently professor in the Linguistics and Cognitive Science Program at Brandeis University.

There seems to be some disagreement about why and when the conflict between Chomsky on the one hand and Lakoff, McCawley, and their colleagues on the other hand started. What's your perception?

It must have been under way by the time I came to MIT in 1965. *Aspects* had just come out and Lakoff was talking about abstract syntax, putting more underlying verbs into deep structure. All that was well under way.

Did you think of that kind of work as being antithetical to the Aspects *model or a development of it?*

I don't think I thought of it as being necessarily antithetical to the *Aspects* model. I just didn't think it was right. I think the key person in motivating that kind of work was actually Postal, even though by the time the dispute got going he was sort of secondary. All the people around MIT who were attracted to a Generative Semantics point of view were people who had been taught by Postal, who left MIT in the spring of '65 or so. He was probably thinking along those lines before anybody else. I think it started with the Katz–Postal theory [Katz and Postal 1964], which had abstract elements like "Q" and "Imp" at the front end of the sentence that triggered obligatory transformations and represented the meaning. I suspect in some way that Postal was the originator of that idea. That means he was the originator of the Standard Theory, too.

I've heard that from several people. How did you see that?

Well, of course, I don't know, because he had already left by the time I came to MIT. But if you look back at *Syntactic Structures*, Chomsky said, "Semantics is semi-systematically connected with syntax – systematically enough that we want to account for it, but not systematically enough that we can use it as a key to determine how the syntax works. We have to do the syntax autonomously." His program was to show we have to (and can) do

98

the syntax autonomously. And he never really worried about a systematic connection to semantics. I think it was really Katz and Postal who forced him to it. So Chomsky bought the idea that deep structure is the input to semantic interpretation, and put it in *Aspects* and it became the Standard Theory. But it seems to me that already in Kuroda's [1965] thesis there were some focus facts in Japanese that indicated there was something wrong with the Katz–Postal theory. In the spring of '66, my second semester at MIT, Chomsky was lecturing on *Aspects*, but he also said, "You know, there are these problems with focus in Japanese." So evidently issues of surface structure interpretation were on his mind.

By my second year at MIT (1966) I was already starting to work on an Interpretive approach. One of the things motivating Generative Semantics analyses was the existence of pro-forms that represent various categories: there's a pro-form for verb phrases and there's a pro-form for sentences and a pro-form for comparatives and so forth – and we want them all to be derived by the same transformation of pronominalization. To express the generalization, all of these things had to become noun phrases in under-lying structure. But in the fall of '66 – that was when Chomsky was away – I was starting to work on Interpretive pronominalization. I worked out an Interpretive version of Equi-Noun-Phrase-Deletion that used some kind of empty category, a precursor of PRO, I forget what I called it. I wrote a paper for Halle [Jackendoff 1966] and showed it to Haj Ross, and Haj said, "But look, that means you'll have to interpret this empty form off the surface structure." That worried me a lot.

When Chomsky returned I showed him the paper and said, "I've been working on pronominalization, but it seems to me that you need surface structure interpretation." And he said, "Oh, yeah, of course you need surface structure interpretation." Just like that, you know. So it must have been on his mind. And his response more or less gave me license to go ahead and develop my approach.

Had you been working with Chomsky before he went away?
No.

And then when he got back?
When he got back I was.

Lakoff seems to feel that, when Chomsky returned from California, he – Chomsky – had already started to perceive the Generative Semanticists as forming an opposition. So I wonder if you saw them as basically fleshing out Chomsky's ideas or as belonging to some other group at this point.
I always felt they were saying, "Look! We're going Chomsky one better." And they were, in a sense, working out the consequences of the Standard Theory. Once you assume that every semantic similarity indicates a simil-arity in underlying structure – which is really what they were trying to do –

that methodology enables you to crank out a certain class of analyses. But at the same time there was also a sense of excitement that grew out of this effect that Chomsky has on lots of people.

What is that?
That he's really threatening because he's so smart. It leads a lot of people into trying to outdo him – either at his own game or by finding another game. And there was a sense of that, I think, among that group. I think for all of us who were, as Morris Halle would say, "the smartest boy in Riga," to come up against the mere existence of Chomsky is really a tough experience. He's the one who conversation always centers around when linguists of our generation get together: what's he up to next? He can become a real obsession. And everybody has their own crazy ways of coming to terms with him – often it's either by getting out of syntax or trying to invent a new kind of syntax. And there is a strong current out in the world of "anything but Chomsky," I think.

How do you mean?
Well, I think that Lakoff and Ross were both great showmen. And, whether or not they intended it, they were grabbed on to by a lot of people, all these structuralists who had had their teeth kicked in, who saw in Generative Semantics a way to get Chomsky. I think there was a point where Lakoff and Ross started playing that role.

But is it Chomsky, or is it just his having been so prominent in the field? Is it possible that just trying to make a place for yourself, which is what any young person wants to do, can be perceived by the person who is already prominent as a personal threat?
Maybe that's what Lakoff and Ross saw themselves as doing, but I think great parts of the world interpreted it another way: "Here's the way to get Chomsky." What was significant about that time was it was the first time that generative grammarians had broken rank. For example, I gave a job talk at Illinois in 1969, in which I attacked Generative Semantics in the course of presenting my own work. And Mike Geis just went for me. He was vicious. At the reception afterwards, Robert Lees pulled us together and said, "Mike, why are you so anxious to get Ray? What's in it for you?" And Mike said, "Well, you know, being a generative linguist is like being part of a family. And it's like being attacked by your own brother." And I think up to that point it really was that way. We saw ourselves as this little enclave of people and it was us against the world. That period was the first time that there was disagreement. Maybe people expected that no matter what you did, Chomsky would approve, because we're all part of this family and we're all working on the same goals. But it was not the case anymore.

Do you see a difference between the kinds of disagreements there were at the time you're discussing and, let's say, those that are going on today?
One difference is that now it's taken for granted that there's going to be

disagreement, and so people's expectations of mutual intellectual admiration are a little bit lower. And that's healthy. It's clear that everybody has to learn to live with everybody else. You're not going to convert anybody, and your opponents are going to be working in the field for a long time. Sometimes people even recognize that there are insights in another framework that they've got to take account of.

Did you attend any of the classes that Lakoff taught at Harvard and Ross taught at MIT at this time?

Ross was giving a class that he and Lakoff sort of team taught. I went to a few sessions of it and gave up on it, I think. I just didn't find it interesting. I had my own axe to grind. Guy Carden had written some papers on quantifier lowering [Carden 1967, 1968], and having started doing some work on quantifiers myself, I thought that was the craziest idea. I started working on arguments against quantifier lowering and negative raising: why those rules wouldn't work purely on distributional grounds [eventually published as Jackendoff 1971]. So when those kinds of transformations were being invoked right and left, I just didn't have any sympathy for it. And I had the feeling that most of the students at MIT felt the same way. By the time we were second and third year students we had seen some really tidy work and there was a real difference.

Was Chomsky talking about "Remarks" at that point?

The fall of '67 would have been when he started talking about "Remarks" – which was not really addressed to Generative Semantics. I think it was only the following year that he started attacking deep structure interpretation. What "Remarks" really addressed was the earlier manifestation of Generative Semantics, wherein transformations could change categories (a possibility utilized widely in Lees [1960] *Grammar of English Nominalizations*). That's really what he was addressing; that and the theory of exceptions developed in Lakoff's thesis, which licensed those sorts of transformations. What Chomsky was saying was that transformations just can't get these derived nominals to come out with the right meaning and the right productivity. Instead, he substituted X-bar theory, which is a way of treating syntax like phonology. You capture generalizations with features. So, "Remarks" was saying, "Here's a different way to organize the syntax so we can get these generalizations without using scads of transformations. Put the power in the base instead." At the same time, he resolved some earlier inherent contradictions in the theory. In *Syntactic Structures*, all embedding was sentential; there was a fantasy that S was the only recursive category. "Remarks" said, "Forget about that; anything can be recursive, and we'll get generalizations about recursion by using syntactic features. We'll constrain phrase structure by means of the X-bar levels, rather than through constraints on embedding transformations. That way there's hope for a syntax that isn't just festering with transformations; we can keep

101

syntax to things that we can really see." Then, of course, Chomsky's paper on *Wh*-movement came along and introduced traces and other things that we can't see . . . .[laughter] But certainly much more of the phrase structure is visible now than it was, and it was possible to achieve less distance between deep and surface structure exactly because of that innovation.[1]

What were the other students at MIT doing at that time?
Well, Joe Emonds was starting work on root transformations pretty early, really trying to constrain rules and say what can move where [Emonds 1970]. And that was the other side of the effort, to work out a typology of transformational rules. My class, I think, was the last one that was taught by Ed Klima at MIT. He did a very careful kind of syntax, where you look at the facts and try out six or seven different ways of handling them and decide which ways are notational variants, so you see the dialectic of giving something here and getting it back there. That was something I really got out of his classes.

That was also the period when Morris Halle was teaching the introductory syntax class, and his approach to it was the same as his approach to phonology. You very carefully lay out the rules one at a time and follow the consequences in great gory detail. That was something I never got out of Generative Semantics, where they would propose a transformation, and you'd try to put it together with the other three transformations of the last three wild papers, and you couldn't do it. It was all well and good in classes and lectures, but when these papers finally came to be published, people started seeing the consequences and interactions more clearly.

What about Ross's analysis of the auxiliary as a right-branching structure [Ross 1969] – were people talking about that at the time?
I think that's one of those kind of things that Klima would try out and say we could do it this way or we could do it that way. I remember Klima spending a whole week on five different versions of *Do*-support.

But the right-branching analysis is one that is basically accepted by everybody who thinks about it these days, and yet at the time it was associated with Generative Semantics, although, as Pullum and Wilson [1977] pointed out, there was really no necessary connection between Generative Semantics and a right-branching analysis of the auxiliary.
The thing was that Ross presented it as the position that auxiliaries are simply verbs. And therefore he was trying to assimilate them to the complement structures of Rosenbaum [1965]. But that was one of the things that was undercut by "Remarks." Ross would ask, "Why do you need this disjunction of categories – auxiliary and verb – in the rule of Subject Inversion, say?" He would express the generalization by just calling them all verbs. But once you have a feature system, as in "Remarks," there's no longer a problem. You just say auxiliaries and verbs share some feature,

and that's that. And so Ross's kind of argument didn't cut much ice anymore.

This was the first time that Chomsky had changed his mind about something that had gotten entrenched, the first time he said, "No, that wasn't right after all," or "I never believed it." If you look back, he always hedges very carefully. He always says, "Well, it's not clear whether it's in the syntax, but if it is in the syntax, it might work like this." So he sets himself up for revisionism if he needs it.

There's something else about this period I've been trying to figure out. Around the period of *Aspects*, Chomsky was the toast of all the intelligentsia. Generative linguistics was the hot new item. People were writing books about Chomsky and all the psychologists were learning generative grammar and all the philosophers were wondering about innateness. But by 1974, that was all gone.

Gone, or established already?
No, gone. Here's my evidence that it's gone; I've discussed this in an essay in *Natural Language and Linguistic Theory* [Jackendoff 1988]. If you look at books written today on psychology, they say, "Well, there was this guy Chomsky who showed us behaviorism was wrong. He invented this theory of generative grammar, but it wasn't a psychological theory because it didn't tell us how to process sentences." Or maybe they go a little farther and say, "The derivational theory of complexity didn't work and that shows that generative grammar is wrong." Or they'll say, "Here's some recent developments in generative grammar," and then they'll talk about Generative Semantics. That is, in these books, the history of linguistics as relevant to psychology stops in the early '70s. They know nothing about the Lexicalist Hypothesis, nothing about Government and Binding theory. Maybe they know a little about Joan Bresnan's Lexical Functional Grammar, because she talked about processing for a while. But they didn't really get very interested in that for long. Instead, what's hot in psychology now is connectionism. They talk about the need for processing but not the need for representations, and certainly not about how you might find out what representations are like. Linguists claim that our rules are about what forms of representation the processor has to work with. But that's not viewed as a possible enterprise. If you read somebody like John Anderson, he says, "The way to find out about representations is to see how the processes work on them." Or Steve Kosslyn will say, "You know, you really can't tell what's in the processor and what's in the structures."

There's some truth to that, don't you think?
Absolutely. But then they go on to say, "We aren't entitled to make any assumptions about structure, and so we'll make the minimal assumptions we can." And then when they're working with language they'll assume something like a simplified version of Case Grammar, which is to say that

they turn their back on practically everything that generative linguistics has discovered. It seems to me that there are more fruitful ways; there could be an interaction.

Here's another part of it. During the period when Generative Semantics was falling apart – '71, '72, '74 – there was an ecological niche left open that was filled by formal semantics.

You're proposing this as a drag chain; but I've heard other people say it was a push chain and point to Barbara Partee and her change of allegiance as being quite early.
I think Barbara wanted to believe Generative Semantics, but was too good a linguist to buy it. But the point is that that was the bandwagon that people jumped on, formal semantics. Hardly anybody ever went back to Lexicalism. I think Fritz Newmeyer is one of the few people to have been a Generative Semanticist who became a Lexicalist.

So people just take a position and then stay with it? Populations change by people coming in and out?
Government and Binding Theory is as predominant as it is only because MIT has been cranking out good Ph.D.s faster than anyplace else. You're to a very great extent a victim of where you did your graduate work and who was there at the time.

Well, of course, you do choose where you go. It's not like your parents, whom you don't get to pick.
Yes, but you don't know anything when you're an undergraduate. If you're coming from one of the major institutions, it's one thing – maybe you do know something. But if you're coming from someplace else, how are you to know? You apply to MIT and Berkeley and they look the same. They're both good linguistics departments.

If one place has money and the other doesn't, of course that will make a difference. The money alone has funneled people to MIT.
Right.

You mentioned a minute ago that it was a down period for Generative Semantics after 1970. Do you think that was true at MIT as well, in syntax? You were working on your X-bar book [Jackendoff 1977] by '72, '73, but I had the impression that you felt you were working basically in isolation, that you weren't exciting Chomsky by it.
I think that may be true. He was asking, "How do we constrain movement rules?," but he hadn't hit on a way to do it. And he was fooling around, trying this and that. Why should we expect even Noam continually to be a fund of brilliant insight? [laughter]

I think there was a lot of consolidation going on. The sense was, "We've bought this theory where we have to interpret surface structure and we can't have pronominalization transformations anymore, and now we've got to put our money where our mouth is." And I have a feeling that a lot of scut work was being laid down, maybe inconspicuously, during that period. I'd done a lot of stuff on pronominalization earlier [Jackendoff 1968b], but somehow it didn't find its way into the literature. What did find its way in was Lasnik's stuff and Fiengo's stuff, which was all about how you can use anaphora to do what movement rules used to do. And that's what was getting laid down then, exploring different structural notions such as c-command, playing with empty elements. And Joan Bresnan was laying out the details of the complement system [Bresnan 1972]. Rosenbaum's theory was all there was on complement structure in '65 when I got to MIT. That was the new hot stuff, and its way of doing embedding formed the basis of Generative Semantics analyses. Joan's more detailed work on comple- mentizers really formed a basic part of what was to come. And then there was Joan's work on the degree system [Bresnan 1975]. She said, "Well, if we want to get rid of unbounded movement rules by COMP to COMP move- ment, then what about the unbounded deletions?" That's one that never got settled, really. It ended up with crucial examples that were completely weird, with Chomsky saying, "They're OK for me," and Bresnan saying, "They're bad for me." And that's where it sat. And nobody's ever come back to that at all.

So, what was the next stage? A lot came out about what linguists have to know about logic, culminating in McCawley's book [McCawley 1981]. We all should learn about modal logic. There's never been a book on what logicians should know about language – but we're the folks who should be writing it. Look at Patty Churchland's [1986] book, *Neurophilosophy*. Churchland is a philosopher, and she said, "To study philosophy of mind, maybe I ought to learn neuroscience." My reaction is, "Well, somebody ought to write a book on phonophilosophy: what learning about phon- ology would teach you about philosophy of mind." That sort of book is really crying out to be written – because all of the standard debates are going on without the participation of linguists [but see now Jackendoff 1994 and Pinker 1994]. They're still worrying about how there can be such things as mental representations; even Jerry Fodor is still worrying about it, still trying to prove that there have to be representations. But in linguistics, we assume that there are representations and that they have properties that are nontrivial – and that you can study them by looking at data from a language. You don't necessarily need reaction time experiments and brain probes. And it seems to me that we've learned a lot about language by assuming that representations exist.

This came up at a talk I was giving at a conference about vision and language. Zenon Pylyshyn said, "Well, there can't be image representations in addition to propositional representations. They don't make any sense. How can you tell which facts have to do with which representation?" And I said to him, "That's exactly what the Generative Semantics– Interpretive Semantics dispute was about: are there two different brands of representation, one for syntax and one for semantics, or is there one?" That's a real intellectual issue. Are the syntactic primitives adequate for semantic description? And Pylyshyn said, "Oh, no, that wasn't what it was about at all. That was just an internal squabble among some people in linguistics. It was just people fighting with each other."

GEORGE LAKOFF
in conversation with John Goldsmith

George Lakoff received his undergraduate degree in Mathematics and English Literature from MIT in 1962 and his Ph.D. in Linguistics from Indiana University in 1965. Between 1965 and 1969, he taught at Harvard. He moved to Michigan in 1969, and to California in 1971, where he has been professor of linguistics at the University of California at Berkeley since 1972. His work at Berkeley has been heavily influenced by developments in psychology, and in particular by the work of Eleanor Rosch on prototype theory and, later, by the connectionist models of Rumelhart and McClelland (Rumelhart *et al.* 1986, McClelland *et al.* 1986). In two important books published in the 1980s, *Metaphors We Live By* (1980, written with Mark Johnson) and *Women, Fire, and Dangerous Things* (1987), he has demonstrated how cognition is strongly affected – organized even – by bodily and social experience. In these and other works he has tried to lay the foundations for a unified theory of conceptual systems whose results not only bear upon grammar, but can be applied in the humanities and social sciences generally. Along with Ronald Langacker, Charles Fillmore, Paul Kay, and Gilles Fauconnier, he has also been arguing for the importance of the notion of linguistic construction. The term "Generative Semantics" first appeared in the title of a paper he wrote in 1963.

I'd like to begin by asking you about the origins of Generative Semantics, from your point of view. What were the ideas, or perspectives, which were crucial in your work as it evolved into Generative Semantics? I'm familiar with a paper of yours that goes back to 1963 – published in 1976 – but if I'm not mistaken, your interactions with Paul Postal were also critical during those early years.

Generative Semantics began with my undergraduate thesis in English Literature at MIT. The thesis was the first generative story grammar. A year later, in 1963, Vic Yngve hired me on his MIT summer project to continue research on story generation. The idea was to go from a story grammar to surface structures using transformational rules. But the output of the story grammar was semantic. If that was to be the input to the sentence grammar, then sentence grammar would have to operate on semantic structures.

At that time, semantics meant logic – there was no other technically viable approach to semantics. I realized that logical forms – structures of the kind used in symbolic logic – could be recast as syntactic trees that could be appropriate inputs to transformational rules.

Of course, I realized that this was a radical proposal. This was 1963, a year before Postal and Katz talked Chomsky into the idea of deep structure and two years before *Aspects* was published. Transformational grammar still meant *Syntactic-Structures*-style transformations, with double-base transformations for complex sentences. And Chomsky was still adamant that semantics be kept out of grammar completely. The idea of introducing logical forms into a grammar was anathema to him. I was only 22, and as an Indiana student was not really even considered a member of the MIT Linguistics community. My only claim to legitimacy was the fact that I had taken some linguistics courses there as an undergraduate. If the idea was to be taken seriously, I would have to have some evidence.

So I tried asking myself if there could be syntactic evidence for having a sentence grammar take logical structures as inputs. I came up with a way of looking for evidence. What I did was list the properties of logical forms, so that I could ask, for each property whether there was evidence that that property of logical form needed to be referred to in a sentence grammar of English. The properties included predicate–argument structure, operator scope, coreference (indicated by identity of variables), binding, propositional functions, inferential relations (to other logical forms), and possible sublexical structure. The last property was the one I fixed on initially. If sentence grammars had logical structures as inputs to transformational derivations, then there might be cases where a surface lexical item might express more than one logical predicate in a single sentence. That would mean that the surface predicate would be decomposable, and its decomposition would occur in the syntax. If so, there might be syntactic evidence for the decomposition.

"Toward Generative Semantics" [G. Lakoff 1976], the paper I wrote in the summer of 1963, took up this question with respect to causative constructions. It was assumed that one of the jobs of a sentence grammar was to show systematic relationships among sentences. I asked how one could account for systematic relationships among stative, inchoative, and causative constructions, such as *The milk is cool, The milk cooled,* and *John cooled the milk.* I posited an underlying logical form with abstract predicates of causation and change, and argued that the intransitive verb *cool* was derived by an inchoative transformation from the adjective *cool* by appending the adjective below the underlying inchoative verb. Likewise, the transitive verb was derived by a causative transformation from the inchoative verb by appending the inchoative *cool* below the abstract causative predicate, thus creating a transitive verb.

A second argument I used concerned sentences like *Yaz doubled to left* and *Yaz doubled off the left field wall.* I asked what the generalization governing *to*-phrases such as *to left* was. I observed that the most normal syntactic use was to express the goal of a moving entity. In these sentences, there is no such moving entity represented in the surface structure, but in the semantic structure there would be a baseball represented as moving "to left" or "off the left field wall." Thus, I argued, a semantic underlying structure would allow the prepositional phrases in such sentences to come under the generalization that such phrases represented goals of moving objects.

During the summer of 1963, while I was writing that paper, Jim McCawley was also working in Yngve's group (he was working on Finnish phonology) and we talked a great deal about the idea of a Generative Semantics. Postal was a corridor away in Building 20, writing *An Integrated Theory of Linguistic Descriptions* [1964] with Jerry Katz. That's was when I first got to know him.

We talked about my Generative Semantics idea, which he was very skeptical about. He was in the process of developing the classical modes of argumentation in generative grammar, and when we talked he pressed me to give him arguments and evidence for my analyses. In the process, I learned syntactic argumentation. But at first, the net effect was conservative. Postal convinced me, after he saw my paper, that the same evidence I used could equally well be used to support the theory he had developed with Katz – the precursor to the *Aspects* idea that there was a syntactic (not logical) deep structure that fully "determined meaning." He convinced me that I should put Generative Semantics aside and try working within transformational grammar. His argument was that English had verb phrases, but logical forms did not, and since transformations could not build structure, there was no way to account for verb phrases on my theory.

During the 1963–64 academic year, I was in Indiana finishing my second year of graduate school and working out the consequences of applying Postal's argument forms and looking for evidence in syntax of the properties of logical forms. During that year, Postal was doing very similar research. When he came out to Indiana to teach at the 1964 Linguistic Institute, we discovered that we had gotten virtually the same results – what came later to be called "abstract syntax." Postal, Ross, and I all worked on abstract syntax, which was formulated within the *Aspects* framework, until we found evidence in 1966–7 that required us to re-adopt Generative Semantics.

During the years when we were working on Generative Semantics, we all shared pretty much the same commitments, but we gave them different priorities. The commitments were these: the *Cognitive Commitment*, which is the commitment to take seriously empirical results about the nature of mind and to make the theory of language fit with those results; the *Generalization/Full Range Commitment*, which is the commitment to seek maximal generalizations over the full range of linguistic data, both within and across all domains of language – syntax, semantics, pragmatics, discourse, phonetics, phonology, morphology, and so on; the *Fregean Commitment*, which is the commitment to characterize semantics using the tools of formal logic – logical forms, model theory, and so on; and finally the *Formal Symbol System Commitment* – the commitment to the central Chomskyan metaphor, namely, that a language is a formal symbol system (in the technical sense).

We did not explicitly name or discuss these commitments. We just took them for granted and assumed that they were consistent with each other. I had my priorities in the order given, with the Cognitive Commitment first, the Generalization/Full Range Commitment second, the Fregean Commitment third, and the Chomskyan Commitment last. What this meant, for me, was that, if empirical data made these commitments incompatible, then the commitments I would hold on to to the end were the Cognitive and the Generalization/Full Range Commitments. The one I was willing to jettison first was the Chomskyan Commitment. I still hold the Cognitive and Generalization/Full Range Commitments in that order, but I have been forced by the empirical data to abandon both the Fregean and Chomskyan commitments.

Ross had the Generalization/Full Range Commitment first, the Chomskyan Commitment second, the Cognitive Commitment third and the Fregean Commitment, if at all, a distant last. That is why Ross, seeking generalizations, was led to squishes, even though they contradicted formal symbol systems. It is also why, when he wasn't looking at squishes, he stuck to generative syntax. He has never tried to follow, or adapt to, the empirical results coming from cognitive science.

Postal also placed the Generalization/Full Range Commitment first and the Chomskyan Commitment second, with the Fregean Commitment a distant third (if at all), and no Cognitive Commitment at all. Paul's Generalization/Full Range Commitment wasn't as broad as mine or Jim's. His did not include semantic or pragmatic generalizations. That is why he has continued to do a version of formal syntax and to look for syntactic generalizations, but not semantic, pragmatic, or cognitive generalizations.

McCawley's story is much more complicated. McCawley had an additional commitment that was (and still is) primary – what we will call the Solid Ground Commitment. McCawley wants to do theoretical linguistics at all times using ideas and representational techniques that he feels are well understood, like formal logic and classical transformational grammar. Jim also had subtler versions of the Fregean and Chomskyan commitments. He would split the Fregean Commitment into two parts: (Frege-1) a commitment to empirically established ideas in logic. (Frege-2) a commitment to the formal mechanisms of existing logic. He ranks (1) above (2).

Here are some of the things that Jim includes as empirically established ideas in logic: predicate–argument structure, operator scope, binding, propositional functions, restricted quantification. I also accept these, though for me they are consequences of the Generalization Commitment. Jim continues to use the existing formal mechanisms of logic as part of the Solid Ground Commitment. I have abandoned them as being inconsistent with the Cognitive Commitment. But since Jim's Solid Ground Commitment is ranked higher than his Cognitive Commitment, Jim still uses them.

Jim also has a subtler version of the Chomskyan Commitment, which again is split into two parts: (Chomsky-1) a commitment to make use of the symbolic representations that have come out of generative grammar to the extent that they are useful for characterizing syntactic phenomena. Among

110

these, he includes trees, derivations, the cycle, and so on. (Chomsky-2) a commitment to the detailed entailments of the mathematics of the theory of formal grammars – among them, that rules of grammar cannot "look at" the meanings of symbols manipulated by grammars.

Jim maintains (Chomsky-1) as a corollary of the Solid Ground Commitment, but does not maintain (Chomsky-2) at all. As a result, Jim is quite happy to have rules of transformational grammar that look at semantic content, even though this technically violates the mathematics of the theory of formal grammars. Accordingly, Jim doesn't believe in generative power arguments, which depend on the strict adherence to the mathematics of theory of formal grammars.

Thus, Jim seems to have the following rankings:

1 Solid Ground
2 Generalization
3 Frege-1 (apparently a consequence of (2))
4 Chomsky-1 (apparently a consequence of (1))
5 Frege-2 (apparently a consequence of (1))
6 Cognitive

Since Jim has the Solid Ground Commitment as his Number 1, he pays less attention to his Cognitive Commitment, since he doesn't see it as providing a solid ground for representing traditional syntactic and semantic phenomena.

Chomsky, not surprisingly, put the Chomskyan Commitment first – ahead of any commitment to generalizations or to empirical evidence about cognition. This meant that *no* evidence based on linguistic generalizations or experiment could conceivably have convinced him that language was not just a formal symbol system. The Chomskyan Commitment has the autonomy of syntax as a consequence. Rules in a formal symbol system cannot, *by definition*, make reference to the meaning of the symbols or to aspects of general cognition.

We were claiming, on the basis of generalizations over the full range of linguistic data, that the meanings of the symbols played a role in syntactic rules. But, for anyone who put the Chomskyan Commitment above the Generalization/Full Range Commitment, such a claim could only be nonsense, since the Chomskyan Commitment *defines* syntax so that only form, and not meaning, can play a role in syntactic rules. For Chomsky, generalization meant generalization over form alone, not over meaning.

Chomsky, in his *Syntactic Structures* days, had a version of the Generalization/Full Range Commitment – he focused on generalizations and was committed to having a grammar generate all and only the sentences of the language. But he backed off of such a Full Range Commitment when he limited the domain of his theories to "core grammar" – which includes only about forty or fifty constructions and limits his theories to the study of a tiny percentage of language. Chomsky gave up on the Full Range part of the commitment, and kept the generalization part secondary to the basic Chomskyan Commitment to formal symbol systems.

Given his commitments, there was no possibility that evidence or arguments that contradicted his theoretical commitments could have convinced him. We did not know this, of course. We thought that he shared our commitments and priorities, and that he was being stubborn or irrational. Likewise, if he thought we shared his commitments, he must have thought of us as irrational or uninformed or just plain stupid. In reality, our theoretical commitments were incommensurable and no amount of evidence or argument would have mattered.

At this point, a very important issue should be brought up with respect to the Chomskyan Commitment to formal symbol systems. At the time I proposed Generative Semantics in 1963, I made a further unstated assumption, namely the *Symbolic Semantics Hypothesis*: all aspects of meaning that are relevant to grammar can be represented symbolically in logical form. This was a feature of Generative Semantics when it was re-adopted in 1967, and many people incorrectly thought that it was a necessary feature of Generative Semantics. It was, however, an incidental feature, and it did not last long. By 1968, it had become clear that the Symbolic Semantics Hypothesis had to be given up, and I abandoned it in my "Counterparts" paper [1986b], on the basis of examples like *If I were you, I'd hate me* versus *If I were you, I'd hate myself* and related examples. These examples indicated to me and McCawley that we needed a possible world semantics and a modified version of David Lewis's notion of counterparts across possible worlds. But "counterpart across possible worlds" is a model-theoretic notion, not a purely symbolic notion. (Technically, it can be symbolized if you include variables over the worlds and axioms constraining what worlds and counterparts are to mean. But that did not seem appropriate to us – especially since variables over worlds had no direct syntactic realizations.) When we adopted possible world semantics in 1968, we implicitly gave up on the Symbolic Semantics Hypothesis, though we didn't make a big deal of it, since we never saw it as essential at all.

Around the same time, we gave up on the Symbolic Semantics Hypothesis for other reasons. In 1969, there was a virtual explosion in pragmatics research. It became clear that grammatical well-formedness was relative to context, and that certain context-based relations among propositions mattered for syntax: entailment relative to context, implicature relative to context, presupposition in a context. These relations were not the kind of relations that could be symbolized as part of logical form without loss of generalization. The Symbolic Semantics Hypothesis could not hold for them. The reason was that, for each particular rule, a different constraint on context had to be stated, and sometimes quantification over context was required. There was no nice way to put all this contextual information into

112

logical forms, though they were needed to characterize certain grammatical phenomena. Let us call the class of such phenomena "non-SSH phenomena." These included indirect speech act phenomena, implicature phenomena, presupposition phenomena, discourse structure phenomena, and so on. Such phenomena could only be stated in theories of the day by transderivational rules, since they had to look at aspects of meaning not representable in the logical forms of sentences. I proposed that they be represented model-theoretically and that model-theoretic relations among propositions be represented as such in transderivational rules.

I did not overtly discuss the Symbolic Semantics Hypothesis and where it failed, because it seemed obvious to me. But, as it turned out, it was not obvious to Interpretive Semanticists, nor even to some Generative Semanticists. For example, Jerry Sadock wrote a paper where it was clear that he did not understand the difference between SSH phenomena (those where a single logical form could represent meaning relations symbolically) and non-SSH phenomena (where meaning relations could not be represented symbolically without loss of generalization). In his "The soft, Interpretive underbelly of Generative Semantics," Sadock [1975] cites non-SSH phenomena (for example, indirect speech acts and entailment in context) and suggests that they could be characterized by logical forms and transformations, without showing exactly how. He then concludes that the treatment of these by transderivational rules was arbitrary. Of course, it was not arbitrary given the existence of non-SSH phenomena. But the fact that I did not overtly discuss the SSH, but took it as obvious, could well have led Sadock not to make the distinction. It could also have led Interpretivists to believe, incorrectly, that we were trying to build all aspects of meaning into syntax, where "syntax" was taken to be characterized by purely formal symbol systems without reference to model-theoretic interpretation. With 20–20 hindsight, I can say that it would have been helpful to have had a public discussion in 1968 of the Symbolic Semantics Hypothesis, where it failed, and why it was extraneous to Generative Semantics.

Interestingly, Interpretivists never tried to handle non-SSH phenomena. They have systematically ignored them since they involve meaning relations not representable in logical form. However, there is a post-Interpretivist tradition in which some non-SSH phenomena are recognized implicitly – the tradition of Discourse Representation Theory. Though DRT theorists don't talk about indirect speech acts and such phenomena, they do recognize that phenomena like conditionals and definite versus indefinite descriptions go beyond the bounds of single logical forms. Interestingly, there has been no condemnation of DRT theorists as having grammars that are "too powerful," even though they are, in essence, making use of transderivational rules in much the same sense in which Generative Semanticists made use of them.

The argument to the effect that Generative Semantics was "too powerful" because it had global and transderivational rules was an argument that presupposed that the Chomskyan Commitment had priority over the Generalization Commitment – a presupposition that I did not share. Generative power is defined, technically, with respect to formal symbol systems, which by definition do not permit any rules manipulating symbols to take the interpretation of the symbols into account. Arguments about generative power can only be made relative to such systems.

Global and transderivational rules came along in 1969. That followed, by a year, my "Counterparts" paper, in which I gave evidence for introducing model theory into Generative Semantics. By 1969, Generative Semanticists had also introduced into semantics other concepts that went beyond mere symbol manipulation – for example, possible worlds, presupposition, and implicature. At that point, we were arguing that syntax did not merely depend upon aspects of semantics that could be coded in logical forms (which kept things to formal symbol systems). Rather, we argued, syntax depended as well on model-theoretical aspects of semantics, on possible world semantics, presuppositions and implicatures (which went beyond logical forms and the limits of formal symbol systems).

Given that we were operating with a system that mixed symbols and their model-theoretic interpretations, arguments about generative power made no sense, because they were limited to formal symbol systems alone. But these arguments did make sense to Interpretive Semanticists, who clung to the Chomskyan Commitment above all else, and so could not admit anything like model-theoretic interpretations that went beyond pure symbol systems.

From our point of view, global rules were the most natural of rules, since they were rules that directly linked semantics and surface form. And transderivational rules were equally natural, since they allowed model-theoretic relations that could not be expressed in logical forms to enter into semantic aspects of rules of grammar. Syntactic transformations, which did not directly link semantics to surface forms were seen as strange and "in the way." Ultimately, theories of construction grammar showed that transformational rules had never really been necessary. Grammatical constructions express the content of many of the old global and transderivational rules.

Of course, one of the ironies about the old "too powerful" arguments is that Interpretive Semantics needed to have semantic principles to do the work of those rules, only since they called them "semantic interpretation rules" their generative power did not count. In general, the "too powerful" arguments were (a) silly, since the Interpretivists did not include their semantic rules in the tally; and (b) irrelevant, since they did not apply to Generative Semantics, which by that time had ceased to be a pure symbol system.

Generative Semanticists had an implicit distinction between a theoretical paradigm and a theory of grammar. Theoretical paradigms included our commitments and our methodology. A particular theory of grammar was just seen as a tool for working in a theoretical paradigm. Thus, for us, real advances within the theoretical paradigm required regularly developing new theoretical tools, that is, new theories of grammar. A new theory of grammar was, for us, like a better microscope. One of the achievements of Generative Semantics was the regular discovery of new phenomena that led to the regular construction of new and better theoretical tools, that is, new theories of grammar. Each time an old theory of grammar was abandoned and replaced by a new one, that was an achievement within the same theoretical paradigm.

Interpretivists, on the other hand, seem to have identified particular theories of grammar with whole theoretical paradigms. To them, it appeared that we were changing theoretical frameworks every six months, rather than developing better theoretical tools every six months. Changes in theories of grammar appeared to them not as developments within a theoretical paradigm but as changes from paradigm to paradigm.

There was another major difference. Chomsky held a view about the philosophy of science that we did not hold – the Quine–Duhem thesis. Quine assumed that a scientific theory was a finite list of axioms in first order predicate calculus, and used the Lowenheim–Skolem theorem to argue that no finite number of counterexamples could falsify any finite number of axioms since a finite number of auxiliary hypotheses could always be added to handle the counterexamples. As Chomsky has said, in the Quine–Duhem spirit, only the theory as whole, once completed with no additional auxiliary hypotheses, can be falsified.

We of course did not subscribe to the Quine–Duhem thesis, since the role of generalization played no role in it. That is, no auxiliary hypotheses, from our perspective, could be adequate if they failed to capture generalizations about content. But, as Chomsky knew well, the theory of formal systems could only state generalizations about form and not content. Since we were concerned with generalizations about content, the Quine–Duhem thesis made no sense to us. But for Chomsky, the Quine–Duhem thesis was important, since it shielded his theories from possible counterexamples.

This was the source of a sad incident at the 1969 Texas Conference. There, after a talk by Chomsky, Ross stepped forward and presented Chomsky with counterexamples to his proposals. At each point, Chomsky cut him off and refused to let him finish, saying that no individual linguistic examples could possibly be counterexamples to his proposals. In retrospect, it appears that he was invoking the Quine–Duhem thesis, saying that only the theory as a whole when ultimately completed could be falsified. But since we did not believe the Quine–Duhem thesis (and had no idea at the time that he did), we thought he was just being dismissive. We saw his treatment of Ross as scandalous and aggressive behavior. From our

115

perspective, Ross was right, since he was correctly presenting counter-examples that revealed inadequate generalizations. But from Chomsky's Quine–Duhem perspective, Ross was talking nonsense.

Unfortunately, all these assumptions were in the background at the time. Had they been discussed openly, it would have become clear that our initial assumptions were incommensurable with Chomsky's, and that all our searching for counterexamples to convince him of the correctness of our theory was in vain.

It has been argued that if we had set up a bunch of Generative Semantics departments at various universities in the MIT model, we would have produced more disciples and taken over the field. I don't believe that for a minute. We were too young, too junior, and did not have Chomsky's authority. Chomsky was just too powerful.

It is remarkable, thinking back, to realize how young and naive we were. In 1967, when Chomsky started attacking us, I was 26, Haj and Jim were 29, and Paul was 30. We were kids, with no position at all, and we got sucked into a fight with the most powerful linguist in history – a fight on his terms. None of us had any older, wiser sympathetic mentors to advise us. We were largely ignorant of the uses of academic power. We saw Chomsky as being out to destroy our careers, as he had done to others we knew. We didn't realize that we would have done much better to have simply gone about our work and set our own terms for any discussion rather than to try to argue on his terms.

After you left Cambridge, how did your ideas change?
When I got to Michigan in 1969, I realized how provincial Cambridge linguistics was. I entered a more open and supportive intellectual environment. McCawley spent a semester visiting Michigan during my first year there, and his students, Jerry Morgan and Georgia Green, came with him. Larry Horn came from UCLA to work with us. It was a great research group. When they left the next year, they were replaced by a great group of Michigan students: John Lawler, Ann Borkin, Deborah James, Rich Rhodes, and Linda Coleman. A lot happened during those two years. I began working on the Natural Logic program, and wrote "Linguistics and natural logic" [1972]. My work on conversational postulates was done there. James's groundbreaking work on interjections and pragmatic particles came out of that period, as did Borkin's work on metonymy and on raising. Generative Semantics took on a very different direction than it had during my Cambridge years. Jim was part of this work for the first year, but Haj and Paul were not part of it at all. Robby and I were taking Generative Semantics in a very different direction – one where logic and pragmatics became central.

In the summer of 1975. I ran an underground Linguistic Institute at Berkeley. I got a National Science Foundation grant to bring eight people to Berkeley for a summer workshop. The word got out and 188 people came. I appointed Ivan Sag as my research assistant, and he set up communes in vacant sorority houses for visitors. It was one of the most exciting and intense intellectual experiences I have ever been involved in. The Institute ground rules were that we had lecture and seminar slots from 10 a.m. to 10 p.m., six days a week, and anyone at all could give a talk or schedule a seminar with three days notice. A number of historic lectures were given that summer. First, there was Eleanor Rosch's first lecture on her basic-level category results. Second, there was Len Talmy's first lecture on his work demonstrating that the primitives for spatial relations concepts were topological and orientational. Third, Chuck Fillmore gave his first lecture on the need for Frame Semantics. And fourth, Paul Kay presented his work with Chad MacDaniel on the neurobiological basis for color categorization.

These works, which have since become landmarks in Cognitive Semantics, showed conclusively, and in different ways, that the techniques of formal logic were inadequate to the task of characterizing natural language semantics. After hearing those lectures, I could no longer believe in formal logic as the right way of doing semantics, even though I had been one of the people who had brought formal logic into linguistics.

Moreover, a year earlier, I had given a paper at CLS – "Syntactic amalgams" – that had shown that there were sentences that did not have any single deep structure or logical form, sentences like: *John invited you'll never guess how many people to you can imagine what kind of a party for God knows what reason* or *John is going to I think it's Chicago for I'm pretty sure it's a conference.* There are a variety of types of such amalgam sentences, and their existence showed that one could no longer maintain a theory in which the surface structures of all sentences were derived in step-by-step fashion from either deep structures or logical forms.

These data disproved *both* Generative Semantics and Interpretive Semantics, since they were inconsistent with (a) the idea of a single derivation linking surface forms with single deep structures or logical forms; and (b) the use of formal logic to characterize natural language semantics. If the Interpretivists had given up and declared Generative Semantics to have "won," I would still have given up on formal logic and transformational derivations and moved on to work on Cognitive Linguistics, and so would be at odds with both Generative Semanticists and Interpretive Semanticists.

Since my highest priorities were the Cognitive and Generalization commitments, I was led by these results to abandon the Fregean and Chomskyan commitments. Other Generative Semanticists (like McCawley, Postal, Sadock, and Morgan) did not share my commitment priorities. They did not put the Cognitive Commitment above all else and so did not draw the same conclusions from these results – indeed, they weren't even interested in these results. Of course, at the time, none of us was aware that we had different priorities. I was mystified as to why my colleagues did not draw the same conclusions from these results as I did. And they must have been equally mystified at my taking them so seriously.

So, what happened to Generative Semantics? To put the question in perspective, one should ask, "What happened to Interpretive Semantics?" By 1980, there was no more Interpretative Semantics. It fragmented into Chomsky's Government and Binding, Bresnan's Lexical Functionalism, Gazdar, Pullum, and Sag's Generalized Phrase Structure Grammar, and Jackendoff's Conceptual Semantics. Today Interpretive Semantics as an active research program is only a dim memory.

There are various metaphors one can use to conceptualize what happened to Interpretive Semantics: if you consider a theory as a constructed physical object (like a building), then Interpretive Semantics fragmented. If you consider a theory as a person, then Interpretive Semantics died. But I think it is more accurate to consider a general theoretical paradigm as a species, with individual theorists' versions of it as subspecies. In this metaphor, Interpretive Semantics evolved into a variety of other theoretical approaches, with its subspecies evolving into distinct species – distinct theoretical paradigms, as GB, LFG, and GPSG were by 1980.

The same could, and I think should, be said of Generative Semantics. It too evolved. Postal went on to develop Relational Grammar with Perlmutter, and then with David Johnson, to develop Arc-Pair grammar. Ross went on to develop the study of squishes. But the greatest evolution came on the West Coast: I went on to to develop Cognitive Semantics and a variety of Construction Grammar; Langacker developed Cognitive Grammar; Fauconnier developed the theory of Mental Spaces; Fillmore developed Frame Semantics, and (with Paul Kay) another variety of Construction Grammar; Robin Lakoff was one of the principal founders of the field of pragmatics, and has gone on to develop approaches to discourse pragmatics and was the founder of the Language-and-Women Movement; Robin's student from the Generative Semantics era, Deborah Tannen, has become the best-known researcher in the pragmatics of interpersonal communication – and the first author of a best-selling linguistics book [1990]; Fillmore's first student, Sandra Thompson, along with former Generative Semantics supporters like Talmy Givón and Wallace Chafe, has gone on to form the Functionalist Movement; Lauri Karttunen and David Dowty were most interested in the focus on logic with Generative Semantics, and they have gone on to do important work in the formal semantics tradition; Ed Keenan and Berkeley student Aryeh Faltz were also mostly interested in the Generative Semantics focus on logic and have gone on to develop a theory of Boolean Semantics. The Mid-West branch has been the least fruitful. There, only Jerrold Sadock has founded a new approach to linguistics: Autolexical Grammar.

In short, the enormous creative energy in Generative Semantics evolved into an incredibly rich variety of traditions – each centrally concerned with different aspects of language. Indeed, the descendants of Interpretive Semantics have provided us with a much narrower set of approaches to language, compared with the richness of the Generative Semantics heritage. If the value of a theory is to be measured by the richness and collective insightfulness of the approaches that it evolves into, then Generative Semantics must be said to have had the more interesting and valuable evolution.

I'm glad the Generative Semantics days are over. Cognitive Linguistics is far more interesting than generative linguistics and logic ever were. Contemporary research on conceptual metaphor systems – and conceptual systems in general – is far more exciting than work on logical forms and grammar ever was. It takes us into the center of what thought is like, to its biological foundations, and to applications throughout the humanities and social sciences. Neither Generative nor Interpretive Semantics could ever have done that.

JOHN ROBERT ROSS
in conversation with John Goldsmith

John Robert "Haj" Ross joined the MIT faculty in 1966, receiving his MIT Ph.D. the following year. His dissertation, "Constraints on variables in syntax," is possibly the most widely cited dissertation in the history of the field. In the early 1970s, he began to study the "squishiness" of linguistic categories, which is to say, the way in which linguistic rules apply not in a yes-or-no fashion in any given case, but in a better-or-worse fashion. Ross's interest in squishes has had much in common with Lakoff's interest in prototypes, and in fact with McCawley's interest in developing a theory of linguistic categories as coalitions of potentially independent features (see McCawley 1982). Ross also became interested in the ways that sound affected structure – even to the extent that degrees of sonority of segments might influence the order of conjuncts in a syntactic phrase. This, in turn, led him to reconsider the nature of poetry from a linguistic point of view, a task in which he is still engaged. He currently teaches in the Department of English, at the University of North Texas.

Did you feel you had a mentor?
One mentor of mine was George Miller. I met him in the summer of 1963 when I was working at the MITRE Corporation in Bedford, Massachusetts, with a bunch of people supervised loosely by Hu Matthews. I had heard of George Miller somehow or other and one Saturday I went and met him. We got to be very good friends. I never took a course with him, but I read quite a few of his papers. He was always interested in my work and in fact, a long time later, in 1975 or thereabouts, when he ran the lab at Rockefeller University, I would come down once every couple of weeks and just shoot the breeze with him.

How did you get to go to MITRE that summer?
Bruce Fraser. To Bruce I owe incalculable amounts of my career. I first applied to MIT when I was in Germany. I had gone to Yale, and then I went to Germany for three semesters. I have no idea why I applied to MIT. When you're just starting, you try to develop a nose for who's supposed to be a hot shit, and somehow people told me about Chomsky. I remember I took a completely incomprehensible course in Germany about automata theory and pushdown stores and phrase structure grammars and the name Chomsky came up. I didn't read anything that Chomsky wrote. But somehow I osmoted that I should go and study with this person. So I applied, and I was rejected.

I was so vain, I actually thought that I had been sent the wrong letter by clerical error. When I came back from Germany – it was April, or something like that – I found Morris Halle. I immediately disliked him, but I realized I would have to give him a chance to apologize for the stupidity of

120

his staff. So I explained my theory to him of clerical error, and he said, "No, I remember your case quite well, Mr Ross. You were the person who was knocking around Europe, and as far as we could see, you've never done a lick of work in your life." And he said, "We have a small group of people here who are interested in language. We don't have time to spoon-feed anyone. Why don't you go away someplace and if you decide you want to start doing some work and study, you might reapply sometime." End of interview. It was a wonderful teaching. It was really terrific. I have Morris to thank for straightening me out on that occasion and on other ones, too. So I went to Penn for a year and a half and worked very hard and discovered syntax.

I knew Bruce Fraser because Bruce and I had grown up together. We were going to rival schools in Poughkeepsie and we had been acquaintances. For some reason, Bruce was amazingly friendly and helpful and he got me this job with Hu Matthews's group. I had also been in Hu Matthews's class at Penn, where he had been a student before he came to MIT. He came down once a week to teach a course in comparative Proto-Siouxan, one of those useful graduate courses. I got to know Hu, and Bruce got me the job at MITRE, and then I got to know Hu some more at MITRE, and Noam, and some other people, and somehow when I reapplied to MIT after a year or so, I was admitted as a special student. I took Morris's course on phonology, and then I sat in on everything and was gung-ho, so then they really let me come to MIT.

What were people doing in syntax? Chomsky was writing Aspects *and people were working on what kinds of problems?*
Well, during that summer I got to be friends with Paul Postal a little bit, although he still thought of me as a complete flake from knowing me at Yale, where I had been your typical fatuous undergraduate and had done zero work. I was somehow interested in language always, but I wasn't interested in working. I was trying to grow up a little bit through the helpful tutelage of playing poker about forty hours a week and football and being on the radio station and in a fraternity and drinking a lot and going to class occasionally and never going to the library or doing any studying. So he had written me off.

You were doing some linguistics?
I was Yale's first linguistics major. I had bombed out of math, and I went to Bernard Bloch and said, "Look, I'd really like to major in linguistics. Can we arrange something?" So, with great kindness and amazing quantities of patience, he arranged some reading courses for me, which I did poorly in because I didn't read the books, and he let me sit in on graduate courses, which I also did poorly in, often walking out of his class in the fall after three-quarters of an hour to go to football practice. The experience of having an undergraduate linguistics major was so traumatic for Yale that they didn't do it again for ten years.

121

Somehow, though, I had already done a lot of work when I got to Penn. I had read an enormous amount of stuff and done work on syntax as much as I could. I'd done work on negation, and I met Ed Klima, and we got along very well. Fodor and Katz's paper had just come out, and we'd been given permission to think about semantics. The big deal was syntactic features. And some version of chapter 3 or 4 of *Aspects* was around. I guess the idea was also around about getting rid of what were called generalized transformations, which were transformations that took two syntactic trees and glued them together. Noam had had the idea of a recursive base structure. All of this was extremely liberating.

Now, *the* major work on English that had been done was Lees's [1960] grammar of English nominalizations. It had phrase structure rules and transformations and so on. What it also had was a whole bunch of things that stuck in Noam's craw. It had lots of transformations which would work for eighteen lexical items, because when you get to nominalizations, things are extremely kinky and nonproductive. Noam's vision of grammar is that English is just like algebra, I think, and you don't have lexical classes of variables in algebra. You don't say addition is commutative except for the characters d and r. This was always a fly in the ointment for Noam. Noam never accepted or liked all of this stuff about lexical irregularity and lexical classes. He hadn't figured out what to do with it. In January of '64, when I came to MIT, I took Paul Postal's course, Linguistic Structure. In it Postal was taking very seriously what no one had done before, which was exceptions, and was using a feature mechanism and had invented the notion of rule feature.

Was Lakoff working on this already?
George got it from Paul, as I understand, but you should check this with him. In the summer of 1964, Paul taught at the LSA Summer Institute at Indiana University, which is where George was a graduate student. Paul presented his stuff on rule features and exceptions, and George became really enthused by it and worked in extremely close coordination with him. George wanted to escape from Bloomington, and eventually got a job with Susumu Kuno at Harvard, who, with Tony Oettinger, had a large project funded by the National Science Foundation on machine translation, mathematical linguistics, syntax. I was on the payroll too when I came to MIT in 1964 or '65. Starting in the fall, George got me a job there. It was a wonderful job. You didn't have to do anything. You just sat and knocked syntax around and if you felt like writing a paper, you could write a paper.

Anyway, from the fall of 1964, which was when I entered the program officially, there was an enormous amount of work on rule features, and it was Paul who was behind all of this. Paul was an extremely reductionist person and had an extremely abstract view of syntax. So he'd say, "Why do we need to have both adjectives and verbs? There's really tiny differences between them in languages. Lots of languages inflect adjectives just like verbs. Why do we have to have both noun phrases and prepositional phrases?" He used to have an underlying structure for *The farmer killed the duckling* which was "by the farmer killed of the duckling." The obligatory rules would strip the preposition off any subject, and, if the verb stayed a verb, its object preposition would get zapped. He had the idea that there was one underlying form which was full and that transformational rules would zap things that show up in the full form. It was like morpho-phonemic syntax.

There was in Postal's work, but not in Klima's or Chomsky's, the idea that you should try to find the irreducible set of syntactic primitives out of which you could build things. For Postal it was nouns and verbs. He later thought that you could get rid of nouns also, that nouns were a kind of predicate, so that a noun like *canoe* derived from something like "one which canoes." His conception of syntax was that basically there were predicates and arguments and a predicate could be a verb, an adjective, or a noun, as in a sentence like *He's a friend of Tom's*, where "a friend" would be a nominal predicate. That was all Postal's idea. I never heard Chomsky refer to it. Nobody on the faculty at MIT really seriously attacked anybody else then, because it was a time of solidifying boundaries, of building solidarity. But I bet that ideas like that were just anathema to Noam. What was anathema to Noam also was thinking about lexical exceptions. My feeling about lexicalism was that functionally it was invented in desperation under pressure from Postal and especially from Lakoff.

Lakoff had rule features of two kinds. One kind he called simple exceptions, which marked verbs like *resemble*, which doesn't undergo passive. But then there were also rules which had to be able to be undergone by a form. For instance, *try* was marked "plus" for the structural description feature of Equi-Noun-Phrase Deletion, because the question was, what are you going to do with **I tried for Tom to leave?* George said it not only had to meet the structural description for Equi, but also had to undergo it.

What did people say before that? What did Rosenbaum say?
My feeling is that nobody knew about the problem with *try*, for instance. Nobody had come up with cases like that. Postal came up with them. Postal never wrote down any of his stuff about rule features. George was Paul's lieutenant, and got all that together. Once you have such powerful features as being able to force things to meet the structural description of a rule and then undergo it, then you can get extremely abstract, but semantically motivated, underlying structures. In other words, you can get to do Generative Semantics, which is what George had been wanting to do since 1963.

All of this was worse than anathema to Chomsky. He never talked about Lakoff's work or Postal's work, but I know it was a thorn in his foot. Lexicalism, I thought of, and think of now, as a huge rug under which to sweep all of this clutter which clearly to Noam's mind had nothing to do with real language; remember, language is like algebra and algebra has no lexical exceptions. What Noam wanted to do is push into something called the lexicon these examples which worked for five verbs, so that he could concentrate on real language, which was exceptionless, pure, beautiful. It had nothing to do with semantics, nothing to do with phonology, nothing to do with lexical classes. It worked structure-dependently.

What were you doing at this point, '64, '65?
In '64, when I came to MIT, I was getting ready for the exams. Then, in the spring of 1965, Ed Klima gave a course called "The Structure of German." That was a huge turning point for me because I knew German somewhat. Klima started working on topicalization in German, resumptive topicalization. Rosenbaum had gotten complement structures more or less, so we knew when we saw an infinitive we didn't go into a tailspin. Something had been known about getting rid of the subject of putative underlying subordinate clauses. So there was a framework, and Klima basically took that framework and said, "OK, let's crank German through it." I was very struck by it. I thought it was very beautiful. Paul Kiparsky was not exactly teaching the course, but he knew German much better than I did and he knew a lot of syntax and so he was helping Ed a lot. Anyway, I got the sentence *Ich habe versucht anzufangen, das Haus zu bauen* "I have tried [= I tried] to begin the house to build." And I thought, "Well, I'll just try topicalizing everything and everything I can think of using the parameters that were given by Rosenbaum." I went through it more or less like a computer would and generated about thirty or fifty sentences which I knew were all crazy. And then I asked Paul and other people and to my astonishment, much more than half of them were OK. Just amazing sentences like *Ich habe das Haus anzufangen versucht zu bauen* "I have the house to begin tried to build" and *Das Haus anzufangen zu bauen, habe ich versucht* "The house to begin to build I have tried [= I tried]." And then, mysteriously, when the *es* of extraposition was there, a lot of them wouldn't work (like *Das Haus habe ich (*es) versucht, anzufangen zu bauen* "The house have I (*it) tried, to begin to build"), and it was real data. It was a set of data. So I wrote a paper which was basically unpublished, although it showed up in some German publication. It was called "Some cyclically ordered rules in German syntax." And it's very funny, you know – one of the things I'm looking forward to wincingly is that future historians will find that . . . well, it's not my fault; no, it was either Klima's or Kiparsky's fault . . . that the origin of COMP to COMP hopping comes from the work on German. Anyway, there's this mechanical thrill of having got this set of rules ordered trickily and you send these constructions through them, and then, by God, here comes this long fucker twenty words long out at the end, and it works! There was this real Gyro Gearloose thrill of linguistics, doing that kind of thing then. And

124

there was also this feeling that we basically knew about 85 percent of the correct answer. There was still some stuff we didn't know about, like maybe superlatives or purpose clauses, but that was peripheral. We'd get to it, and the basic stuff was in place and if we twiddled the knobs a little bit . . .

Where did that feeling come from? I'm remembering a feeling from my first year at MIT, a feeling that I was living next to a genius. Mystical and magical.
And we were. We certainly were. And it was magical. Even when *you* were there. You came in 1972, which was a tough time for MIT and the world. It's funny, the Vietnam War, in its horror and nastiness, ran very much parallel with the horribleness of the syntax wars. It was in that period that occurred an instructive event for me. George was giving a Generative Semantics workshop in San Francisco at the LSA winter meeting. There were a couple of hundred people in the audience. George gave his talk and then there were questions, and one of the Interpretivists, with whom George had been into Donnybrooks before, started asking questions, and the questioning got more and more heated. Finally, George, from the podium, said to the questioner, who we'll call X, "Well, fuck you, X." And X looked as if he'd been slapped in the face, and then said, "Well, fuck you, George." And that was the end of that.

Another thing happened in 1969 or so. There was a conference in Austin, Texas, and I went down there with Noam. We sat next to each other on the plane. Noam was giving a paper, and I was going to read Morris Halle's paper, because Morris had been invited but couldn't come for some reason. At the meeting, after Noam's talk, there was a question period, and I was asking a question from the back of the room and Noam was at the podium. Noam wouldn't let me say the end of the question. He started drowning me out from the podium. He had a microphone and I didn't. So I had to sit down.

Do you remember what you were trying to ask?
Oh, something about whether semantics is generative or not. It's just something that was really anathema to Noam. I remember I talked to him about it afterwards. I can't remember exactly what he said, but it was something like, "I just couldn't take it. Here these people were saying wrong things." I don't remember him saying he was sorry, exactly, he was just trying to explain why he had to do what he did.

PAUL M. POSTAL
in conversation with John Goldsmith and Geoffrey Huck

Paul M. Postal received his Ph.D. from Yale in 1963 and taught at MIT until 1965, when he moved to the City University of New York. In 1967, he was appointed to a research position at IBM, where he remained a research staff member until 1994. In work done jointly with David Perlmutter in the early 1970s, Postal developed a nontransformational theory of grammar which has had a major, although indirect, impact on current syntactic analysis. Their theory of Relational Grammar has assumed that grammatical relations such as Subject, Direct Object, and Indirect Object are primitive and are not further definable in terms of other syntactic relationships. Many of their ideas – for example, those involving clause union and the bifurcation of intransitive clauses into "unergatives" and "unaccusatives" – have become coin of the realm in syntax.

What is your view today of the significance of the Generative Semantics–Interpretive Semantics dispute?
That it's of very marginal scientific relevance. There were a few things there that linguists should take account of. But it only has larger significance internal to Chomsky's biography. Because Chomsky was then, and has remained, such a dominant figure, anything that relates to him takes on a certain importance. But that is independent of the importance of the content. For example, in reading contemporary papers in the Chomskyan framework I am struck by how much talk there is about how language is "modular." But this seems to mean no more than that there are different principles. Once that is said, what difference does it make that one is in one supposed "module" and one is in another? What is at stake here? Nothing, as far as I can see. And yet it's thrust forth aggressively, as if there were some content to calling the system modular. I think there's been lots of stuff like that where there's very little to dispute.

Chomsky has always been seen as taking a position radically different from everyone else's, and this combativeness has attracted people to his work. Did it attract you, for example? How did you find out about Chomskyan linguistics in the first place?
I was a graduate student in the anthropology department at Yale, but I was interested in linguistics. I was in the anthropology department because I didn't want to study Greek or Latin, which you had to do in the linguistics department. It was dumb since I had to study other things which were ultimately of no interest or use to me. But anyway, I first came to know about Chomsky through those two reviews that he wrote in IJAL [Chomsky 1957b, 1957c]. And Lees's review of *Syntactic Structures* [Lees 1957] appeared about simultaneously, and I was very attracted by what I read. The linguistics that was being taught at Yale was this really very dogmatic American structuralism – with great pretensions about being scientific,

although they really didn't know anything about modern science or the philosophy of science. They had a homemade notion of science as classifying data and being very empirical and were very suspicious of theory or theorizing about which they really knew very little. So Chomsky really shone compared to them. I had studied the philosophy of science somewhat in college and I had read things like Quine and so forth, which people at Yale had never heard of. So when Chomsky would refer to these things, I understood him and it seemed to me that he was in tune with modern thought, whereas the people at Yale were really not. So I was pretty attracted by that. The first time I saw him, I think, was when he came to give a lecture at Yale. I don't remember the year, 1958 or 1959? He lectured about English stress, which he and Morris Halle had been working on. He really performed very badly. He was obviously nervous, given the then prestigious but naturally presumed hostile audience, Bernard Bloch, Rulon Wells, and so on; he hemmed and hawed, and he was not very well organized, especially at the beginning. But it was clear that he had intellectual control of this strange material, which was totally different from anything done at Yale. The reaction was really negative. Everybody there disliked what he said and objected to it. I think I must have met him personally because I somehow got invited after that to come to a seminar at MIT that Chomsky and Halle were giving about their stress work. I was writing a paper about simplicity in phonology, and I sent it to Halle. Maybe that was it, too. But anyway, I was invited, and I went there and talked with them a bit. And then they offered me a job a year or two later – starting in the summer of 1961. I hadn't finished my thesis. I actually wrote it the first year I was at MIT.[2]

Who was there at MIT at that point?
There was not a linguistics department in the sense of a Ph.D. program. There was a research group in the Research Laboratory of Electronics, and that's who we worked for. Chomsky and Halle had positions in the modern language department, but I don't know exactly what they were teaching then. Jerry Katz and Jay Keyser came at the same time I did. I think we all had roughly the same kind of position.

What were you working on? What were the ideas that were around? You were getting involved in the semantic aspects of grammar . . .
Not then, no. I was working on my thesis that first year and nothing else, essentially. I finished it in the summer of '62. Maybe I worked on phonology a bit, also, because I gave a few talks on phonology. And it was only after that that I started thinking about English. And then Katz and I started working together a little bit on semantics.

What were the sorts of questions that people worried about?
Finding arguments for transformations, rule ordering. The dominant issue

127

was showing that transformational grammar and generative grammar were right and that the structuralists were wrong. There was a strongly dominant way of thinking, at least it seemed that way, in both America and Europe, which was quite antithetical to the ideas that Chomsky was introducing. And I think that there was a feeling among those who accepted Chomsky's ideas of being an embattled minority and that if one didn't do something combative, one would be squashed. Most of the active "theoretically oriented" linguistic community believed in structuralism. They believed in finding procedures for getting the right analyses, and their grammars really didn't have any place for anything like transformations, which for them seemed very abstract and unreal. Their notion of reality was to be very close to the data or they were very suspicious.

What about Harris? He had transformations.
I never knew Harris; although Chomsky or Halle or maybe Robert Lees once introduced me to him at an LSA conference, in Philadelphia, I think. He gave me a minute or two lecture on something, maybe the importance of biuniqueness in phonology (which Halle was then challenging), but I am not at all sure of my memories here. I looked at some of his work, but never really studied it carefully, because I found it impenetrable. And I never worried at that point about what the relationships between Chomsky's and Harris's ideas were. This has been something of an issue in certain narrow circles and Chomsky is sensitive to suggestions that he may have insufficiently credited Harris for transformational grammar [see Katz 1981: ch. 1, Chomsky 1986b: 50]. But I never worried about where these ideas came from. I assumed there was some relation, since they were using the same words, like "transformation" and "kernel sentence," and so forth. I guess I implicitly assumed that Chomsky was the basic intellectual source for these ideas.

Were you working with Chomsky at that point, 1962?
No. The only sense in which I ever worked with him was that I would sometimes go to him and say, "I'm worried about this," and "What do you think about that?" But it was very rare that I would actually get to talk to him. There would always be people hanging around or coming into his office who would interrupt or turn the conversation and I doubt that we ever spoke together for five minutes alone. And I remember being basically frustrated in such discussions. (Note that we never carried out or published any joint work.) Also remember that I was working on Mohawk, which people there seem to have considered slightly comic for some reason.

So when you started teaching at MIT, how was the actual content of the courses worked out? You taught a course on Mohawk?
No, I never did. I started teaching in 1963. I was given the job of teaching structural linguistics, for example, the ideas of Bloomfield, Bloch, Harris,

Martinet, and so on. Chomsky didn't want to talk about that, so as the maximally junior faculty member, I naturally got assigned to do it. Then the other course I think I had was on English syntax.

Were you just beginning to think about that?
Yeah. It was very painful for me, because I didn't know anything about it; preparing for every class was like torture.

Do you remember what the constructions were then that you were working on?
I only taught there two years, 1963–4 and 1964–5, and my memories do not divide up things by years, but I do remember talking about comparatives and how they seemed to be obeying what later came to be called "island constraints." I thought that was an important discovery, and I remember talking about it in class. I don't remember why I thought it was important, or what my analysis was, except that it involved positing movements in comparatives.

By the end of the 1960s, the distinction between what would come to be known as grammatical relation changing rules versus long-distance rules was already in the lore . . .
That distinction, no. Well, you might be right, but not having heard you say that, I would have said that the date for that was 1972 to 1974. And that David Perlmutter and I cooked that up by ourselves and that nobody had said that before. You could show me to be wrong, but that's my internalized remembrance of it.

As you recall it, what was the conventional wisdom as to how to break constructions up – what were the core things to look at? If grammatical relation changing rules didn't form a natural subclass, how were things divided up?
I don't think those considerations played any role until 1967 or 1968. Haj Ross had begun to develop those divisions in his thesis [Ross 1967b], where he had long-distance and ripping rules that obeyed the island constraints and things like passives that didn't. I would suspect that that is the origin of any such thinking and I had a similar elaborated typology in my cross-over stuff which I was working on in 1968. And I don't think anybody had ever talked in those terms before. But there was no assumption of anything like relation changing rules at that point. I believe Perlmutter and I developed that (what seems to me now, confusing and confused) terminology in 1972 and 1973 and introduced it in our lectures in 1974.[3] It was quite a change in thinking and marks for me the beginning of Relational Grammar.

Going back to the period when you were at MIT, what about things like pronominalization and reflexivization? Were those central questions?
They were of some interest. The material about reflexives was used extensively, especially the argument about the way reflexives interact with

129

imperatives. That was considered a major argument in favor of transformational grammar.

Were those the terms in which you were taking it at that time?
Absolutely. I think that the dominant idea of the early 1960s was to show that transformational grammar was right. There was not really that much interest in – well, this would be disputed, but, thinking back on it, we were not talking in terms of "How can we understand pronominalization or reflexives?" We tended more to think, "How can we derive from this an argument that transformational grammar is better than nontransformational approaches?'

Did you see a shift in 1962, 1963, when Chomsky was beginning to concentrate on those things that would culminate in Aspects*?*
No, I don't . . . You have to remember that throughout that period – this may sound strange – but some time in that period, Chomsky had already, to a significant extent, in my opinion, lost interest in syntax and transformational grammar. He was concerned with other things. Throughout that period he was working on the phonology book with Halle [Chomsky and Halle 1968], constantly revising it, rewriting it. So that took a certain amount of time, probably most of it Halle's, but Chomsky was involved to a certain extent. And then he did that stuff, which was published in 1963, with George Miller [Chomsky and Miller 1963, Chomsky 1963, and Miller and Chomsky 1963]. He could have done great amounts of grammatical work if he wanted to. He didn't do any. *Aspects* was basically just some ideas he had from his spring course. There were, of course, always problems in trying to get a good version of transformational grammar. And problems would always arise in his course. The stuff about features was a central part of the spring course, as I remember.

Was the use of features new there?
It was new in syntax. He took it from phonology and saw that it could be used to deal with certain issues that he hadn't had a good way to deal with. He had also bought – one of the very few times that he ever bought anything – the stuff that Katz and I had in our book [Katz and Postal 1964] about the way semantics was related to all this.

I have heard a rumor, which I think you have just put to rest, from people who were around MIT at the time that you were very centrally responsible for the idea that deep structure is a single tree.
That is not true. Jerry and I didn't have that idea in our book, as I remember. I think the first place that it appeared was in *Aspects*.

By Aspects, *Chomsky takes the innateness hypothesis to be pretty well established. How did you feel about it? When you arrived at MIT, did you believe in innateness?*
I don't remember any discussion of this before 1963, probably. Innateness

was not a topic I remember anybody talking about when I first got to MIT. When I first got there, the issues were technical ones. For example, in phonology, Halle had formulated this argument about biuniqueness and there was a lot of interest in generative phonology, features, rules, and rule ordering, and that's what phonology was about. And then there was also interest in finding arguments for transformations. I suppose the real issue is when Chomsky started citing the Cartesians and Humboldt and so forth. It was certainly not prevalent in 1961 and 1962. Well, there was talk about mentalism. One of the structuralists' accusations was that Chomsky was bringing back mentalism, and that must have been related to innateness in some way: if linguistic rules are real psychological things, then that leaves open the question of what is innate and what's not.

There was another hypothesis that Chomsky had of course accepted long before, and that was the autonomy hypothesis, which was later challenged by views which I think had their origins in your work with Katz. Was that at all an issue for you?
I have never had any interest in that issue, which didn't seem like something one could really work on. When I have read things about it, they have always tended to put me to sleep. And again, I don't think this was an issue at the beginning. Chomsky had had the idea that all the basic distinctions in syntax were independent of semantics, that the kind of vague semantic tests people had proposed were completely wrong and didn't give the right results. But basically there was no clear notion of semantics to be independent *from* until Katz and Fodor wrote their article.[4] And Chomsky never really bought that. The closest he came was his acceptance of the view that the semantic component would operate on the output of the syntactic component. But he never did any work in that framework. And he was never emotionally committed to it, which showed up when, very quickly, he was able to jettison it.

How did you get into the work that resulted in An Integrated Theory of Linguistic Description *?*
I guess just from talking with Katz. Basically what we did in that book was that he restated his ideas about semantics and I wrote the part about hooking it up to the syntax.

And then there's the next step, of relating logical formulas to natural language, and apparently this was first suggested by George Lakoff. . . .
My memory is that the first ideas of that order came from McCawley. Lakoff also said the same sorts of things. I don't know about the priority between them.

Did you work with Lakoff when he was an undergraduate at MIT?
I think I talked with him. But worked with him, no.

We've heard that Lakoff tried to interact with Chomsky, but that there was a great difference in personalities.

No, that's wrong. There's a great similarity in personality.

I only saw them interact together once, I think, at Indiana. Chomsky was giving a talk which included claims about coordination; his analysis was kind of dopey because it ended up giving you binary structures and only binary structures. George pointed that out from the floor. I think that basically it came off all right; Chomsky took it well and accepted that this was wrong and he would have to fix it up somehow.

The impression I have is that the ideas you were talking about at the 1964 Linguistic Institute were very central to Lakoff's development at that point.
We talked a lot then. But I understood myself just to be spreading standard received opinion at MIT. I gave two courses there. In fact, the directors originally only wanted me to give one (syntax) course, but I insisted on a phonology course as well, because I said you wouldn't get the whole picture if you didn't see the phonology. As I remember it, the syntax course was just arguments for transformational grammar, dreary stuff about why you needed transformations and so forth. The phonology course was just Mohawk phonology. So whatever he got out of that couldn't have been anything much more than what was received material at MIT.

Lakoff, in his thesis, which he wrote in 1964, 1965, hooks up the properties of certain verbs and their ability to govern rules. That isn't something you see in Chomsky. You do see it in your work, though.
Certainly we talked a great deal about that, I remember. I had thought a lot about that. It was all drivel, as far I am now concerned. Nothing I ever said about it made any real sense. George worked on these issues a great deal and made his thesis out if it. And I talked about it in courses I gave at City University when I was there. But it was awful, because I could never make real sense out of it to myself, still less to anyone else.

How does that differ from what you think now? It's a point of view that I very much associate with you. The idea, for example, that there could be a rule which is very general and obligatory, say, in Swahili, is general but has some exceptions in English, and then applies to three verbs in French, but it's the same thing, somehow, across languages. That's an idea I associate with you, and I don't think anyone else puts it quite that way.
Well, maybe I had that idea. I wouldn't put it that way now, because I don't believe in that kind of rule. I would now say what's common is the construction, the structures themselves, and the rules might allow a certain structure with all the verbs of the sort not inherently incompatible with it in one language and with most verbs of that sort in another language and with one verb in French. But what would be common would be the structures themselves rather than the rule. Twenty years ago I would certainly have been talking in terms of rules.

Lakoff has said that the Generative Semantics movement was never a coherent

*movement in the sense that its members really shared the same agenda. It was
basically a coincidence that at a particular time in history your concerns and
McCawley's concerns and Lakoff's concerns coincided sufficiently that you saw some
commonalities, but that you were each coming from really very different points of
view.*

I think that's true. The others were interested in a lot, especially George,
that I was never interested in or could say anything serious about –
pragmatics, for example. All the things about presupposition that George
was interested in I always felt were beyond my ken. I knew I would never
have anything to say about such issues nor could I work on them. Thus I
was never very interested in them. And in so far as that became associated
with Generative Semantics, I really had nothing to do with it. I always felt
there was a central core of facts that one could work on and maybe
understand and that the issue was what's the best theory for the central
facts, leaving it open as to what could be said about the other stuff, which
seemed mostly beyond comprehension. And my position is not much
different today.

I'm not sure about the others, but I think my work has been consistent
in *not* dealing with certain things. Even semantic things I have basically not
dealt with. I only made one attempt to deal with semantics – in a paper
about comparatives and lowering [Postal 1974a]. That was really the last
thing I ever did that could be said to have anything to do with Generative
Semantics. My feeling about it was that there was something right in what
I was saying; but it had so many problems that I never saw how to pursue it.

*I'm wondering whether you were surprised at the opposition that developed to some of
these ideas. Even as early as 1966, I suppose, I take it that there was some strong
negative reaction.*

I do remember, probably in those years, George and Haj telling me that
they would go to Chomsky's course and hassle him, make novel proposals,
and claim to have counterexamples to his accounts. They were quite
disturbed that he didn't seem to accept their ideas. I remember telling
them that I thought Chomsky was probably behaving reasonably: did they
really have strong arguments? Wasn't he just being reasonably resistant? So
at that point I felt that the participants were carrying on a reasonable
discussion, and that George and Haj were right in bringing up problems
which they were really working on intensively. Although he was resistant to
their ideas, which I suppose I largely approved of, it seemed to me the
resistance was appropriate. There was no reason for them to be upset. My
view was that when their arguments really were good enough, he would
accept them.

Do you think you were right in those respects?
No.

If you could go back and advise them, what would you be saying now?
I would tell them that there is no point in talking to him.

What caused this change in your thinking?
Several things which are well represented by Chomsky's behavior at that conference in Texas and the paper which resulted from it.[5] Consider the former. After his verbal presentation, there was an opportunity for the audience to use a microphone, up toward the front. Those who wanted to ask a question or comment had to raise their hand and be called on by whomever was in charge. Haj Ross did that, took the microphone, started to talk, hadn't finished and Chomsky interrupted him. Quite brutally. Haj just turned around and walked away while Chomsky went on with his interruption. Ross's gesture signaled that this was a breakdown of communication, that he felt that Chomsky had broken the rules. Which I believe he had.[6]

But in general, Chomsky and the other people at MIT do train people well. And they do continue to attract good students and others who are already in the field.
Yes, they attract good people. At MIT the students tend to be very smart. But it seems to me that they come out of there not questioning much. Perhaps the notion is somehow transmitted to them that their job is basically to fill in little cracks in an already existing edifice of some magnificence.

This reminds me of something that Haj Ross said, that there was already a feeling at that point, around 1964, that all the work was done. And it was just a question of filling in the gaps.
I think that's right. There clearly was the unfounded idea that great success had been achieved. I certainly never felt that way. None of the things I worked on ever worked out really right. My basic feeling had always been more one of lack of success than of success. I had noticed that already in working on Mohawk. Most of the phenomena I recorded I could never understand or construct any rules for. The real problem was to extract some tiny subpart from the confusion that I could actually write down and make a thesis out of. So the idea that we're really finished, I could never have taken that seriously.

So the linguistic world is divided into two groups: those who think that with the current state of knowledge in linguistics we're basically there, and those who think that this is a very small shadow of what there is to know.
I believe that Chomsky has now fully accepted the latter position. But when I began to talk that way, it was not popular at MIT. Morris Halle explicitly chided me that it was bad to talk this way because it would discourage the students.[7]

If the generative revolution in linguistics which overthrew structuralism was in your

eyes basically a good thing, and if the majority of generative grammarians today are not doing the kind of work you find worthwhile, where did things go wrong?
First, I think that the basic intellectual ideas of transformational generative grammar – I'm leaving out phonology because I don't know anything about it – are fundamentally wrong. After a while, that became clearer and clearer, and although there have been many changes in the instantiations of transformational grammar, the relics remain. But I think that Chomsky is basically wedded to the original ideas in some form or another. That's one reason why things went bad. Facts uncovered in the relevant work of course remain interesting, like the island facts. That was surely a tremendous discovery. But the various proposals to account for them in some general way have never worked out well. The goals could not be met. So it was inevitable that – well, take Newtonian physics. Although that was a serious theory in the way that transformational grammar never has been, nevertheless it had to be supplanted.

So you see a fairly radical discontinuity between the work you started doing in 1971 and 1972 and what you did before?
I view the early work in Relational Grammar as a way of escaping from the various transformational assumptions, which took a long time for me. The early Relational Grammar work was a not very clear amalgam of relational ideas and transformational ideas.

But when the final break occurred, you're suggesting it was a break of significant proportions?
I think there are two answers to this. One is that the transformational ideas were inherently flawed. And the other is that Chomsky cannot conceive of a framework that isn't his. Can you imagine him, for example, writing in someone else's framework? The idea is ludicrous.[8]

Can you imagine doing that yourself?
No, I can't imagine doing it at this point in my life. But of course earlier I did. I wrote lots of articles in his framework. Now I'm just too intellectually lazy, I think, to do the work to internalize somebody else's framework.

There's something else, though. If one person's name is writ so large on the field, isn't that as much a fact about the field?
I don't think there's any real issue here. It's like Casey Stengel said when his team won its fifteenth pennant or whatever: "I couldn't have done it without the players." Chomsky needed certain "material" to mold, but at the same time he was very effective in molding it.

One thing I'm impressed by is that if one reads in other fields generally considered serious and sees what is taken as a result, it is quite different from linguistics. In pure mathematics a result is the proof of a significant theorem. So there is something one can get one's hands on. In natural science, there are discoveries of phenomena or formulations of laws or

IDEOLOGY AND LINGUISTIC THEORY

theories which entail certain known physical effects. And these results stay. But there is by and large very little like that in generative linguistics. And yet people speak about great contributions. In other words, in evaluating the status of linguistic work, I think people need to be more skeptical.

You've been holding mathematics up as a discipline that linguistics should emulate a bit more than it has. Is that something you believed in the 1960s?
No. Although this was something that Chomsky believed in the 1950s and in effect said at the beginning of *Syntactic Structures* [Chomsky 1957a: 5]. He has this little story, several paragraphs long, about the importance of formalization and how vague ideas are bad for several reasons. It is really a beautiful section, but despite his denials I think he has largely repudiated it. I think there has been an evolution in Chomsky's views in the wrong direction and that his work now much more closely represents what he contrasted "the search for rigorous formulation" with in 1957 than such a search itself.[9]

I'd guess most linguists today would say that linguistics is closer to psychology than to mathematics, so perhaps your position is not widely shared.
My thinking about the abstract character of linguistics, which is certainly not widely shared, arises entirely from Jerry Katz's work over the last six or seven years, specifically his 1981 book.[10] The central argument of this work is that languages and sentences are abstract objects, hence, neither external physical nor psychological objects. A key argument for this conclusion is that natural language sentences embody *necessary* truths – that analytic statements like *All the white bunnies are white* are not (only) certainties, or things that people believe very strongly, they're necessities. But if language were a contingent phenomenon, which follows from the psychological claim, rather than a necessary one, how could this be the case? Since, Katz argues, the analyticity of such sentences devolves totally on the structure of the sentences, if sentences were contingent, they could not determine necessary properties. Interestingly, Chomsky himself also accepts the analyticity facts and agrees that natural language sentences embody necessary truths [see, e.g. Chomsky 1977b: 35, 1979: 145, 1988: 33]. But he failed to recognize the foundational implications, that a contingent psychological structure could not determine anything to be necessary. One of Chomsky's (social) triumphs is the broad current consensus that linguistics is a psychological field. But I can't make any sense out of it nor out of Chomsky's latest version of conceptualism, which has driven him to make (to me) bizarre statements, such that languages aren't real.[11]

Let me go back to a question that I have been wanting to ask. In the very last part of the 1960s and early 1970s, there was a sense of great fatigue and exhaustion on the part of the people who were mainly involved in Generative Semantics . . .
That's probably right. I was fatigued in the sense that, we were not idiots, we knew we had lost.

136

I'm not sure I understand. You felt that you had lost a battle with Chomsky?
Sure.

An intellectual battle or a social battle or both?
Mostly a propaganda battle.

How could you tell? Newmeyer said that at one point most people in the field were convinced by the Generative Semantics position. I don't know how he can tell.
I don't know either although I probably share his view. That is, I suspect he was right that in the late 1960s Generative Semantics seemed to the majority of linguists in the generative camp like the wave of the future. But from the time of the Texas conference on, I think it turned around.

And whose mind was it that was being changed? Or was it the production of enthusiastic young people, coming out of MIT?
In terms of capturing the hearts and minds of MIT students, it was really quite clear. It was n to zero for some ever increasing n. Those people went away, and they got jobs. They influenced students. And it was clear who had won. It really was not in doubt, on the social level, anyway.

At MIT, sure, the facts go that way. But in the field at large? Why did people drift away from Generative Semantics to, say, Montague Grammar?
Well, Montague Grammar had a certain inherent appeal to it. It comes with the backing of logic, a brilliant logician who had real triumphs in logic. It has all the trappings of a powerful formalism. It's rather impenetrable at first. It really looks good from that point of view. And it managed to establish its own kind of fervor that resists contact with linguistic reality, in my experience. Note that the Montague type of semantics was already shown clearly to be a false theory in 1977, since it determines that all necessary truths have the same meaning and that all necessary falsehoods have the same meaning [see Katz and Katz 1977].[12] Supporters of Montague Grammar know about this problem. But their defense tends to involve vague promises about future revisions and irrelevancies like, "The advantage of this approach is that it has a precise, highly developed formalized semantics." Precision and formal development are undeniable virtues, but not ones capable of overcoming the flaw of false consequences.

Earlier, you said you felt it was essential for linguists to use terms which are well defined and well understood; and, of course, when talking about semantics, linguists have always felt that they were on slightly soft ground and that it's therefore nice to be able to refer to this tradition that goes back through Carnap and Russell to Frege and others who have achieved what are clearly results in philosophy.
Well, Montague semantics meets that criterion admirably. It just doesn't meet the criterion of avoiding infinitely many crashingly false consequences. What could be a clearer falsification of a theory of meaning than a

demonstration that it claims that *All white bunnies are white* and *Two and two are four* mean the same thing?[13]

I'm not going to defend it, but there's a sense of being part of a larger movement when you join Montague Grammar, because there's a tradition outside of linguistics, as you say.
Jerry Katz has a saying about this, which he calls "busy hands." A framework will be attractive independently of its substance in so far as it provides graduate students with a technically clear thing that they can keep busy on and get theses out of.

Moving to another topic, what do you think today of your 1974 book, On Raising?
I view it, as I view everything I wrote in transformational terms, as a mixture of the silly and the not silly. I brought up there a lot of facts which have to be taken into account in describing these constructions. I think that I had the right analysis in an abstract sense, namely, a raising analysis into object position, but it should be interpreted relationally. The actual form of the arguments in terms of transformations seems to me rather silly. My remark goes back to the question of why Generative Semantics faded away. In a sense, I think that was a good thing, because after all, it was a dispute about the *right form* of transformational grammar. And to me, there is no right form of that theory, any more than there is a right form of phlogiston theory. The bad thing is not that Generative Semantics disappeared but that the other branch of transformational theory didn't disappear.

One of the core premises of Generative Semantics is that there are semantic representations and that the rules that relate them to surface structure are of one general sort. That first premise has been taken over now in Chomsky's Government and Binding Theory, although with a lot of reservations.
Well, no, I don't think . . .

But the question I wanted to ask – you can answer that – but I did want to ask why that part of the premise seems not to have been pursued in the work that you've done over the last ten, fifteen years.
No, it hasn't been pursued. I still sort of vaguely believe it. But now I think it's wrong to say that that's been adopted in GB Theory. They have no notion of semantics whatever. They have adopted some notations that *look* like the predicate calculus and use terms like "logical form," but in reality none of it has anything to do with the representation of meaning. They're pretty explicit about that, that there is no requirement that sentences with the same meaning have the same logical form, for example. And their so-called logical forms are filled with all sorts of things that have nothing to do with logic, like actual words from particular languages, and so forth. I said this contentiously some years ago, that it was just a new level of syntactic representation. But Chomsky now says that explicitly.

138

But where does meaning representation come in in recent work? If it's not central to Chomsky, and if it isn't something that you've pursued, isn't that a big part of Generative Semantics that has pretty much been just dropped?

Well, yes, I suppose so. Maybe this is why Montague Grammar seems attractive to many people once involved in transformational grammar: it seems to offer some hope of dealing with this issue. I don't think it does for the reasons I mentioned.

When you said that Chomsky today is basically saying that his grammar is all syntax, including those elements which incorporate things that in other theories might be called semantics, this reminds me of something that George Lakoff said. He said that at the time that they were constructing these rules to relate surface structure and what's now semantic representation, at least some of the Generative Semanticists thought they were doing syntax, too – basically that this was all syntax.

I think that's right. I think I viewed it that way. And I still do. I don't use the term "syntax" in the way some people do, that there's "syntax" and "semantics." I never liked that terminology. It seems to me that there are just relations between different kind of objects. And you want the maximally general theory to talk about them. I have never seen any satisfactory argument that these were divided up into two different, very different things. I guess what Chomsky believes is that it just turns out to be a funny fact that the syntactic part of it has some properties that other people thought the semantic part had, namely variables and quantifiers. And he seems to believe that real semantics is in a different realm. He doesn't believe in logical forms in the sense that Generative Semanticists did or that Katz does. He doesn't believe that there are real structures over which one can define actual semantic properties like sameness of meaning or meaning inclusion or analyticity or semantic entailment. But I believe that and that the relations between that and surface structure are all part of one thing; at least, I would like that hypothesis to be investigated. So in a vague sense I still think I believe in the Generative Semantics idea. I would suggest that, as incarnated in transformational grammar, it had a lot of baggage that it didn't need and couldn't overcome.

One other point. Current Chomskyans are more and more making explicit their acceptance of some other crucial Generative Semantics ideas, like lexical decomposition. At a conference in Iowa that I went to in October, David Pesetsky gave a very explicit talk about Japanese causative verbs. Although these verbs are, morphologically, just individual verbs, he argued that they have to be treated as syntactically complex, as in Generative Semantics lexical decomposition. This was just anathema ten years ago. So I think there's some real substance to the idea that Generative Semantics is now . . .

Part of conventional wisdom?

Yes. Which would suggest that the opposition to it was never really intellectual but personal. That the important thing was not whether the idea was good or bad, but whose idea it was.

Do you really believe that?
Not a hundred percent, but I think, yes, to a significant extent.

But why would the field as a whole respond to it? Why did the whole field pick up on one person?
But isn't that the way social movements work? I haven't studied it seriously, but there's a relevant book which looks at end-of-the-world movements [Festinger, Riecken, and Schachter 1956]. Involved are historical cases where a charismatic figure comes along and says, "Wake up, the world's going to end." And he would give an actual date. The members of the religious group he influenced would get together and pray and try to expiate their sins. Then the day would come, the world would not end, and one might figure that the movement would collapse, right? But no, quite the contrary. The fervor of the group members became even greater. They would go out and proselytize, passionately trying to get more members. A new date would be set. When that date would arrive, the prediction would again obviously be falsified and one would assume that the movement would this time surely collapse. No. Again, there was increased proselytization, increased fervor, and it was only with the third date, I think, that such movements really collapsed. What I find interesting about that phenomenon from the point of view of what goes on in an intellectual field like linguistics is that the ability of people to handle disconfirmation without giving up their ideas is really quite enormous. Obviously, the force of the disconfirmation of end-of-the-world predictions is immeasurably greater than that relevant to any imaginable disconfirmation in linguistics. And yet it is possible for otherwise sane people to deal with such disconfirmations without giving up the essentials. People's ability to "save" their ideas from even the most devastating counterexamples is thus extraordinary. I suspect that that fact goes a long way towards helping us understand what goes on in a field like linguistics.

You suggested a few minutes ago that so much of the rancor of the late 1960s period had to do with some problems that originated in relations between particular people. But those problems, or those tensions, were then taken on by the field as a whole. And that's a very different kind of mechanism than the ability to survive a counterexample. The investment of individuals in X's being correct needs to be explained.
Well, but who are the messianic followers? What is their standing independent of a messianic leader and his doctrine, whatever it is? The relation between the leader and the follower is such that the follower's status is in significant part dependent on the leader's status. Would the follower get his or her job, get tenure and be invited to give talks *et cetera* independent of the prestige of the leader, just on his or her own? Doesn't

this person get a tremendous advantage by being a member of this prestige-ful group?

One has to separate two questions. One is whether they would get those things. And the other is whether they believe it. And, of course, if they believe they wouldn't have gotten the benefits without their commitment, that's enough to explain it. I would like to believe that they would have, whichever way they committed themselves, but that almost doesn't matter.

One thing I think we should say is that the timing is at least correct. That the beginning of all this kind of explicit hassling significantly corresponds with Chomsky's public involvement in the anti-Vietnam War movement. There is a certain case to be made that the emotional fervor and sense of rightness that was involved in that political antiwar movement somehow migrated over to linguistics independent of the content. In other words, there is in his kind of linguistics over the last ten or fifteen years a kind of emotional and moral fervor, as if he were battling for the right.

Wasn't that there in 1961, '62, '63?

Perhaps; if so, it seemed reasonable to me then because there was a strong opposition that was clearly in control and I agreed with the right/wrong judgment. But it seems to me Chomsky is now still defending his position as if it were threatened when in fact it is overwhelmingly accepted.[14] He continues to rewrite the same book, as if he didn't notice that he had actually won that war. But on the other hand, he has good reasons for being insecure because he cannot fail to have noticed that he has few substantive results in the sense that these are understood in more serious fields such as logic, mathematics, computer science, or physics. And it is striking how elements of his position which were once considered to be profound contributions now have vanished or become enormously marginalized. Where are syntactic rule ordering, the principle of cyclic application, the A-over-A Principle, etc.? Many of the principles and accomplishments touted in recent years are almost embarrassing in their inadequacy and shoddiness. Consider one example. Chomsky [1981: 193] has argued that Principle C of his so-called Binding Theory explains the strong crossover phenomenon first discussed in Postal 1971. Roughly, this principle claims that a "referring expression" cannot be bound. The claim is thus that the crossover facts can be deduced from this principle. But this account fails resoundingly. First, since the Binding Theory only characterizes noun phrases, Chomsky's Principle C treatment entails that no strong crossover effects can be induced by extraction of prepositional phrases, thereby falsely distinguishing the equally impossible *To whom did he say I gave the book and *Who did he say I gave the book to, where he and who or "whom" are supposed to be coreferential.[15] Second, Chomsky's supposed explanation also ignores the fact that there is an asymmetry in the phenomenon. Roughly, it only exists when an antecedent is extracted, not a pronominal form; thus, a Principle C approach fails to distinguish *Jerome, I convinced him I would hire* (where *Jerome* and *him* are supposed to be coreferential) from *Myself, I can't begin to understand,* wrongly blocking *both*.[16] There are other problems. My experience is that "results" in Chomskyan linguistics tend more often than not to be of the character of his Principle C treatment of crossover phenomena. The significant point then is that there is an extraordinary contrast between the paucity of genuine results in Chomskyan linguistics and the forests of paper which have been, and continue to be, devoted to the linguistic ideas involved.

NOTES

1 INTRODUCTION

1 For some varying views on this and related questions in the linguistic literature, see Wasow 1985 and the reply by Halle and Higginbotham (1986).
2 The following characterizations seem to us representative:

> The rapid decline in the fortunes of Generative Semantics in the early 1970s was in part a consequence of the vagueness with which its proposals were formulated and in part a consequence of the fact that many of its specific empirical claims about the syntax–semantics interface were disconfirmed.
>
> (Newmeyer 1990: 167)

> [Generative Semantics] failed for two reasons. One difficulty was technical: the proposed analyses were by and large shown to be syntactically and/or semantically incorrect. More importantly, the theory led to far too unconstrained a theory of universal grammar; the language learner's choices were so cast as to render language learning impossible.
>
> (Jackendoff 1983: 241–2)

> Generative Semantics was ultimately unsuccessful, however, because of a failure to distinguish between syntactic and non-syntactic properties of sentence structure and an unwillingness to subject the [Katz–Postal] Hypothesis to empirical scrutiny.
>
> (van Riemsdijk and Williams 1986: 88)

3 The closest anyone has come to such a critique is Morgan (1973a), who showed that the set of propositions separately considered to be plausible by Generative Semanticists was not internally consistent (see Chapter 2 below); but Generative Semantics was hardly unique in this regard, as we will show (see also McCawley 1976b: 225).

2 GAPS IN THE PARADIGM: MEDIATIONAL AND DISTRIBUTIONAL THEMES IN THEORETICAL SYNTAX

1 Cf. the following statement by Perlmutter (1980: 196):

> It is important to distinguish between a *framework* and elements of a *theory*. A framework offers certain concepts for use in the construction of grammars

of individual languages and the statement of universals, and claims that this set of concepts, when appropriately refined, augmented by others, etc. will be adequate for the construction of a theory that can provide an adequate answer to [the question, "In what ways do natural languages differ, and in what ways are they all alike?"]. Because of the vagueness of the claims involved, it is probably impossible to falsify a framework. Elements of a theory, on the other hand, make falsifiable empirical claims.

2 One striking example of "whatever" can be found in *The Generative Enterprise* (Chomsky 1982), where Chomsky mentions that he stopped doing phonology and mathematical linguistics because his energies were taken up by antiwar activities (p. 57).

3 Or students: these data constitute the first problem in Merrifield *et al.*'s (1971) popular text.

4 This issue, which was never satisfactorily resolved by descriptivists, continues to be a problem in contemporary theories as well. Since the appearance of the earliest work in generative phonology, critics have questioned the basis for deciding that there is something to be explained regarding the difference in pronunciation found in, say, the English words *omen* and *ominous*, or the first syllable of *hypocrisy* and *hypothesis* (both examples from Kiparsky 1982). Something having to do with meaning is obviously involved, since no one would take seriously the proposal that *wit* is derived from *it* (or *win* from *in*) by /w/-insertion, or that a rule of /k/-insertion derives *quit* from *wit*, or *quick* from *wick*, or *daiquiri* from *diary*. McCawley (1986) addresses this difficult question, which has received precious little consideration in the past twenty-five years relative to its importance.

5 See Goodman (1943). It is worthwhile bearing in mind that some of the basic elements of the philosophical study of knowledge have changed over the last fifty years in ways that are quite radical. One fundamental question in modern epistemology is how we are to deal with the arbitrary character of our subjectivity, and with the way that this subjectivity seems to envelope any propositional statement of our knowledge. Indeed, this question permeates contemporary studies of many domains, including ethics and aesthetics, to name just two outstanding examples. In the context of scientific knowledge, the question emerges in a number of guises. One is this: a scientific statement (or even a conjecture) will necessarily be stated using some technical vocabulary; this is both natural and unavoidable. Is it possible to establish antecedently an objective account of language – that is, one that is in no way dependent on the biography and the historical-cultural background of the person using the vocabulary and making the statement? Most contemporary thinkers answer this question with a "No"; among the works that are often cited in this vein are Rorty (1979) and Feyerabend (1975). This, indeed, is one of the principal reasons why the study of language has come to be central for many concerned with epistemology: if all statements are statements in a particular language, is it possible to speak of something like a propositional content which is fully independent of the choice of languages? Again, the contemporary answer to this is predominantly "No".

Contemporary scientists, or contemporary linguists, have only three choices when facing this negative answer. They can put their faith in the belief that someday, somehow, an objective language, one independent of all history and cultural context, will be established; this faith would be one that recapitulated the faith of the dominant philosophies of science in the first decades of this century. They could, alternatively, abandon hope in the notion of objectivity and the possibility of transcending individual subjectivity, and in this wretched state they would at least be comforted by being surrounded by many others of the same persuasion, and they would be in a position where any interpretation (being totally subjective) was as good as any other interpretation. Finally, they could attempt to establish the notion of objectivity not as an absolute, but rather as a context-dependent notion, in the sense that while it may never be possible to find an absolute and subjectivity-free language, it will always be possible, when two scientists confront each other, to establish a common language which they can agree upon – though of course the issues that separate the two scientists (presumably coming from different sets of assumptions and beliefs) will not be immediately resolved just by finding some perhaps minimal common linguistic ground. The point is that the disappearance of an absolute objectivity is replaced in contemporary thought by the belief that for any given pair of subjectivities S_i and S_j, a common conceptual ground $CG(i, j)$ can be formulated, but as the indexing suggests, the choice of the common conceptual ground is dependent, not independent, of the choice of interlocutors. Finding a common ground is not an easy task, and in many cases it can be made all the harder by the combativeness of the participants. A common ground must be constructed, not merely discovered. In the case at hand that we are studying in this book, the task was arguably not carried through to completion.

In any event, fifty years ago, such a point of view would not have been taken seriously, and it would have been seen as inadequate as a basis for a science. It was generally taken for granted that a common (and thus objective) theoretical ground would be established, and devising scientific theories that were formal in character was taken to be an important step in that direction. And while Goodman did not go as far as Chomsky would have liked (as Chomsky 1975c observes), he did demonstrate that some aspects of complexity (which might seem like an important but subjective characteristic) were formal, and hence entirely subject-independent.

6   For an account of the relation between Harris's conception of transformation and Chomsky's, see Chomsky 1975c: 41ff. Chomsky (p.c., May 1993) has emphasized that his idea of transformations goes back to traditional grammar, which described passive sentences as being derived from active sentences, and so on. Harris, however, departed from the traditional understanding of this concept to the extent that he used it as a device for normalizing texts for discourse analysis. *LSLT*, on Chomsky's understanding, took a view closer to the traditional one, although there transformations were mappings of underlying phrase markers to others rather than equivalence relations on surface forms.

There has been much speculation concerning what portion of his ideas Chomsky owes to predecessors, his supporters sometimes seeking to diminish his debt and his antagonists to exaggerate it. In this study we have not been especially concerned with this issue – perhaps even to the point of giving a misleading impression as to our view of it. Our view is that Chomsky's work is overall remarkably original. The arguments that some have given to show that Chomsky's work is derivative are less than fully convincing. To take just one interesting example, Chomsky (1975c: 47) has maintained that, at the time he wrote his master's thesis at the University of Pennsylvania (1951), he was unaware of Bloomfield's (1939) "Menomini morphophonemics," a paper that to a certain extent anticipates his approach in that thesis. The fact that

Chomsky (1975c: 25) has also mentioned that, in 1947, he read the proofs for Harris's *Methods in Structural Linguistics*, which in its published version (Harris 1951: 237) includes an appendix that briefly summarizes some of the morphophonemic rules in Bloomfield's paper, has been taken by some as possibly bearing on Chomsky's claim, even though so far as we know there is no evidence that the appendix in Harris's book had been written in 1947. This points to a problem inherent in the historiographic practice (which we have occasionally employed in this book) of citing works according to two dates – the dates they were published and the dates they were reportedly written (as, for example, one might refer to "Z. Harris 1951 [1947]").

7 The terminology had a natural origin in algebra, where the inverse image of the null set in the range of a mapping M is traditionally called the *kernel* of M; here, we are encouraged to think of the mapping in question as one that maps a sentence onto a structure in the range composed of the non-obligatory transformations that are involved in the sentence's derivation.

8 Some suggestions along this line appear in G. Lakoff (1970 [1965]). Lakoff and Ross (1976 [1967]: 162) had explicitly noted the similarity between "semantic interpretations, if these are conceived of (roughly) as formulas in predicate calculus, and deep syntax" of the kind they were proposing.

9 See, e.g. Katz and Fodor (1962).

10 As should be clear from the text, we take the orientational propositions in this and the other sketches to be ordered; whether or not the core propositions are also ordered, or whether there were additional core propositions, we leave open. At the same time, we should underscore that there are certain propositions that have been associated with Generative Semantics that seem to us less plausible as candidates for the core of that program. For example, Fritz Newmeyer (p.c., May 1992) has suggested to us that Lakoff and Ross's conclusion about the lack of motivation for a level of deep structure distinct from semantic representation must have been a core proposition of Generative Semantics. Clearly, Generative Semanticists felt that the proposition that there was such a level between semantic representation and surface structure as described in Chomsky's *Aspects* had been empirically refuted; but as regards whether or to what extent there might be syntactic conditions on surface structure which might require mechanisms roughly analogous to postulating such level, Generative Semanticists were generally silent (an issue to which we will return later in this chapter). In fact, the role played by deep structure in Generative Semantics argumentation was quite similar to that played by global rules in Interpretive Semantics argumentation: in both cases the proponents of the programs argued strongly against ideas packaged in a particular way that in other guises they might have been more willing to accept.

There were two other propositions associated with Generative Semantics – namely, that sentences that are paraphrases must share the same semantic representation, and that the highest verb in any semantic representation must be a performative verb – that were generally assumed to have been shown to be false. But whether or not they have been falsified, not all Generative Semanticists accepted these propositions; e.g. McCawley evidently never accepted either as a core proposition, and from the outset had rejected the first of them as even an auxiliary hypothesis.

11 Similar ideas underlie the general program of *LSLT*, although they are expressed there with rather less force and clarity. Cf. the following passage from *LSLT*:

> [Linguistic research] aims to provide for each language a theory of the
> structure of that language (i.e., a grammar), and at the same time to develop

a general theory of linguistic structure of which each of these grammars will present a model. The particular grammars and the general theory must be closely enough related so that some practical technique is available for deciding which of two proposed grammars better exemplifies the general theory.

(Chomsky 1975c: 80)

12 The fact that antecedents of the psychological view can be found in Chomsky's early writings is not really the issue here. What we are interested in is what was unambiguously highlighted in the literature that was made available to the larger group of professional linguists – which seems to us a fair indication of the centrality of these propositions in his mind at the time.

13 The technical argument is as follows. Any set of sentences, considered as a subset of the grammatical sentences of a language, is compatible with an infinite number of grammars that might have generated that subset. To take a mathematical example, the strings *aba*, *aabaa*, *aaabaaa*, and *aaaabaaaa* could have been generated by a grammar that is constructed so as to produce only strings consisting of an equal number of *a*s on either side of a *b*. But then again it might have been merely happenstance that the strings picked for the subset contained letters arranged in just this way. How would one know that the string *bababbbbbaaaaabbb* was not also in the language? Similarly, a child cannot conclude, just because he or she has never heard an adult utter a sentence of a certain type, that that sentence is not in the language (nor, of course, that all sentences so uttered are in the language).

14 That is, there is no induction problem to be solved as regards the syntax. There still would remain important questions about how the child acquires semantic competence. (See, e.g. J. A. Fodor 1980.)

15 For example, Chomsky (1975a: 92) formulated "a thesis of 'absolute autonomy of formal grammar'", which implies that

> the formal conditions on "possible grammars" and a formal property of "optimality" are so narrow and restrictive that a formal grammar can in principle be selected (and its structures generated) on the basis of a preliminary analysis of data in terms of formal primitives excluding the core notions of semantics, and that the systematic connections between formal grammar and semantics are determined on the basis of this independently selected system and the analysis of data in terms of the full range of semantic primitives.

A "weaker version" was also suggested which holds "only conditionally, with certain parameters, perhaps localized in the dictionary."

Although Chomsky noted that this definition "assume[s] an initial bifurcation of primitive notions into semantic and formal in some way" he went no further in marking out the primitives of the former sort than to say that "we might take such notions as 'synonymous,' 'significant,' 'denotes,' 'satisfies,' 'refers to concrete objects' to be core notions of semantics" (1975a: 91). But no set of formal definitions that would effect a clear bifurcation in all cases was given, suggesting that the hypothesis was not meant to be tested so much as to guide the construction of more particular auxiliary hypotheses. Developing a set of satisfactory definitions would of course be a significant challenge, since – as Partee (1975) noted – there are no independent or extratheoretic criteria for determining what are syntactic and what are semantic primitives.

Like the autonomy hypothesis, the innateness hypothesis has depended on an "initial bifurcation" of primitive notions – this time into those that are

147

domain specific and those that are domain general. But no clear formulation of such notions has been attempted (see Chomsky 1980). One strategy that has emerged in the literature has been, roughly, to say: show me a general learning theory, and I'll show you that it cannot account for the linguistic data by itself (see, e.g. Chomsky 1959, 1969: 64, 1975b). While there is nothing wrong with this strategy so far as it goes, it does not rule out the possibility of a general learning theory any more than the fact that no current phonological proposals can account for all the phonological data rules out the possibility of a general phonological theory: the force of the argument is governed entirely by the willingness of the reader to accept the presumption that future (not to say current) developments in the study of faculty-independent strategies for learning will be barren, or at best insignificant (an imprudent presumption, in our opinion, as some of our recent work has illustrated in phonology; see Goldsmith and Larson 1992, Goldsmith 1994, and other work cited there).

16 There has, however, been legitimate discussion – primarily by philosophers – of the logic of Chomsky's arguments; for example, see the papers in Hook 1969, Stich 1975, and Block 1981 concerning the innateness hypothesis.

17 The Generative Semanticists' diffidence when it came to speculating about the genetic basis of specific linguistic abilities needs to be distinguished from the plausibility or coherence of their arguments in support of the particular linguistic principles they hypothesized, given what was then assumed about the process of language acquisition. In most cases, the one had little to do with the other. For example, one type of counterargument that Interpretivists had used to advantage against Generative Semantics positions took the following form:

> Anyone who hypothesizes a principle P as part of an adult's native grammar ought to be able to show that it is possible to acquire P in the normal course of language acquisition, consistent with current knowledge of the acquisition process. If P is not universal, then evidence supporting P must be available to the language learner. But if *negative* evidence (correction, etc.) would be required to learn P, then P is falsified, since current theories of language acquisition suggest that children do not generally learn via negative evidence.

But Chomsky himself had early on shown the weakness of such an argument. That is, if P seems to be inconsistent with the learning theory of the day, that could be the fault of P – but it could also be a consequence of the way the problem is characterized in the context of the learning theory. In his attack on Skinner, Chomsky had discounted the possibility that the linguistic principles he had adduced from the empirical evidence could be wrong and shifted the burden to behaviorism. In a similar fashion, an advocate of P might challenge the chain of inferences that had led to the conclusion that P is unlearnable. As an example, consider the observation by Green (1974b) and C. L. Baker (1979) that adult speakers of English have somehow acquired the knowledge both that there is a rule that relates sentences like *John gave a million dollars to the museum* with *John gave the museum a million dollars* and that this rule does not apply in the case of verbs like *donate* – i.e., one would not say **John donated the museum a million dollars*. The paradox is then how a child learns the exception in the absence of negative evidence. But it may not be either the generalization about dative alternations nor the skepticism about negative evidence that requires reconsideration: as Pinker (1989) shows, one can maintain both by modulating the learning theory to accommodate the acquisition of certain types of semantic information that bear on the application of syntactic rules.

For arguments that Interpretivists had made not nearly as much progress in their attempt to restrict the class of theories available to the language learner as they had sometimes claimed, see Peters 1981, Gazdar 1981.

18 It is worth emphasizing that, on Chomsky's rather loose characterization of the distinction between syntax and semantics cited earlier, just about everything called "semantics" in linguistic work – including the Katz–Fodor–Postal proposals, virtually all of the analyses by linguists of quantifiers, modals, and anaphora, and even the more abstract semantical apparatus employed by philosophers like Donald Davidson to analyze events – could be considered pure syntax. Thus, what Chomsky has referred to, in his own theory or in others, as a level of "semantic representation" or "semantic interpretation" is entirely syntactic in this sense. The resulting terminological confusion no doubt contributed to the difficulty Interpretivists and Generative Semanticists had in arriving at a common understanding.

19 Newmeyer (1980: 114, 1986: 107), for example, characterizes "Remarks" as "the principal document of [Chomsky's] counteroffensive" against Generative Semantics, although Chomsky himself would evidently dispute that characterization. In personal communication (January 1992), Chomsky has maintained that "Remarks" was not written in response to Lakoff's work, which he says he scarcely knew of, but rather had been primarily motivated by longstanding disagreement with his former student Robert Lees, whose 1960 MIT dissertation‘ on nominalizations Chomsky had supervised. In fact, although work by Lakoff, McCawley, Postal, and Ross is referred to at various points in "Remarks," Generative Semantics is never mentioned. Nevertheless, in subsequent work, Chomsky (e.g. 1972a: 158–62) did make clear that he believed that his arguments in "Remarks" had identified significant and deep-seated problems for the Generative Semanticists' conception of "pre-lexical" syntax, and he certainly has never done anything to discourage such an interpretation of this paper. See also note 20.

20 Actually, the transformational position was not a creature of Generative Semantics. As Chomsky (1970: 188) noted, "[i]n the earliest work on transformational grammar (cf. Lees 1960)," its correctness "was taken for granted." Moreover, in *Aspects*, Chomsky had explicitly endorsed the kind of derivation he was now arguing against:

> Where derivational processes are productive, they in fact raise no serious difficulties. Consider, for example, nominalization transformations of the sort that form the sentences "their destruction of the property . . . ," "their refusal to participate . . . ," etc. Clearly, the words *destruction, refusal*, etc., will not be entered in the lexicon as such. Rather *destroy* and *refuse* will be entered in the lexicon with a feature specification that determines the phonetic form they will assume (by later phonological rules) when they appear in nominalized sentences. A nominalization transformation will apply at the appropriate stage of derivation to the generalized Phrase-marker containing the configuration "they destroy the property" . . .
>
> (1965: 184)

Although Chomsky had suggested in a footnote in *Aspects* a lexical alternative to the transformational position (1965: 219–20), he also pointed out in "Remarks" that he himself had been responsible for some of the subsequent arguments against that alternative. It is then no wonder that Generative Semanticists and others found the very strong position on lexicalism that Chomsky took in "Remarks" somewhat puzzling.

21 The precise nature of this process – one of the most commonplace in transformational studies – remains controversial. See, for example, Chapter 1 of Ruwet 1991.

22 Chomsky (1972a: 161–2), arguing against Lakoff (1971), claimed that Lakoff's proposal that "the regularities noted 'are instances of constraints on shallow or surface structure' . . . is untenable, since these regularities do not appear at the level of shallow or surface structure, but only at a more 'abstract' level." But the only facts to which this argument could possibly have applied were those involving the unproductiveness and semantic idiosyncracy of derived nominals, as opposed to their internal structure. Since neither Chomsky nor Lakoff had provided grounds for assuming that a transformational solution would necessarily require output constraints in these other cases (see above), this particular argument was in fact irrelevant to the question of whether a lexical approach to derived nominals was to be preferred to a transformational one.

23 Chomsky briefly entertained an argument in "Remarks" (1970: 217, n. 11) against such an approach. Chomsky's claim was that the noun phrase *John's intelligence* has at least the readings "the fact that John is intelligent" and "the extent to which John is intelligent," since it can substitute in either the context ____ *is undeniable* or the context ____ *exceeds his foresight.* But, as Chomsky also pointed out, there are cases like *John's intelligence is his most remarkable quality,* where "[i]t is difficult to find a natural source for the nominal": then *John's intelligence, which is his most remarkable quality, exceeds his foresight,* which Chomsky assumed was fully grammatical, could not be derived, since "in general the identity of structure required for appositive clause formation to take place goes even beyond identity of the given phrase-markers, as was pointed out by Lees (1960: 76)." But Chomsky's argument could have applied only in case the forms are ambiguous rather than simply vague as to the relevant properties. Since Chomsky provided no grounds for the assumption that these properties had to be specified in underlying structure, his argument had no bearing on the Bach–McCawley approach.

24 For example, Chomsky and Halle provided rules for predicting the the phonological properties of the nouns *advocacy, condensation,* and *compensation* by deriving them from abstract underlying phonological forms involving (the forms underlying) the verbs *advocate, condense,* and *compensate,* plus affixes (1968: 370). While it is not logically necessary that the syntax of these words pattern on their phonology (or, rather, there is no reason why the relevant analysis could not be undertaken in the lexicon, as Chomsky had proposed, rather than in the syntax), by Occam's razor one would, other things equal, prefer the grammar which had the tighter connection. In an interesting twist, the Generative Semanticists generally supported the Natural Phonology approach to the phonological analysis of such nominalizations, which postulated underlying phonological representations for these words much closer to their surface phonetic representations.

25 See Chomsky 1975c: 84:

> It is certainly correct that logic is indispensable for formalizing theories, of linguistics or anything else, but this fact gives us no insight into what sort of systems form the subject matter for linguistics, or how it should treat them. Neither from this fact, nor from the indisputable fact that work in logic has incidentally led to important insights into the use of language, can it be argued that the study of the formal (or semantic) properties of natural languages should model itself on the study of the formal (or semantic) properties of logic and artificial languages.

26 This latter suggestion, which appeared in a response to Chomsky's published criticism, was not exactly ingenuous, since what Chomsky had argued was that the interpretation of sentences containing *realize* depends on both the surface

150

structure and the semantic interpretation of the complement (Chomsky 1971: 197). That is, McCawley was offering the possibility of a Generative Semantics version of Chomsky's solution. In neither case, however, were these ideas developed in a definitive fashion.

27 Cf., e.g. Barbara Partee's (1971: 3) statement that "Lakoff, McCawley, Postal, and others have accepted the hypothesis that transformations preserve meaning and extended it to the position that all and only sentences which are paraphrases of each other should have the same deep structures."

28 McCawley (1975a: 45) provided a test of the following sort: a sentence X is said to differ in meaning from a sentence Y if "Z realizes that X but doesn't realize that Y" is not contradictory. By this test he concluded that alternates involving order of conjunction and some optional ordering transformations share the same meaning; i.e. he found the following sentences contradictory:

(i) Ted realizes that Marty and Zelda are engaged, but he doesn't realize that Zelda and Marty are engaged.

(ii) Max realizes that Santa Claus gave Johnny a toy guillotine but he doesn't realize that Santa Claus gave a toy guillotine to Johnny.

Chomsky's arguments appear to have committed him to the position that neither (i) nor (ii) is contradictory.

McCawley's appeal to this particular sort of test might have been thought ironic, given that it had been just such sentences that had led Chomsky to his conclusion about Generative Semantics. In fact, McCawley was simply pushing the dispute back one level. That is, he evidently did not intend that this test be an empirical test in the sense that the factual existence of someone who assents to a sentence like (i) or (ii) would falsify his claim about conjunction.

29 Later developments showed that the issue was quite complex. See, e.g. McCawley 1970a, 1978, 1981, Partee 1973, Postal 1974a, Jackendoff 1975, and Fauconnier 1985, among others.

30 "We will say that a node A 'commands' another node B if (1) neither A nor B dominates the other; and (2) the S-node that most immediately dominates A also dominates B" (Langacker 1969: 167).

31 The Katz–Postal hypothesis in its original form presumed a decidedly "Harrisian" conception of transformations as rules specifying relations between (surface structure) sentences. Given such a conception, one can legitimately ask whether an active sentence has the same meaning as its passive counterpart, and so forth. The equivalent notion in Generative Semantics could only involve a relation between derivations: are the two sentences mapped onto the same or perhaps mutually entailing semantic representations? One then might investigate which local transformations in Generative Semantics "preserve meaning" to the extent that no global rule constrains their output, but that would be the only sense in which the Katz–Postal hypothesis could have an application in that theory. Looking at Katz–Postal through a Harrisian lens has inevitably led to some peculiar interpretations of its relevance to Generative Semantics, such as that it is maintained there "in an uncomfortably artificial way [via global rules]; indeed by entirely circular means" (R. Harris 1993: 175).

32 For example, Ross (1972: 106) proposed what he called " The principle of semantic relevance": " Where syntactic evidence supports the postulation of elements in underlying structure which are not phonetically manifested, such elements tend to be relevant semantically." Ross conceived of underlying structure as mediating between surface structure and meaning; his hypothesis then sought to limit the relation between those levels by specifying a restriction

NOTES

on one way that underlying structure might differ from surface structure. Such a hypothesis could trivially have been formulated as a global rule, but one that itself further limited the scope of global operations: in accord with this hypothesis no rule, global or local, could be written that had the effect of deleting semantically irrelevant constituents. See also Lakoff 1971: 283.

33 Jackendoff's argument had been that a sentence like (i) is three-ways ambiguous:

    (i) I assigned three problems to many students.

On the first reading, I assigned a group of three problems to a group consisting of many students. On the second reading, I assigned one problem to one group consisting of many students, a second problem to a different group consisting of many students, and a third problem to yet a third group of many students. On the third reading, I assigned three problems to one student, three possibly different problems to another student, and so on, until I had assigned many students three problems each. Jackendoff claimed that "traditional logical notation is insufficient" to express these three readings (Jackendoff 1972: 308). It is true that G. Lakoff (1972: 558) at the time admitted uncertainty about how the "group" reading of quantifiers should be represented, but that fact in itself hardly demonstrated a deficiency of the Generative Semantics program. In any case, by 1981 McCawley at least had accepted a role for second–order mechanisms like set variables and branching quantifiers, which could be used to capture the ambiguity in question (see, e.g. McCawley 1981, ch. 14). A device something like set variables is employed in Heim, Lasnik, and May (1991) for a similar purpose.

34 Other positions are possible. Cooper (1982) proposes that multiply-quantified sentences need not be given alternative semantic representation to represent ambiguity. Higginbotham (1985: 582) offers a critique of that position.

35 For further perspectives on the issue, primarily from a semantic point of view, see especially Katz 1977a, Kempson and Cormack 1981, 1982, K. Bach 1982, and Gil 1982. See also McCawley (1992) for a syntactic argument that global rules are not required to explain the nonsynonymy of multiply-quantified sentences.

36 The Interpretivist position was of course that the Generative Semanticists had not given a well-articulated account, since they had not responded to the objections.

37 Hale and Keyser take pains to distance themselves from the Generative Semantics analyses that their analyses resemble and try to show that their work is not subject to the arguments that J. A. Fodor (1970) assembled against Generative Semantics. As Wasow (1976) had pointed out, the Interpretivists' dispute with Lakoff's and McCawley's claim that *John killed Bill* and *John caused Bill to die* are both to be transformationally derived from essentially the same underlying source was not over whether the meanings of lexical items could be decomposed into their constituent semantic elements; what the Interpretivists denied was that that relationship was systematic and could be described and explained by syntactic rule. Thus, when Hale and Keyser (1987: 9), working within the Interpretivist tradition, later attempted to specify such a rule, they found it necessary to point out that their analysis "is not inconsistent with the position developed by J. A. Fodor (1970) in his criticism of the analysis of *kill* as deriving from the complex source *cause to die*," because they have added a technical device to mark lexical causatives like *kill* as denoting a single event. But they offer no citations of the Generative Semantics accounts with which they are comparing their own (citing only Fodor's critique of them), nor do

152

they discuss in what respects their technical device might or might not be consistent with such accounts. In fact, McCawley (1978) – as we will see below – had already proposed something similar in a Generative Semantics framework. It could hardly be said, then, that Hale and Keyser have tried to draw a genealogical connection between those accounts and their work. Hale and Keyser's perspective is not unusual (see also M. Baker 1988: 449, 459 and Li 1990: 400, fn. 1), and examples of the sort could be multiplied.

If our argument is valid, then citations – at least in linguistics – are not an especially accurate guide to the rise, flow, and fall of concrete and substantive positions taken. That is, linguists' citation practices during this period are evidently more indicative of their allegiance to their respective research programs than of the source of the ideas they discuss. Compare, for example, the observation of De Mey (1982: 131):

> Whereas upholders of the quantitative approach consider references as unobtrusive measures of genuine affinity and intellectual descent, easily tapped and processed, opponents look upon them as highly ambiguous and poorly understood artefacts of the scientific literature which are easily misused. They find it rather simpleminded to think of references which in scholarly papers are provided in footnotes, as footprints indicating the route along which the author has reached his results. Not only are there different ways of citing, such as negative versus positive citations, which mean very different positions toward the cited document, i.e. rejection or support. Many crucial items and influences are not cited at all and many of those that are cited bear only a superficial relation to the work presented in the paper.

A related argument concerning research traditions in phonology can be found in Goldsmith (1992), where the relation of Firthian work to contemporary phonological theory is discussed.

38 What Chomsky had made clear was that all things would not be equal unless a theory's predictions about what grammars are possible are taken into account. But once facts about "universals," mode of acquisition, and so on are considered, the issue of the power of a theory becomes entirely an empirical one.

39 Katz and Bever (1976) purport to advance such a criterion, arguing that:

> what makes a phenomenon grammatical is the fact that the principles that explain it are all required to explicate the properties and relations that have been systematically interrelated by the laws and concepts originally devised to account for speakers' intuitions about rhyme, alliteration, ellipsis, word order, synonymy, ambiguity, etc.
>
> (p. 40)

This suggestion fails for several reason. The et cetera clause may be filled in as liberally or as conservatively as the reader wishes, leading to radically different views of grammaticality; indeed, a grammatical theory committed to explicating relations of synonymy and ambiguity opens the door to analyses that incorporate all the semantic information that linguists can measure. At the same time, the criterion fails to leave any methodological room for phenomena which *next* year's theory of syntax will explain but which this year's does not. Katz and Bever's position commits them to classifying as being not grammatical any phenomenon whose explanation (whatever that may mean) is not based on principles that have already been established. It may seem a benign enough conclusion from this that the new range of data explained by the latest theoretical modification was not till then "grammatical," but then it is no longer possible to criticize an opponent's theory for casting its net too widely,

NOTES

into the realm of the extragrammatical – the criteria having once again become useless in this regard.

The problem is simply restated in an alternative suggestion by Koster (1978: 567) to the effect that extragrammatical principles are just those that have the properties that "they are less general across languages, and – within the language in which they occur – they are subject to lexical idiosyncracies and are responsible for variance in judgment about the sentences they produce." Since this criterion depends on a prior analysis of the data, it might be applied to any data whatever, as Koster himself (1978: 580 fn. 48) is evidently aware: "Because of this very heterogeneous character of language phenomena, it is entirely pointless to list arbitrary data from arbitrary languages. . . . Violation of a principle as such tells us very little about its validity, because virtually all principles can be violated."

40 Cf. also E. Bach (1974: 168): "The truth is that we don't know what is a matter of competence and what performance unless we provide both a theory of competence and a theory of performance."

41 How relevant Emonds's work in fact was to the Generative Semantics–Interpretive Semantics dispute is arguable. Emonds in both his thesis (1970) and his book (1976) generally assumed Chomsky's Extended Standard Theory as the context for his investigations, and Chomsky cited these works as providing evidence for a set of surface structure conditions which, "if warranted, would be an interesting and suggestive supplement to the proposal that properties of surface structure play a distinctive role in semantic interpretation" (1972a: 117). But McCawley (1975a: 66) saw no such connection between Emonds's arguments and Chomsky's arguments for surface structure interpretation. In fact, although McCawley (1982: 1) classified Emonds as a representative of the Interpretive Semantics community, he also felt comfortable in adopting an "alternative" to Emonds's version of structure preservation in which "base rules" are treated as combinatoric restrictions on surface structure (McCawley 1982: 112; see also McCawley 1988: 290–1).

Nevertheless, what made Emonds's work a significant contribution to the Interpretivist program was its demonstration that a wide variety of distributional facts could be explained as the result of a few far-reaching syntactic principles independent of semantics. McCawley's willingness to embrace an analogous set of syntactic conditions on surface structure suggests that his conception of the organization of grammar was not so different from that of the Interpretivists as has been sometimes supposed. See below.

42 Cf. also Newmeyer (1980: 169–70, 1986: 135):

Probably no metatheoretical statement by a Generative Semanticist did more to undermine confidence in that model than Paul Postal's paper "The Best Theory" . . . Postal contrasted two hypothetical models, one with just As and another with both Bs and Cs, where A, B, and C are distinct components or rule types . . . . If for Postal, A, B, and C had been constructs of equal complexity and generality, then no one would have objected to his characterization. But for Postal and the other Generative Semanticists, A came more and more to be nothing but an unconstrained rule of grammar, while for Interpretivists, B and C were highly constrained rule types of definite form and specific function. Thus, it is the latter alternative which is preferable, not the former. . . . Interpretivists, at least in principle, were committed to constraining (or at least characterizing) B and C, whereas Generative Semanticists steadily weakened the content of A by ever increasing the type of data that it had to cover.

Aside from the fact that he somewhat mischaracterizes Postal's argument, Newmeyer bases his conclusion upon a premise that, on the face of it, is flatly false. It would be far more accurate to say that, as things stood around 1969, when Postal and Chomsky were writing their papers, the semantic interpretation rules that Interpretivists had proposed constituted an unconstrained rule type of no definite form or function. While Generative Semanticists did not have a tightly constrained theory of the relation between surface structure and semantic representation, they certainly had proposed more constraints on that relation than Interpretivists had.

The issue was sometimes confused, as we have suggested, by comparisons of the full Generative Semantics grammar with the Interpretive Semantics syntax. Conceived as a device that specifies the set of sentences of the language along with their (surface-)structural descriptions, a Generative Semantics grammar with global rules would clearly be less constrained than an Interpretive Semantics syntax without global rules. But conceived as a device that associates surface forms with meanings, no Interpretive Semantics theory proposed at the time had an advantage over Generative Semantics theories, i.e. was better able to predict the kinds and limits of associations found in natural languages.

43 This is not to say that there were not serious attempts (both within and without the Interpretivist tradition) to develop a theory of performance; in addition to the work of Bever, see also Kean 1975, Frazier 1977, and Rochemont 1978.

44 On both the weak and strong versions, the Synthetic Conjecture can be understood either as a methodological canon or as a statement about the nature of language. As a statement of methodology, the strong version is that inquiry into distribution and inquiry into the manner in which language encodes meaning will lead the scientist to the same conclusions regarding the grammar of the language. As a statement about the nature of language, the strong version is that the analytic constructs identified by scientific analysis determine both the distribution of grammatical forms and the relation of those forms to meaning.

Several weaker versions of the Synthetic Conjecture are conceivable (including the neoautonomist position, discussed below), and have undoubtedly played a role in recent syntactic developments. Again, both methodological and analytical versions can be formulated, although in these cases the methodological version may be the more natural.

45 Compare this with the following statement from (Green 1974a: 186): "The innovation of Generative Semantics was to attempt to translate meaning into form . . . all aspects of meaning (whatever that is) which determine aspects of surface form must be represented structurally, either in underlying structure of that form, or in some other structural representation which serves a similar purpose. . . . "

46 This is not to say that May's rule was strictly homomorphic with the Lakoff–McCawley rule. But May's rule quite evidently owed its existence to the observation, originally exploited by the Generative Semanticists and later endorsed by Chomsky, that quantifier scope could be insightfully analyzed in a theory that had a level of semantic representations related to surface structure via transformational rules. In fact, May (1985: 158) explicitly distinguished his Quantifier Rule from Lakoff and McCawley's Quantifier Lowering only to the extent that on his view the latter "would give rise to structures containing unbound traces." The way this passage is phrased makes it clear that May considered his rule to be an Interpretive version of the Generative Semanticists' rule, but it also confuses the latter with the former. That is, the Generative Semanticists' rule of Quantifier Lowering would have given rise to

unbound traces only if it were imported into Interpretivist theory as a rule relating Interpretivist deep structure (with quantifiers in "raised" position) and Interpretivist surface structure with traces. But of course Generative Semanticists had no need for traces in their theory. The relevant comparison would rather have been between May's rules mapping surface structure to LF and the inverse of the Generative Semanticists' rules now mapping surface structure to semantic representation (instead of the reverse), where the movement would be upward in both cases. But in that domain the issue of unbound elements is no more relevant to the one than to the other.

47 To take a random example, in their two substantive papers in *Linguistic Inquiry* vol. 7, no. 1, Bresnan (1976a) and Jackendoff (1976) compare their respective Interpretive approaches with corresponding approaches by Generative Semanticists, but no work by Lakoff, McCawley, or Ross after 1972 is cited in either case.

48 From an Interpretivist standpoint, Green's data might have been approached in any of several different ways. Thus, given the oddness of sentences like **It's strange/I regret that very important to the Japanese is the . . .* , it might have been claimed that exceptions to the root hypothesis concerning APP are lexically governed. Or one might have attacked Green's acceptability judgments as dubious and/or her analysis as vague and insufficiently rigorous. Or, if APP is just a "stylistic" rule in the sense of Rochemont 1978, it might have been maintained that Green's data are essentially irrelevant to the more central issues of syntax.

We take it that Green herself would have found none of these potential responses particularly compelling, however. The lexical exception strategy would fail to account for the alternation involving stressed and unstressed *think*, and the facts do suggest that something unlike what is predicted by Emonds's root hypothesis is going on. Although not formalized, Green's suggestions at the very least provide a starting point for an investigation of these facts. And since the distinction between root and other transformations rests crucially on whether rules like APP can apply in subordinate clauses (as well as on the essentially *a priori* assumption that the structures associated with rules like APP are not produced in the base of the grammar), Emonds's important larger claim that major nonroot syntactic rules are structure-preserving is called directly into question.

49 See Horn 1978 for some complications.

McCawley evidently continued to hold with Morgan that an adverb like *almost* could modify either the cause part or the result part of a semantically complex simple lexical causative like *kill*. That is, for the purposes of this argument it is essential to distinguish between directness of causation and semantic complexity: the use of *kill* implies direct causation (or, perhaps, in Hale and Keyser's terms, a single event), but the semantic representation underlying that lexical item still consists of a cause part and a result part.

50 This problem had two facets: (a) given the great power of transformations to delete, copy, and permute, why do surface structures not differ from underlying structures more radically than they do? And (b) if underlying forms represent the meaning of surface forms, why should surface forms *not* be a simple reflection of their putative underlying forms? The Interpretivist answer to the second question was that there were independent restrictions on the relation between deep structure and surface structure; hence, they were naturally more interested in the first question. The Generative Semanticists accepted the idea of constraints on transformations and hence assumed that the answer to the first question would be provided by an empirically satisfactory

theory of such constraints. As to the second question, they appealed (rather vaguely) to the efficiency of the code, as suggested above.

51 Actually, the fact that exceptions to Predicate Raising had to be stipulated in Green's theory hardly constituted an argument against it, since the same facts would have required an equivalent stipulation in Oehrle's theory, as Oehrle admitted. The only substantive question, once the facts had been established, was which approach could account for them most economically.

52 Although in his thesis Oehrle provided semantic characterizations for dative constructions that in some (but not all) cases are more precise and complete than the ones Green had provided, he was less forthcoming about exactly how such representations might be related to syntactic structure. At one point (1976: 91) he suggested that "what one would like is a substantive theory of semantic structure which would deal with various degrees of paraphrase, semantic shifts, certain universal aspects of metaphor, and so on," but he himself did not attempt to offer one.

53 As Oehrle himself noted in the conclusion to his thesis, "in certain respects, the two alternative hypotheses formulated here are equivalent . . . [I]t is evident that each theory will be able to deal with a wide variety of facts in the same fashion, e.g., selectional similarity."

3   RHETORICAL STRATEGIES AND LINGUISTIC ARGUMENTATION: THREE CASE STUDIES

1 This assumption ultimately proved difficult to justify (see, e.g. the critique in Berman 1974 of McCawley's (1970a) paper arguing for an underlying VSO order in English). In later work, McCawley adopted a position in which linear precedence was not necessarily defined for the leaves of trees in underlying structure.

2 As Anderson (1985: 320) points out, the Halle-style argument was familiar to Bloomfieldians well before Halle introduced his version of it; "similar facts had already been noted by researchers within the American structuralist tradition without provoking a rejection of the biuniqueness principle." Anderson attributes the persuasiveness of Halle's demonstration to its "timeliness" and to its being embedded in a "comprehensive" and "elegant" theory of phonology which was closely associated with the most "sophisticated" work then being done on speech acoustics. Anderson also suggests that "a predisposition to take the theory seriously may have contributed to the acceptance of its basic premises" (p. 321). (See also note 3 below.)

3 Wasow (1976: 288) attempted a criticism of McCawley based on this observation, comparing McCawley's argument unfavorably with Halle's, but in fact Halle's argument was equally susceptible. Hamp (1953), as Anderson (1985: 320) points out, had used Halle-type facts to argue for a revision of phonemic theory, not a rejection of it, and Bloomfield (1939) and Bloch (1941) had both considered cases of "complete overlap" and retained a phonemic level as part of preferred solutions. For the Bloomfieldians, there were issues concerning the generality and centrality of such facts that prevented them from constituting crucial evidence against a phonemic level. If authentic candidates for a treatment involving complete overlap were few and far between, then they might indicate an interesting twist at the periphery, but hardly provide reason to jettison a system that was insightful over central cases. Perhaps as importantly, Bloomfieldians were, as Anderson (1985: 321) emphasizes, much more interested in the consequences of proposing various representations

NOTES

(phonemic, morphophonemic, etc.) than in the consequences of proposing
rules relating those representations:

> in American structuralist phonemics . . . in which only the representations
> of forms have "real" status, [a Halle-type] argument is nonsensical or at best
> irrelevant: the principles relating one representation to another (the rules)
> are simply parts of the definitions of individual elements of representations,
> and have no independent status whatsoever in the grammar. If they can be
> formulated in a simple and concise way, so much the better; but the notion
> that the elements of representations themselves should be chosen for the
> convenience of the rules was inconceivable.
>
> (Anderson 1985: 321)

4 G. Lakoff (1971: 273–6) usefully summarized McCawley's argument and
Chomsky's response. As McCawley had, Lakoff pointed out that the position
Chomsky attributed to McCawley was one that the latter had actually rejected.
Drawing on the language of Chomsky 1971, Lakoff concluded that:

> Chomsky's claim . . . that McCawley has not proposed anything new in his
> paper is based on an equivocation in his use of the term "deep structure"
> and collapses when the equivocation is removed . . . . [I]t should be clear
> that McCawley's argument, if correct, would indeed provide a Halle-type
> argument against the *Aspects* notion of "deep structure," as was McCawley's
> intent.
>
> (G. Lakoff 1971: 276)

Although both McCawley in his personal correspondence and Lakoff in his
article had made unmistakably clear that they believed Chomsky had misrepresented McCawley's argument, Chomsky 1972a: 147–8 responded to Lakoff in a
way that simultaneously suggested that Lakoff's interpretation may have been
incorrect and that McCawley's argument was confused:

> Since Lakoff gives no argument at all for this claim (specifically, no
> reference to McCawley's text) and does not indicate in what respect my
> reconstruction, which was based on cited comments from McCawley's text,
> is inaccurate, I cannot comment on his claim – though it may be correct, for
> as I noted there explicitly, it is quite difficult to reconstruct McCawley's
> argument.
>
> (Chomsky 1972a: 147)

These comments, however, are inapplicable to the published version of
Lakoff's paper (Lakoff 1971), which is rife with specific references.

The whole exchange would have been comical if it were not that it bore
serious scientific consequences. In any case, Chomsky then added a slightly
new twist to his counterargument, suggesting that because McCawley had not
given a precise characterization of the rule T, his conclusion did not
necessarily follow (Chomsky 1972a: 147). But of course, this counterargument
reduces to a question of whether there is a form of this rule that can be
demonstrated to be empirically correct. McCawley and Lakoff had argued that
the evidence supported the supposition that there is, while Chomsky was
obviously wagering that there is not, although he had no empirical evidence to
offer in the matter. Thus, the dispute had been taken to a point where logic
was powerless to resolve it.

5 More generally, noun phrases denoting sets of individuals cannot be transformationally derived from conjunctions of noun phrases, each denoting an
individual. Among McCawley's examples supporting this conclusion were phrases

158

like *approximately fifty books, an enormous number of persons,* and so on; moreover, it would seem absurd to assume a deep structure with 63,428 conjuncts to accommodate the phrase *the 63,428 persons in Yankee Stadium.*

6 We assume that a Generative Semantic theory of Set B adverbs would require a global rule to ensure that the right interpretation went with each surface structure. But then it is not clear that there would have been much to choose between such a theory and a theory, say, like Trace Theory in which semantic interpretation rules determined the scope of Set B adverbs from the position of their traces at surface structure and the scope of Set A adverbs from their actual position at that structure. It should be pointed out, however, that traces had not at the time been motivated for anything other than moved nominals.

7 In his lengthy review article on Postal's book, Emmon Bach (1977) considered in detail both Postal's hypothesis and the competing non-Raising hypothesis of Chomsky and concluded (p. 652) that, although the evidence seemed to weigh in favor of a rule of Raising into superordinate object position, no general result could be extracted about the nature of language, in large part because both theories had had to leave so much to the imagination. See also the critique in Bresnan 1976b and Postal's (1977) reply, as well as Postal 1993 and the work cited there. Arguments assuming an analysis in which the "Raised" subject of the embedded verb is the surface direct object of the matrix verb can be found in a variety of contemporary theories. For the most part, however, those working in the Intepretivist tradition have followed Chomsky in the assumption that there is no rule of Raising to Object, although the reasons that have been advanced to support such an assumption have changed as the theory in which it has been embedded has changed. For example, as pointed out to us by Paul Postal (p.c.), by the mid-1970s, Chomsky had begun to argue that grammars contain a limited number (one or two) of entirely general rules rather than large numbers of specific rules. If so, then there could be no question of having to "motivate" a rule of Raising to Object; instead, specific restrictions had to be postulated to prevent Move-alpha from raising complement subjects everywhere they were encountered. Where a complement subject was observed to have certain properties of main clause direct objects (e.g. objective case), Chomsky recommended that additional mechanisms (e.g. Exceptional Case Marking) be postulated to account for these effects.

In more recent work, Chomsky (1992) has suggested a scheme in which a noun phrase that is the subject of a complement clause at surface syntactic structure may be raised out of its clause and into the matrix clause at the level of LF, where it would function as the direct object of the main verb – precisely the inverse of Postal's proposal. Since it is difficult to imagine anyone wishing to make a case that complement subjects are not also *logical* subjects, this suggestion illustrates as vividly as anything can that, however much LF was to be "a representation of meaning," Chomsky has never accepted the criteria of adequacy that would make it such on the understanding of the Generative Semanticists.

4 WHAT HAPPENED TO GENERATIVE SEMANTICS?

1 For example, in G. Lakoff 1972, presuppositions, entailments, and implicatures were not directly represented in the initial phrase marker in underlying structure but were accounted for in a separate context set that was paired with it. Elements of the context set could be accessed transderivationally by the grammar.

NOTES

2 That Halle's remarks accurately characterize the atmosphere at MIT during the first half of the 1970s is suggested by the following remark by Richard Oehrle, which appears in the acknowledgment section of his MIT dissertation (Oehrle 1976):

> Whatever there is of value in this thesis is for the most part a direct product of the research and teaching establishment created by Morris Halle, his colleagues, and their students, a place where the distinction between friend and mentor disappears in the face of common problems.

3 The Lakoffs and McCawley left a legacy at Michigan, however. In the early 1970s, Michigan students were very productive members of the Generative Semantics community. Important contributions to Generative Semantics were also coming out of Illinois, Texas, Ohio State, UCLA, and (particularly after the arrival of the Lakoffs) Berkeley.

4 See McCawley 1973a, 1974b, 1975a, 1975b, 1975c, 1975d, 1976b, 1976c, 1976d, 1976e, 1976f, 1977a, 1977b, 1977c, 1977d.

5 See, e.g. McCawley 1979: viii: "For further discussion of [theoretical issues] to be productive, the disputants need a much broader and deeper understanding of the relevant factual areas than any of them (myself included) had around 1970." McCawley had expressed his concern in print that linguists should be paying attention to a far wider range of facts than many were accustomed to as early as 1972 (see McCawley 1972).

6 Developing and improving abstract theories of grammar was far from a central interest of the nongenerativist faculty under whom many of these students had come to the university to study. Perhaps more importantly, only a portion of the Chicago students during this period were supported by general fellowship, although money was available for research on a number of languages taught there. Because McCawley refused, in virtue of his anarchist/libertarian political views, to apply for government funding for his work, or to participate in reviewing or writing letters of support for government grant proposals, students had no financial incentive to pursue his theoretical interests.

5 CONCLUSION

1 See Hull 1988, which argues that research programs do not have conceptual "essences," but are defined solely by social criteria. (Hence the resemblance of research programs to political parties.)

2 The cultural appeal of Chomsky's program should also not be discounted. Chomsky had repeatedly argued that Bloomfieldians were involved only in a kind of dull, classificatory exercise and that his program was by far the more scientifically interesting. Needless to say, this contest over the definition of Bloomfieldianism perplexed and disturbed the Bloomfieldians, who saw many similarities between Chomsky's goals and methods and their own and in general considered him a member of their research community. Nevertheless, Chomsky's view of Bloomfieldianism as something worthy of disparagement clearly prevailed among the younger linguists who were entering the field in large numbers in the 1950s and 1960s.

3 See Kuhn 1970: 157–8:

> But paradigm debates are not really about relative problem-solving ability, though for good reasons they are usually couched in those terms. Instead the issue is which paradigm should in the future guide research on problems

160

many of which neither competitor can yet claim to resolve completely. A decision between alternate ways of practicing science is called for, and in the circumstances that decision must be based less on past achievement than on future promise. The man who embraces a new paradigm at an early stage must often do so in defiance of the evidence provided by problem-solving. He must, that is, have faith that the new paradigm will succeed with the many large problems that confront it, knowing only that the older paradigm has failed with a few. A decision of that kind can only be made on faith.

APPENDIX: CONVERSATIONS WITH RAY JACKENDOFF, GEORGE LAKOFF, JOHN ROBERT ROSS, AND PAUL M. POSTAL

Ray Jackendoff

1 Note that this interview took place in 1987, before the work of Baker, Pollock, and Larson changed the picture again.

Paul M. Postal

2 Note that my verbal answer did not address the first question, as to whether I was originally attracted by Chomsky's combative characteristic of taking radically different positions. I do not know if I originally found that attractive . . . quite possibly so. I have often been accused of having similar characteristics myself. Currently, I would tend to see it as a kind of compulsive self-aggrandizement, which leads *inter alia* to vast attention being paid to what are often largely trivia, as with the "modularity" issue mentioned above. After all, the goal of research is to develop insightful true positions, not positions which clash with those of others.

3 The reference is to lectures David Perlmutter and I gave at the Summer Institute of the Linguistic Society of America, held at the University of Massachusetts, Amherst, Massachusetts in 1974. These became the basis for the development of what we called Relational Grammar.

4 Katz and Fodor 1963. The semantic ideas first laid out here have been refined and expanded over nearly thirty years with particular attention to their philosophical foundations. See *inter alia* Katz 1972, 1977b, 1986, 1990, and many other references therein.

5 At issue is the conference on the goals of linguistics held in the fall of 1969 at the University of Texas at Austin; see Peters 1972.

6 To better understand this incident dating back nearly a quarter of century, one must stress the clash between the lack of civility manifested and the relations between the participants. While Chomsky's behavior would have been reprehensible no matter who was speaking, Ross was not a random person from the audience but (1) a colleague of Chomsky's; (2) however, a very junior colleague; (3) someone who had done his Ph.D. work under Chomsky; (4) a colleague who had done extensive work in Chomsky's framework; (5) someone who had always treated Chomsky and his work (both verbally and in print) in laudatory terms; and (6) a person for whom rudeness or bullying others was unthinkable. That Chomsky was willing to publicly exploit his academic/professional dominance and temporary control of the forum to treat someone standing in such a close relation to him with contempt before a large and important

linguistic meeting had to communicate several important lessons to anyone who was aware of what was going on. One clear implication was that disagreeing with Chomsky, even then the most renowned and influential person in the field, would have a high price. A second was that the controversies which had arisen were not being treated by Chomsky as (only) technical matters to be resolved in normal scientific ways but as somehow sufficiently threatening to induce strongly emotional responses and even clear violations of normal standards. Although I no longer remember anything of the substance of either Ross's comment or Chomsky's reply, the moment when Chomsky interrupted Ross and continued his interruption as the latter walked away from the podium marks for me a key point. It became crystal clear that the disputes over linguistic ideas linked to Generative Semantics had degenerated into bickering at the level of political campaign propaganda and that the two sides were divided not only by technical differences but by differences of values. Imagine the difference in atmosphere if, instead of continuing, Chomsky had said: "I am sorry Haj, I didn't mean to interrupt you; please come back and continue." In later years, Chomsky would blame others for the acrimony of the disputes which took place. But I place a considerable amount of the responsibility on his own attitudes, about which this incident is quite revealing. Assigning blame in this way is independently plausible, I should add. For those with the most power/influence are, obviously, most likely to see their attitudes prevail. And no one doubts that Chomsky was far and away the most influential figure in this dispute.

7   In retrospect this episode reveals several less than healthy attitudes. On one side, there is the assumption that student mentalities are too frail to be told what the instructor really believes. On the other is the implication that the instructor should say something different than what he believes, as a service to some larger cause.

8   I confess to seeing no link between question and answer here.

9   The issue of Chomsky's retreat from his original view of formalization is raised in a partially humorous context in Pullum 1989, reprinted in Pullum 1991 with a few additional comments. Chomsky (1990: 145–7) denies that there has been any change in his position with respect to the role of formalization in linguistics. But materials independent of those cited by Pullum indicate that this is false. Thus contrast Chomsky's position in Chomsky 1979: 133–4 and Chomsky 1977a: 124–5, which is that formalization is a *necessary* condition of true explanation, with positions like that of Chomsky 1990, which take it merely to be a sometimes useful tool whose desirability has to be determined on a case by case basis.

10   See Katz 1981 and also Katz 1984, 1990, Katz and Postal 1991.

11   Denials of the reality of languages (as contrasted with psychologically real grammars) occur in, for example, Chomsky 1986b: ch. 2, 1987: 32–7, 1991: 9–10.

12   The reader inclined to entertain even briefly that, for example, *All white bunnies are white* and *Two and two are four* have the same meaning might consider that such a position entails that the two sentences provide equivalent answers when they fill in the blank in B, a reply to a parent's question, A, about the content of a young child's math class:

A: What did you learn in class today?
B: We learned that _____.

13   In this connection, one should consider the end-of-the-world falsifications mentioned below.

14   Chomsky's tendency to picture himself as part of an isolated minority at a point

where he is actually the dominant figure in a broad-based and extremely influential movement is treated somewhat humorously is Pullum 1984, reprinted in Pullum 1991.

15 Postal 1971 documented that prepositional phrase extraction induced strong crossover effects; see, for example, p. 157 of that book. The same page even affirmed the generalization:

> The fact is that in every case crossing restrictions are unaffected by whether or not a preposition travels with its following N[oun] P[hrase] under the operation of either WH-Q movement or by WH-REL movement . . . .

This problem for Chomsky's Principle C account is noted in Koster 1987: 82; Koster, a linguist far more sympathetic to Chomsky's views than I am, takes it to be "crucial."

16 The asymmetry issue is equally documented in Postal 1971: 143. Kuno (1987: 81–2) concludes that the asymmetry facts undermine the Principle C account.

REFERENCES

Anderson, Stephen R. 1971. *On the Linguistic Status of the Performative/Constative Distinction.* Bloomington, IN: Indiana University Linguistics Club.
—— 1985. *Phonology in the Twentieth Century: Theories of Rules and Theories of Representations.* Chicago: University of Chicago Press.
Aronoff, Mark. 1974. "Word-structure." MIT dissertation.
—— 1976. *Word Formation in Generative Grammar.* Cambridge: MIT Press.
Bach, Emmon. 1968. "Nouns and noun phrases." In Bach and Harms 1968, 91–122.
—— 1974. "Explanatory inadequacy." In David Cohen (ed.), *Explaining Linguistic Phenomena.* Washington, DC: Hemisphere Publishing. 153–71.
—— 1977. "Review of *On Raising,* by Paul M. Postal." *Language* 53. 621–54.
Bach, Emmon and Robert T. Harms (eds) 1968. *Universals in Linguistic Theory.* New York: Holt, Rinehart & Winston.
Bach, Kent. 1982. "Semantic nonspecificity and mixed quantifiers." *Linguistics and Philosophy* 4. 593–605.
Baker, C. L. 1979. "Syntactic theory and the projection problem." *Linguistic Inquiry* 10. 533–81.
Baker, C. L. and Michael Brame. 1972. "Global rules: a rejoinder." *Language* 48. 51–77.
Baker, Mark. 1988. *Incorporation.* Chicago: University of Chicago Press.
Benwick, Sir Lancelot of, Morgan le Fay, and The Green Knight. 1976 [1968]. "Camelot, 1968." In McCawley 1976a, 249–74.
Berman, Arlene. 1974. "On the VSO hypothesis." *Linguistic Inquiry* 5. 1–38.
Bever, Thomas. 1974. "The ascent of the specious or, there's a lot we don't know about mirrors." In David Cohen (ed.), *Explaining Linguistic Phenomena.* Washington, DC: Hemisphere Publishing. 173–200.
Binnick, Robert I. 1969. "Non-high neutral vowels in Modern Mongolian." *Papers from the Fifth Regional Meeting of the Chicago Linguistic Society.* Chicago: Chicago Linguistic Society. 295–301.
—— 1970. "Studies in the derivation of predicative structures." University of Chicago dissertation.
Bloch, Bernard. 1941. "Phonemic overlapping." *American Speech* 16. 278–84. Repr. Joos 1957, 93–6.
—— 1948. "A set of postulates for phonemic analysis." *Language* 24. 3–46.
Block, Ned (ed.) 1981. *Readings in the Philosophy of Psychology,* vol. 2. (Language and thought series.) Cambridge, MA: Harvard University Press.
Bloomfield, Leonard. 1926. "A set of postulates for the science of language." *Language* 2. 153–64. Repr. Hockett 1987, 70–80. Also repr. Joos 1957, 26–31.

—— 1931. "Review of *Was ist ein Satz?*, by John Ries." *Language* 7. 204–9. Repr. Hockett 1987, 153–61.

—— 1933. *Language.* Chicago: University of Chicago Press.

—— 1939. "Menomini morphophonemics." *Travaux du Cercle Linguistique de Prague* 8. 105–15. Repr. Hockett 1987, 243–54.

—— 1943. "Meaning." *Monatschrifte für Deutschen Unterricht* 35. 101–6. Repr. Hockett 1987, 271–6.

Booth, Wayne. 1974. *Modern Dogma and the Rhetoric of Assent.* Chicago: University of Chicago Press.

Bowers, John. 1976. "On surface structure grammatical relations and the structure-preserving hypothesis." *Linguistic Analysis* 2. 225–42.

Bresnan, Joan. 1972. "Theory of complementation in English syntax." MIT dissertation.

—— 1975. "Comparative deletion and constraints on transformations." *Linguistic Analysis* 1. 25–74.

—— 1976a. "On the form and functioning of transformations." *Linguistic Inquiry* 7. 3–40.

—— 1976b. "Nonarguments for raising." *Linguistic Inquiry* 7. 485–501.

Carden, Guy. 1967. "English quantifiers." Harvard master's thesis.

—— 1968. "English quantifiers." In Susumo Kuno (ed.), *Mathematical Linguistics and Automatic Translation.* Report NSF-20. Harvard Computation Laboratory.

Chomsky, Noam. 1951. "Morphophonemics of Modern Hebrew." University of Pennsylvania master's thesis.

—— 1955. "Semantic considerations in grammar." *Monograph no. 8.* Washington, DC: Institute of Languages and Linguistics, Georgetown University. 141–53.

—— 1957a. *Syntactic Structures.* (Series minor, 4.) The Hague: Mouton.

—— 1957b. Review of *A Manual of Phonology*, by Charles F. Hockett. *International Journal of American Linguistics* 23. 223–34.

—— 1957c. Review of *Fundamentals of Language*, by Roman Jakobson and Morris Halle. *International Journal of American Linguistics* 23. 234–42.

—— 1958. "Linguistics, logic, psychology, and computers." In John W. Carr, III (ed.), *Computer Programming and Artificial Intelligence: An Intensive Course.* Ann Arbor, MI: University of Michigan College of Engineering. 429–54.

—— 1959. "Review of B. F. Skinner, *Verbal Behavior.*" *Language* 35. 26–58. Repr. *The Structure of Language: Readings in the Philosophy of Language.* Englewood Cliffs, NJ: Prentice-Hall, 1964. 546–78.

—— 1963. "Formal properties of grammars." In Luce, Bush, and Galanter 1963, 323–418.

—— 1964. *Current Issues in Linguistic Theory.* (Series minor, 38.) The Hague: Mouton.

—— 1965. *Aspects of the Theory of Syntax.* Cambridge, MA: MIT Press.

—— 1969. "Linguistics and philosophy." In Hook 1969, 51–94.

—— 1970 [1967]. "Remarks on nominalizations." In Jacobs and Rosenbaum 1970, 184–221. Repr. Chomsky 1972b, 11–61.

—— 1971 [1968]. "Deep structure, surface structure, and semantic interpretation." In Danny Steinberg and Leon A. Jakobovits (eds), *Semantics: An Interdisciplinary Reader in Philosophy, Linguistics, and Psychology.* Cambridge: Cambridge University Press. 183–216. Repr. Chomsky 1972b, 62–119.

—— 1972a [1969]. "Some empirical issues in the theory of transformational grammar." In Peters 1972, 63–130. Repr. Chomsky 1972b, 120–202.

—— 1972b. *Studies on Semantics in Generative Grammar.* The Hague: Mouton.

—— 1973 [1971]. "Conditions on transformations." In Stephen R. Anderson and

Paul Kiparsky (eds), *A Festschrift for Morris Halle.* New York: Holt, Rinehard & Winston. 232–86. Repr. Chomsky 1977b, 81–162.

—— 1975a. "Questions of form and interpretation." *Linguistic Analysis* 1. 75–109. Repr. Chomsky 1977b, 25–62.

—— 1975b. *Reflections on Language.* New York: Pantheon.

—— 1975c [1955–6]. *The Logical Structure of Linguistic Theory.* Chicago: University of Chicago Press.

—— 1976. "Conditions on rules of grammar." *Linguistic Analysis* 2. 303–51.

—— 1977a. "On wh-movement." In Peter W. Culicover, Thomas Wasow, and Adrian Akmajian (eds), *Formal Syntax.* New York: Academic Press. 71–132.

—— 1977b. *Essays on Form and Interpretation.* New York: North Holland.

—— 1979 [1976]. *Language and Responsibility: Based on Conversations with Mitsou Ronat.* New York: Pantheon.

—— 1980. "Rules and representations." *Behavioral and Brain Sciences* 3. 1–61.

—— 1981. *Lectures on Government and Binding.* (Studies in generative grammar, 9.) Dordrecht: Foris.

—— 1982. *On the Generative Enterprise: A Discussion with Riny Huybregts and Henk van Riemsdijk.* Dordrecht: Foris.

—— 1986a. *Barriers.* Cambridge, MA: MIT Press.

—— 1986b. *Knowledge of Language: Its Nature, Origin, and Use.* (Convergence.) New York: Praeger.

—— 1987. *Language in a Psychological Setting.* Tokyo: Sophia University.

—— 1988. *Language and Problems of Knowledge.* Cambridge: MIT Press.

—— 1990. "On formalizations and formal linguistics." *Natural Language and Linguistic Theory* 8. 143–7.

—— 1991. "Linguistics and adjacent fields: a personal view." In Asa Kasher (ed.), *The Chomskyan Turn.* Oxford: Blackwell.

—— 1992. *A Minimalist Program for Linguistic Theory.* MIT Working Papers in Linguistics.

Chomsky, Noam and Morris Halle. 1968. *The Sound Pattern of English.* New York: Harper & Row.

Chomsky, Noam and Howard Lasnik. 1977. "Filters and control." *Linguistic Inquiry* 8. 425–504.

Chomsky, Noam and George A. Miller. 1963. "Introduction to the formal analysis of natural language." In Luce, Bush, and Galanter 1963. 323–418.

Churchland, Patricia Smith. 1986. *Neurophilosophy: Toward a Unified Science of the Mind-Brain.* Cambridge: MIT Press.

Cole, Peter (ed.). 1978. *Pragmatics. Syntax and Semantics,* vol. 9. New York: Academic Press.

Cooper, Robin. 1982. "Binding in wholewheat* syntax (*unenriched with inaudibilia)." In Pauline Jacobson and Geoffrey K. Pullum (eds), *The Nature of Syntactic Representation.* Dordrecht: D. Reidel. 59–77.

Davidson, Donald, and Gilbert Harman. 1972. *The Semantics of Natural Language.* (Synthese library, 40). Dordrecht: D. Reidel.

Davison, Alice. 1972. "Performative verbs, felicity conditions, and adverbs." University of Chicago dissertation.

—— 1983. "Linguistic or pragmatic description in the context of the performadox." *Linguistics and Philosophy* 6. 499–526.

De Mey, Marc. 1982. *The Cognitive Paradigm.* Dordrecht: D. Reidel.

Duhem, Pierre. 1954 [1905]. *The Aim and Structure of Physical Theory.* Princeton: Princeton University Press.

Emonds, Joseph. 1970. "Root and structure preserving transformations." MIT dissertation.

167

REFERENCES

—— 1976. *A Transformational Approach to English Syntax.* New York: Academic Press.

Fauconnier, Gilles. 1985. *Mental Spaces.* Cambridge, MA: MIT Press.

Festinger, Leon, Henry W. Riecken, and Stanley Schachter. 1956. *When Prophecy Fails.* New York: Harper & Row.

Feyerabend, Paul. 1975. *Against Method.* London: Verso.

Fillmore, Charles. 1963. "The position of embedding transformations in a grammar." *Word* 19. 208–31.

Fillmore, Charles, Paul Kay, and Catherine O'Connor. 1988. "Regularity and idiomaticity in grammatical constructions: the case of *let alone.*" *Language* 64. 501–38.

Fodor, Janet. 1977. *Semantics: Theories of Meaning in Generative Grammar.* Cambridge, MA: Harvard University Press.

Fodor, Janet, Jerry A. Fodor, and Merrill F. Garrett. 1975. "The psychological unreality of semantic representations." *Linguistic Inquiry* 6. 515–31.

Fodor, Jerry A. 1970. "Three reasons for not deriving 'kill' from 'cause to die'." *Linguistic Inquiry* 429–38.

—— 1979. *The Language of Thought.* Cambridge: Harvard University Press.

—— 1980. "Fixation of belief and concept acquisition." In Massimo Piattelli-Palmarini (ed.), *Language and Learning: The Debate between Jean Piaget and Noam Chomsky.* Cambridge: Harvard University Press. 143–9.

Frazier, Lynn. 1977. "On comprehending sentences: syntactic parsing strategies." University of Connecticut dissertation. Distributed by Indiana University Linguistics Club.

Fries, C. C. 1961. "The Bloomfield 'school'." In C. A. Mohrmann, A. Sommerfelt, and J. Whatmough (eds), *Trends in European and American Linguistics 1930–1960.* Utrecht: Spectrum. 196–224.

Fujimura, Osamu (ed.) 1973. *Three Dimensions of Linguistic Theory.* Tokyo: TEC Corporation.

Gazdar, Gerald. 1979. *Pragmatics: Implicature, Presupposition, and Logical Form.* New York: Academic Press.

—— 1981. "On syntactic categories." *Philosophical Transactions of the Royal Society* (Series B) 295. 267–83.

Gil, David. 1982. "Quantifier scope, linguistic variation, and natural language semantics." *Linguistics and Philosophy* 5. 421–72.

Goldberg, Adele E. 1992. "Argument structure constructions." University of California dissertation.

Goldsmith, John A. 1978. "Complementizers and the status of root sentences." In Mark J. Stein (ed.), *Proceedings of the Eighth Annual Meeting of the Northeastern Linguistic Society.* Amherst, MA: Department of Linguistics, University of Massachusetts. 89–96.

—— 1980. "Meaning and mechanism in grammar." *Harvard Studies in Syntax and Semantics* 2. Cambridge, MA: Harvard University Linguistics Department.

—— 1981. "Complementizers and root sentences." *Linguistic Inquiry* 12. 541–74.

—— 1992. "A note on the genealogy of research traditions in phonology." *Journal of Linguistics* 28. 149–63.

—— 1994. "Grammar within a neural net." In Pamela Dowling, Sue Lima, and Gregory Iverson (eds), *The Reality of Linguistic Rules.* Philadelphia: John Benjamins. 95–113.

Goldsmith, John and Gary Larson. 1992. "Using networks in a harmonic phonology." *Papers from the Twenty-eighth Regional Meeting of the Chicago Linguistic Society,* vol. 2. Chicago: Chicago Linguistic Society. 94–125.

Goodman, Nelson. 1943. "On the simplicity of ideas." *Journal of Symbolic Logic* 8. 107–21.

Gordon, David, and George Lakoff. 1971. "Conversational postulates." *Papers from the Seventh Regional Meeting of the Chicago Linguistic Society.* Chicago: Chicago Linguistic Society. 63–84.

Green, Georgia. 1969. "On the notion 'related lexical entry'." *Papers from the Fifth Regional Meeting of the Chicago Linguistic Society.* Chicago: Chicago Linguistic Society. 76–88.

—— 1970a. "How abstract is surface structure?" *Papers from the Sixth Regional Meeting of the Chicago Linguistic Society.* Chicago: Chicago Linguistic Society. 270–81.

—— 1970b. "Review of Robin Lakoff, *Abstract Syntax and Latin Complementation.*" *Language* 46. 149–67.

—— 1974a. "The function of form and the form of function." *Papers from the Tenth Regional Meeting of the Chicago Linguistic Society.* Chicago: Chicago Linguistic Society. 186–97.

—— 1974b. *Semantics and Syntactic Regularity.* Bloomington, IN: Indiana University Press.

—— 1976. "Main clause phenomena in subordinate clauses." *Language* 52. 382–97.

Grice, H.P. 1975. "Logic and conversation." In Peter Cole and Jerry L. Morgan (eds), *Speech Acts. Syntax and Semantics,* vol. 3. New York: Academic Press. 45–58.

—— 1978. "Further notes on logic and conversation." In Cole 1978, 113–27.

Hale, Ken, and Jay Keyser. 1987. *A View from the Middle.* Lexicon Project Working Papers #10. Cambridge, MA: Lexicon Project, Center for Cognitive Science, MIT.

Halle, Morris. 1959. *The Sound Pattern of Russian.* The Hague: Mouton.

—— 1987. "Preface." In M. A. Browning, Ewa Czaykowska-Higgins, and Elizabeth Ritter (eds), *MIT Working Papers in Linguistics,* vol. 9. Cambridge: Department of Linguistics, MIT. v–vii.

Halle, Morris, and James Higginbotham. 1986. "Wasow on scientific linguistics." *Natural Language and Linguistic Theory* 4. 291–4.

Hamp, Eric. 1953. "The morphophonemes of the Keltic mutations." *Language* 27. 230–47.

Harris, Randy Allen. 1993. *The Linguistics Wars.* Oxford: Oxford University Press.

Harris, Zellig S. 1940. Review of Louis H. Gray, *Foundations of Language. Language* 16. 216–23.

—— 1951. *Methods in Structural Linguistics.* Chicago: University of Chicago Press.

—— 1954. "Distributional structure." *Word* 10. 146–62.

Heim, Irene, Howard Lasnik, and Robert May. 1991. "Reciprocity and plurality." *Linguistic Inquiry.* 22: 63–101.

Heringer, James. 1969. "Indefinite noun phrases and referential opacity." *Papers from the Fifth Regional Meeting of the Chicago Linguistic Society.* Chicago: Chicago Linguistic Society. 89–97.

—— 1976. "Idioms and lexicalization in English." In Shibatani 1976, 205–16.

Higginbotham, James. 1985. "On semantics." *Linguistic Inquiry* 16. 547–93.

Hockett, Charles F. 1948. "A note on 'structure'." *International Journal of American Linguistics* 14. 269–71. Repr. Joos 1957, 279–80.

—— (ed.) 1987. *A Leonard Bloomfield Anthology: Abridged Edition.* Chicago: University of Chicago Press.

Hook, Sidney (ed.) 1969. *Language and Philosophy: A Symposium.* New York: New York University Press.

Hooper, Joan, and Sandra Thompson. 1973. "On the applicability of root transformations." *Linguistic Inquiry* 4. 465–97.

Horn, Lawrence, R. 1970. "Ain't it hard (anymore)." *Papers from the Sixth Regional Meeting of the Chicago Linguistic Society.* Chicago: Chicago Linguistic Society. 318–27.

—— 1978. "Lexical incorporation, implicature, and the Least Effort Hypothesis."

Papers from the Parasession on the Lexicon. Chicago: Chicago Linguistic Society. 196–209.

Hornstein, Norbert. 1984. *Logic as Grammar*. Cambridge: MIT Press.

Hull, David L. 1988. *Science as a Process*. Chicago: University of Chicago Press.

Hymes, Dell, and John Fought. 1981. *American Structuralism*. (Series minor, 102.) The Hague: Mouton.

Ioup, Georgette. 1975. "Some universals of quantifier scope." In John Kimball (ed.), *Syntax and Semantics*. New York: Academic Press. 37–58.

Iwakura, Kumihiro. 1978. "On root transformations and the structure preserving hypothesis." *Linguistic Analysis* 4. 321–64.

Jackendoff, Ray S. 1966. "The erased NP in relatives and complements." Unpublished paper, MIT.

—— 1968a. "Quantifiers in English." *Foundations of Language* 4. 422–42.

—— 1968b. *An Interpretive Theory of Pronouns and Reflexives*. Bloomington, IN: Indiana University Linguistics Club.

—— 1971. "On some questionable arguments about quantifiers and negation." *Language* 47. 282–97.

—— 1972. *Semantic Interpretation in Generative Grammar*. (Current studies in linguistics.) Cambridge, MA: MIT Press.

—— 1975. "On belief-contexts." *Linguistic Inquiry* 6. 53–93.

—— 1976. "Toward an explanatory semantic representation." *Linguistic Inquiry* 7. 89–150.

—— 1977. *X-bar syntax*. Cambridge: MIT Press.

—— 1983. *Semantics and Cognition*. (Current studies in linguistics.) Cambridge, MA: MIT Press.

—— 1988. "Topic . . . Comment: Why are they saying these things about us?" *Natural Language and Linguistic Theory* 6. 435–42.

—— 1994. *Patterns in the Mind*. New York: Basic Books.

Jacobs, Roderick A. and Peter S. Rosenbaum (eds) 1970. *Readings in English Transformational Grammar*. Waltham, MA: Ginn.

Joos, Martin. 1950. "Description of language design." *Journal of the Acoustical Society of America* 22. 701–8. Repr. Joos 1957, 349–56.

—— (ed.) 1957. *Readings in Linguistics*, vol. I. Chicago: University of Chicago Press.

Karttunen, Lauri. 1974. "Presupposition and linguistic context." *Theoretical Linguistics* 1. 3–44.

Katz, Jerrold J. 1970. "Interpretive Semantics versus Generative Semantics." *Foundations of Language* 6. 220–59.

—— 1972. *Semantic Theory*. New York: Harper & Row.

—— 1977a. "The real status of semantic representation." *Linguistic Inquiry* 8. 559–84.

—— 1977b. *Propositional Structure and Illocutionary Force*. New York: T. Y. Crowell.

—— 1981. *Language and Other Abstract Objects*. Totowa, NJ: Rowman & Littlefield.

—— 1984. "An outline of platonist grammar." In Thomas G. Bever, John M. Carroll, and Lance A. Miller (eds), *Talking Minds: The Study of Language in Cognitive Science*. Cambridge: MIT Press. Repr. Katz 1985.

—— (ed.) 1985. *The Philosophy of Linguistics*. Oxford: Oxford University Press.

—— 1986. *Cogitations*. Oxford: Oxford University Press.

—— 1990. *The Metaphysics of Meaning*. Cambridge: MIT Press.

Katz, Jerrold J. and Thomas Bever. 1976 [1974]. "The fall and rise of empiricism." In Thomas Bever, Jerrold J. Katz, and D. Terence Langendoen (eds), *An Integrated Theory of Linguistic Ability*. New York: Crowell. 11–64.

Katz, Jerrold J. and Jerry A. Fodor. 1962. "What's wrong with the philosophy of language." *Inquiry* 5. 197–237. Repr. Jerry A. Fodor and Jerrold J. Katz (eds), *The Structure of Language: Readings in the Philosophy of Language*. Englewood Cliffs, NJ: Prentice-Hall, 1964. 1–18.

—— 1963. "The structure of a semantic theory." *Language* 39. 170–210. Repr. Jerry A. Fodor and Jerrold J. Katz (eds), *Structure of Language: Readings in the Philosophy of Language*. Englewood Cliffs, NJ: Prentice-Hall, 1964. 479–518.

Katz, Jerrold J. and Fred M. Katz. 1977. "Is necessity the mother of intention?" *Philosophical Review* 86. 70–96.

Katz, Jerrold, J. and Paul M. Postal. 1964. *An Integrated Theory of Linguistic Descriptions*, Cambridge, MA: MIT Press.

—— 1991. "Realism vs. conceptualism in linguistics." *Linguistics and Philosophy* 14. 515–54.

Kean, Mary-Louise. 1975. "The theory of markedness in generative grammar." MIT dissertation.

Kempson, Ruth M. 1975. *Presupposition and the Delimitation of Semantics*. Cambridge: Cambridge University Press.

Kempson, Ruth M. and Annabel Cormack. 1981. "Ambiguity and quantification." *Linguistics and Philosophy* 4. 259–309.

—— 1982. "Quantification and pragmatics." *Linguistics and Philosophy* 4. 607–18.

Kiparsky, Paul. 1982. "Lexical morphology and phonology." In The Linguistic Society of Korea (ed.), *Linguistics in the Morning Calm: Selected Papers from SICOL-1981*. Seoul: Hanshin Publishing Company. 3–91.

Koster, Jan. 1978. "Conditions, empty nodes, and markedness." *Linguistic Inquiry* 9. 551–93.

—— 1987. *Domains and Dynasties*. Dordrecht: Foris.

Kuhn, Thomas. 1970. *The Structure of Scientific Revolutions*. 2nd edn. Chicago: University of Chicago Press.

Kuno, Susumu. 1971. "The position of locatives in existential sentences." *Linguistic Inquiry* 2. 333–78.

—— 1987. *Functional Syntax*. Chicago: University of Chicago Press.

Kuroda, Sige-Yuki. 1965. "Generative grammatical studies in the Japanese language." MIT dissertation.

Lakatos, Imre. 1970. "Falsification and the methodology of scientific research programs." In Imre Lakatos and Alan Musgrave (eds), *Criticism and the Growth of Knowledge*. Cambridge: Cambridge University Press. 91–196.

Lakoff, George. 1968a. *Deep and Surface Grammar*. Bloomington, IN: Indiana University Linguistics Club.

—— 1968b. "Counterparts, or the problem of reference in transformational grammar." Unpublished paper, Harvard University.

—— 1969. "On derivational constraints." *Papers from the Fifth Regional Meeting of the Chicago Linguistic Society*. Chicago: Chicago Linguistic Society. 117–39.

—— 1970a [1965]. *Irregularity in Syntax*. (The Transatlantic Series in Linguistics.) New York: Holt, Rinehart.

—— 1971. "On Generative Semantics." In Danny Steinberg and Leon Jakobovits (eds), *Semantics*. Cambridge: Cambridge University Press. 232–96.

—— 1972. "Linguistics and natural logic." In Davidson and Harman 1972, 545–665.

—— 1974. "Syntactic amalgams." *Papers from the Tenth Regional Meeting of the Chicago Linguistic Society*. Chicago: Chicago Linguistic Society. 321–44.

—— 1976 [1963]. "Toward Generative Semantics." In McCawley 1976b, 43–61.

—— 1987. *Women, Fire, and Dangerous Things*. Chicago: University of Chicago Press.

Lakoff, George and Mark Johnson. 1980. *Metaphors We Live By*. Chicago: University of Chicago Press.

REFERENCES

Lakoff, George and John Robert Ross. 1976 [1967]. "Is deep structure necessary?" In McCawley 1976, 159–64.

Lakoff, Robin. 1968. *Abstract Syntax and Latin Complementation.* Cambridge: MIT Press.

——— 1971. "Passive Resistance." *Papers from the Seventh Regional Meeting of the Chicago Linguistic Society.* Chicago: Chicago Linguistic Society. 149–62.

Langacker, Ronald. 1969. "On pronominalization and the chain of command." In Reibel and Schane 1969, 160–86.

Langendoen, D. Terence. 1973. "The problem of grammatical relations in surface structure." In Jankowsky (ed.), *Georgetown University Roundtable on Language and Linguistics.* Washington, DC: Georgetown University.

——— 1976. "Review of David Cohen (ed.), *Explaining Linguistic Phenomena.*" *Language* 52. 690–5.

——— 1979. "More on locative inversion sentences and the structure preserving hypothesis." *Linguistic Analysis* 5. 421–37.

Langendoen, D. Terence and Paul M. Postal. 1985. "Sets and sentences." In Katz 1985.

Laudan, Larry. 1977. *Progress and its Problems: Toward a Theory of Scientific Growth.* Berkeley, CA: University of California Press.

Lees, Robert B. 1957. "Review of Noam Chomsky, *Syntactic Structures.*" *Language* 33. 375–408.

——— 1960. *The Grammar of English Nominalizations.* The Hague: Mouton.

LeGrand, Jean E. 1975. *"Or* and *any:* the semantics and syntax of two logical operators." University of Chicago dissertation.

Levi, Judith. 1975. "The syntax and semantics of nonpredicating adjectives in English." University of Chicago dissertation. Published 1976, as *The Syntax and Semantics of Complex Nominals.* New York: Academic Press, 1976.

Li, Yafei. 1990. "X^0-binding and verb incorporation." *Linguistic Inquiry* 21. 399–426.

Lieber, Rochelle. 1992. *Deconstructing Morphology.* Chicago: University of Chicago Press.

Luce, R.D., R. Bush, and E. Galanter (eds) 1963. *Handbook of Mathematical Psychology,* vol. 2. New York: John Wiley.

McCawley, James D. 1968a. "Review of Thomas Sebeok (ed.), *Current Trends in Linguistics*", vol. 3. *Language* 44. 556–93. Repr. McCawley 1973c, 167–205.

——— 1968b [1967]. "The role of semantics in a grammar." In Emmon Bach and Robert T. Harms (eds), *Universals of Linguistic Theory.* New York: Holt, Rinehart. 124–69. Repr. McCawley 1973c, 59–98.

——— 1968c. "Lexical insertion in a transformational grammar without deep structures." *Papers from the Fourth Regional Meeting of the Chicago Linguistic Society.* Chicago: Chicago Linguistic Society. 71–80. Repr. McCawley 1973c, 155–66.

——— 1968d [1966]. "Concerning the base component of a transformational grammar." *Foundations of Language* 4. 243–69. Repr. McCawley 1973c, 35–58.

——— 1970a. "Where do noun phrases come from?" In Jacobs and Rosenbaum 1970, 166–83. Repr. McCawley 1973c, 133–54.

——— 1970b. "Semantic representation." In Paul M. Garvin (ed.), *Cognition: A Multiple View.* New York: Spartan Books. 227–47. Repr. McCawley 1973c, 240–56.

——— 1970c. "English as a VSO language." *Language* 46. 286–99. Repr. McCawley 1973c, 211–28.

——— 1972. "A program for logic." In Davidson and Harman 1972, 498–544. Repr. McCawley 1973c, 285–319.

——— 1973a. "Syntactic and logical arguments for semantic structures." In Fujimura 1973, 259–376.

——— 1973b [1968]. "The annotated respective." In McCawley 1973c, 121–32.

—— 1973c. *Grammar and Meaning: Papers on Syntactic and Semantic Topics.* Tokyo: Taishukan/New York: Academic Press.

—— 1974a. "Review of Noam Chomsky and Morris Halle, *The Sound Pattern of English.*" *International Journal of American Linguistics* 40. 58–88.

—— 1974b. "On identifying the remains of deceased clauses." *Language Research* 9. 73–85. Repr. McCawley 1979, 84–95.

—— 1975a. "Review of Noam Chomsky, *Studies on Semantics in Generative Grammar.*" *Studies in English Linguistics* 3. 209–311. Repr. McCawley 1982, 10–127.

—— 1975b. "Verbs of bitching." In D. Hockney, W. Harper, and B. Freed (eds), *Contemporary Research in Philosophical Logic and Linguistic Semantics.* Dordrecht: D. Reidel. 313–32. Repr. McCawley 1979, 135–50.

—— 1975c. "The category status of English modals." *Foundations of Language* 12. 597–601. Repr. McCawley 1979, 96–100.

—— 1975d. "Lexicography and the count–mass distinction." *Papers from the First Annual Meeting of the Berkeley Linguistics Society.* Berkeley, CA: Department of Linguistics, University of California, Berkeley. 314–21. Repr. McCawley 1979, 165–73.

—— (ed.) 1976a. *Notes from the Linguistic Underground. Syntax and Semantics,* vol. 7. New York: Academic Press.

—— 1976b. "Madison Avenue, si, Pennsylvania Avenue, no!" In Peter Reich (ed.), *The Second LACUS Forum.* Columbia, SC: Hornbeam Press. 17–28. Repr. McCawley 1979, 223–33.

—— 1976c. "Some ideas not to live by." *Die neuen Sprachen* 75. 151–65. Repr. McCawley 1979, 234–46.

—— 1976d. "Morphological indeterminacy in underlying syntactic structures." In Frances Ingeman (ed.), *1975 Mid-America Linguistics Conference.* Lawrence: Linguistics Department, University of Kansas. 317–26. Repr. McCawley 1979, 113–21.

—— 1976e. "Notes on Jackendoff's theory of anaphora." *Linguistic Inquiry* 7. 319–41. Revised version published under the title "How to get an Interpretive theory of anaphora to work", in McCawley 1982, 128–58.

—— 1976f. "Remarks on what can cause what." In Shibatani 1976, 117–29. Repr. McCawley 1979, 101–12.

—— 1977a. "Lexicographic notes on English quantifiers." *Papers from the Thirteenth Regional Meeting of the Chicago Linguistic Society.* Chicago: Chicago Linguistic Society. 372–83. Repr. McCawley 1979, 179–90.

—— 1977b. "Evolutionary parallels between Montague Grammar and Transformational Grammar." *Proceedings of the Seventh Annual Meeting of the Northeastern Linguistic Society.* Cambridge, MA: Department of Linguistics, MIT. 219–32. Repr. McCawley 1979, 122–32.

—— 1977c. "Remarks on the lexicography of performative verbs." In A. Rogers, R. Wall, and J. Murphy (eds), *Proceedings of the Texas Conference on Performatives, Implicatures, and Presupposition.* Washington, DC: Center for Applied Linguistics. 13–25. Repr. McCawley 1979, 151–64.

—— 1977d. "The nonexistence of syntactic categories." *Proceedings of the Michigan State Conference on Linguistic Metatheory.* East Lansing, MI: Michigan State University Linguistics Department. Revised version in McCawley 1982, 176–203.

—— 1978. "Logic and the lexicon." In Donka Farkas, Wesley M. Jacobson, and Karol W. Todrys (eds), *Papers from the Parasession on the Lexicon.* Chicago: Chicago Linguistic Society. 261–77.

—— 1979. *Adverbs, Vowels, and Other Objects of Wonder.* Chicago: University of Chicago Press.

—— 1980. "An un-syntax." In Moravcsik and Wirth 1980, 167–93.

REFERENCES

—— 1981. *Everything that Linguists Have Always Wanted to Know about Logic but Were Ashamed to Ask*. Chicago: University of Chicago Press.

—— 1982. *Thirty Million Theories of Grammar*. Chicago, University of Chicago Press/London: Croom Helm.

—— 1985. "What price the performative hypothesis?" *University of Chicago Working Papers in Linguistics* 1. 1–22.

—— 1986. "Today the world, tomorrow phonology." *Phonology Yearbook* 3. 27–45.

—— 1988. *The Syntactic Phenomena of English*. Chicago: University of Chicago Press.

—— 1992. "The cyclic principle as a source of explanation in syntax." *Papers from the Twenty-eighth Regional Meeting of the Chicago Linguistic Society*, vol. 2. Chicago: Chicago Linguistic Society. 158–80.

McClelland, James L., David E. Rumelhart, and the PDP Research group. 1986. *Parallel Distributed Processing: Explorations in the Microstructure of Cognition*, vol. 2, *Psychological and Biological Models*. Cambridge, MA: MIT Press.

McCloskey, Donald N. 1983. "The rhetoric of economics." *Journal of Economic Literature* 21. 481–517.

Mates, B. 1950. "Synonymity." *University of California Publications in Philosophy*. 201–26.

May, Robert. 1977. "The grammar of quantification." MIT dissertation. New York: Garland, 1990.

—— 1983. *Logical Form as a Level of Linguistic Representation*. Bloomington, IN: Indiana University Linguistics Club.

—— 1985. *Logical Form: Its Structure and Derivation*. (Linguistic Inquiry Monographs, 12.) Cambridge: MIT Press.

Merrifield, William R., Constance M. Naish, Calvin R. Rensch, and Gillian Story. 1971. *Laboratory Manual for Morphology and Syntax*. Santa Ana, CA: Summer Institute of Linguistics.

Miller, George A., and Noam Chomsky. 1963. "Finitary models of language users." In Luce, Bush, and Galanter 1963, 419–92.

Montague, Richard. 1973 [1970]. "The proper treatment of quantification in ordinary English." In J. Hintikka, J. Moravcsik, and P. Suppes (eds), *Approaches to Natural Language*. Dordrecht: D. Reidel. 221–42.

Moravcsik, Edith A. 1980. "Introduction: on syntactic approaches." In Moravcsik and Wirth 1980, 1–18.

Moravcsik, Edith A. and Jessica R. Wirth (eds) 1980. *Current Approaches to Syntax. Syntax and Semantics*, vol. 13. New York: Academic Press.

Morgan, Jerry. 1969. "On arguing about semantics." *Papers in Linguistics* 1: 49–70.

—— 1970. "On the criterion of identity for noun phrase deletion." *Papers from the Sixth Regional Meeting of the Chicago Linguistic Society*. Chicago: Chicago Linguistic Society. 380–9.

—— 1973a. "How can you be in two places at once when you're not anywhere at all?" *Papers from the Ninth Regional Meeting of the Chicago Linguistic Society*. Chicago: Chicago Linguistic Society. 410–27.

—— 1973b. "Presupposition and semantic representation: prolegomena." University of Chicago dissertation.

Mufwene, Salikoko. 1977. ". . . Which one was the father of Jesus Christ?" *Papers from the Thirteenth Regional Meeting of the Chicago Linguistic Society*. Chicago: Chicago Linguistic Society. 439–58.

Newmeyer, Frederick J. 1971. "The source of derived nominals in English." *Language* 47. 786–96.

—— 1980. *Linguistic Theory in America: The First Quarter-century of Transformational Generative Grammar*. New York: Academic Press.

—— 1986. *Linguistic Theory in America*. New York: Academic Press. (2nd edn of Newmeyer 1980.)

—— 1990. "Competence vs. performance; theoretical vs. applied: the development and interplay of two dichotomies in modern linguistics." *Historiographia Linguistica* 17. 167–81.

Oehrle, Richard T. 1976. "The grammatical status of the English dative alternation." MIT dissertation.

—— 1977. "Review of Georgia Green, *Semantics and Syntactic Regularity*." *Language* 53. 198–208.

Parrett, Herman. 1974. *Discussing Language*. (Series Maior, 93.) The Hague: Mouton.

Partee, Barbara. 1971. "On the requirement that transformations preserve meaning." In Charles J. Fillmore and D. Terence Langendoen (eds), *Studies in Linguistic Semantics*. New York: Holt. 1–21.

—— 1973. "The semantics of belief-sentences." In J. Hintikka, J. Moravcsik, and P. Suppes (eds), *Approaches to Natural Language*. Dordrecht: Reidel. 309–36.

—— 1975. "Comments on C. J. Fillmore's and N. Chomsky's papers." In Robert Austerlitz (ed.), *The Scope of American Linguistics*. Lisse: Peter de Ridder. 197–209.

Perlmutter, David M. 1980. "Relational Grammar." In Moravcsik and Wirth 1980, 195–229.

Peters, Stanley (ed.) 1972. *The Goals of Linguistic Theory*. Englewood Cliffs, NJ: Prentice-Hall.

—— 1981. "Comments." In C. L. Baker and John McCarthy (eds), *The Logical Problem of Language Acquisition*. Cambridge: MIT Press. 22–9.

Pinker, Steven. 1989. *Learnability and Cognition: The Acquisition of Argument Structure*. Cambridge: MIT Press.

—— 1994. *The Language Instinct*, New York: Morrow.

Postal, Paul. 1969. "Anaphoric islands." *Papers from the Fifth Regional Meeting of the Chicago Linguistic Society*. Chicago: Chicago Linguistic Society. 205–39.

—— 1970. "On the surface verb 'remind'." *Linguistic Inquiry* 1. 37–120.

—— 1971 [1967]. *Crossover Phenomena*. New York: Holt, Rinehart & Winston.

—— 1972. "The best theory." In Peters 1972, 131–70.

—— 1974a. "On certain ambiguities." *Linguistic Inquiry* 5. 367–424.

—— 1974b. *On Raising*. Cambridge: MIT Press.

—— 1976 [1967]. "Linguistic anarchy notes." In McCawley 1976a, 201–25.

—— 1977. "About a 'nonargument' for raising." *Linguistic Inquiry* 8. 141–54.

—— 1993. "Some defective paradigms." *Linguistic Inquiry* 24. 347–64.

Pullum, Geoffrey K. 1984. "Chomsky on the Enterprise." *Natural Language and Linguistic Theory* 2. 349–55. Repr. Pullum 1991, 38–46.

—— 1989. "Formal linguistics meets the Boojum." *Natural Language and Linguistic Theory* 7. 137–43. Repr. Pullum 1991, 47–55.

—— 1991. *The Great Eskimo Vocabulary Hoax and Other Irreverant Essays on the Study of Language*. Chicago: University of Chicago Press.

Pullum, Geoffrey K. and Deirdre Wilson. 1977. "Autonomous syntax and the analysis of auxiliaries." *Language* 53. 741–88.

Reibel, David A. and Sanford A. Schane (eds). 1969. *Modern Studies in English: Readings in Transformational Grammar*. Englewood Cliffs, NJ: Prentice-Hall.

Reinhart, Tanya. 1976. "The syntactic domain of anaphora." MIT dissertation.

—— 1983. *Anaphora and Semantic Interpretation*. Chicago: University of Chicago Press/London: Croom Helm.

Rochemont, Michael S. 1978. "A theory of stylistic rules in English." University of Massachusetts–Amherst dissertation.

Rogers, Andy. 1971. "Three kinds of physical perception verbs." *Papers from the Seventh Regional Meeting of the Chicago Linguistic Society*. Chicago: Chicago Linguistics Society. 206–22.

REFERENCES

Rorty, Richard. 1979. *Philosophy and the Mirror of Nature*. Princeton: Princeton University Press.

Rosenbaum, Peter S. 1965. "Grammar of English predicate complement constructions." MIT dissertation. Published Cambridge: MIT Press, 1967.

Ross, John Robert. 1967a. "On the cyclic nature of English pronominalization." *To Honor Roman Jakobson*. The Hague: Mouton. 1669–82. Repr. Reibel and Schane 1969, 187–200.

—— 1967b. "Constraints on variables in syntax." MIT dissertation. Published as *Infinite Syntax*, Norwood: Ablex, 1986.

—— 1969. "Auxiliaries as main verbs." *Studies in Philosophical Linguistics* 1. 77–102.

—— 1970. "On declarative sentences." In Jacobs and Rosenbaum 1970, 222–72.

—— 1972. "Act." In Davidson and Harman 1972, 70–126.

—— 1973. "Nouniness." In Fujimura 1973, 137–258.

—— 1979. "From Cognitive Grammar, via linguistic Gestalts, to unmetaphoring." Unpublished paper read at the Conference on Current Approaches to Syntax, University of Wisconsin–Milwaukee, 16 March 1979.

Rumelhart, David E., James L. McClelland, and the PDP Research Group, 1986. *Parallel Distributed Processing: Explorations in the Microstructure of Cognition*, vol. 1, *Foundations*. Cambridge: MA: MIT Press.

Ruwet, Nicolas. 1991. *Syntax and Human Experience*. Chicago: University of Chicago Press.

Sadock, Jerrold. 1970. "Whimperatives." In Jerrold Sadock and Anthony Vanek (eds), *Studies Presented to Robert B. Lees by his Students*. Edmonton: Linguistic Research. 223–39.

—— 1971. "Queclaratives." *Papers from the Seventh Regional Meeting of the Chicago Linguistics Society*. Chicago: Chicago Linguistics Society. 223–31.

—— 1974a. "Read at your own risk: syntactic and semantic horrors you can find in your medicine chest." *Papers from the Tenth Regional Meeting of the Chicago Linguistic Society*. Chicago: Chicago Linguistic Society. 599–607.

—— 1974b. *Toward a Linguistic Theory of Speech Acts*. New York: Academic Press.

—— 1975. "The soft, interpretive underbelly of Generative Semantics." In Peter Cole and Jerry L. Morgan (eds), *Speech Acts. Syntax and Semantics*, vol. 4. New York: Academic Press. 383–96.

Scheffler, I. 1955. "On synonymy and indirect discourse." *Philosophy of Science* 22. 39–44.

Schmerling, Susan F. 1971. "Presupposition and the notion of normal stress." *Papers from the Seventh Regional Meeting of the Chicago Linguistic Society*. Chicago: Chicago Linguistic Society. 242–53.

Selkirk, Elisabeth O. 1982. *The Syntax of Words*. Cambridge: MIT Press.

Shibatani, Masayoshi (ed.) 1976. *The Grammar of Causative Constructions. Syntax and Semantics*, vol. 6. New York: Academic Press.

Shopen, Tim. 1972. "Logical equivalence is not semantic equivalence." *Papers from the Eighth Regional Meeting of the Chicago Linguistic Society*. Chicago: Chicago Linguistic Society. 340–50.

Siegel, Dorothy C. 1974. "Topics in English morphology." MIT dissertation.

Stich, Stephen P. (ed.) 1975. *Innate Ideas*. Berkeley: University of California Press.

Stockwell, Robert P. 1980. "Summation and assessment of theories." In Moravcsik and Wirth 1980, 353–81.

Suppe, Frederick. 1977. "Afterword – 1977." In Frederick Suppe (ed.), *The Structure of Scientific Theories*. Urbana, IL: University of Illinois Press. 617–730.

Tannen, Deborah. 1990. *You Just Don't Understand: Women and Men in Conversation*. New York: Morrow.

Trager, George L. 1953. Review of F. G. Lounsbury. *Oneida verb morphology*. *Studies in Linguistics* 14. 77–81.

REFERENCES

Trager, George L., and Henry Lee Smith, Jr 1951. *An Outline of English Structure.* (Studies in Linguistics, Occasional Papers, 3.) Norman, Oklahoma: University of Oklahoma Press.

van Riemsdijk, Henk, and Edwin Williams. 1986. *Introduction to the Theory of Grammar.* Cambridge, MA: MIT Press.

Wasow, Thomas. 1976. "McCawley on Generative Semantics. Review of James D. McCawley, *Grammar and Meaning.*" *Linguistic Analysis* 2. 279–301.

—— 1985. "The wizards of ling." *Natural Language and Linguistic Theory* 4. 485–91.

Weinreich, Uriel. 1966. "Explorations in semantic theory." In Thomas Sebeok (ed.), *Current Trends in Linguistics,* vol 3. The Hague: Mouton. 395–478.

Wilson, Deirdre. 1974. "Presupposition and non-truth-conditional semantics." MIT dissertation.

177

INDEX

abstract, elements 98; performatives
79; syntax 98, 109, 122; theory 22
acceptability, facts 41; judgments,
Generative semantics and 80–1,
131, 139; of sentences 26, 46–7
Adjective Phrase Preposing (APP) 46
Adverb Preposing 71
allophony, rules of 61, 70
amalgams, syntactic 40, 117, 135
ambiguity 17, 19, 35, 65; adverbs and
21, 40; and quantified sentences 38;
scope 39, 46; semantic 16–17; of
warm 54
American Structuralism 8–12, 84, 126
analogical rules and transderivational
constraints 40
analyticity 18, 136, 139
anaphora 16, 19, 44, 105
Anderson, John 103
Anderson, Stephen R. 79–80, 157nn.
2, 3
anomalies 6, 16–17, 81
A-over-A Principle 141
Aronoff, Mark 30
Autolexical Grammar 118
automata theory 120
autonomy hypothesis 13, 23, 25–6,
44–5, 48, 131, 147 n. 15; and syntax
19, 98–9
auxiliary hypothesis 6, 14, 19–20, 86,
92, 115
auxiliary propositions 6, 143–4n. 1

Bach, Emmon 30, 154n. 40, 159n. 7
Baker, C.L. 58, 148n. 17
Baker, Mark C. 30, 40, 153n. 37
Bever, Thomas 2, 35, 40–2, 153n. 39

Binnick, Robert I. 52, 83, 85
biuniqueness, phonology and 61, 128
Bloch, Bernard 10, 121, 127–8, 157n. 3
Bloomfield, Leonard, followers of 10,
61, 62; ideas about meaning 8–10,
12; and "complete overlap" 157n. 3;
theories 25, 71, 128; *A set of
postulates for the science of language*
21–2; *Language* (1933) 8
Booth, Wayne 59
Bowers, John 47
Brame, Michael, K. 80
Bresnan, Joan 80, 105, 159n. 7; *Lexical
Functional Grammar* 103

Carden, Guy 101
Case Grammar 103
causative, constructions 108; lexical
47; subject 54; verbs 139
c–command 105
Chicago Linguistic Society 52, 75, 83,
85–7
Chomskyan program, core
propositions of 12–14, 19;
development of 3, 62; innateness
hypothesis 25; psychological
reorientation of 21–6
Chomsky, Noam 93; correspondence
with McCawley 30–3, 59–61, 63–6,
69; debt to predecessors 145–6n. 6;
deep structure 99, 107; Extended
Standard Theory 72–3; and
Generative Semantics 26–7, 31,
34–6, 39, 42, 53, 88, 92, 104, 149n.
19; and Interpretive Semantics 1,
21, 44, 53, 63, 94; *kernel* sentences
and 15, 17, 128; on language

179

135, 138; relations 16; rules 29,
69–70, 102, 107, 123, 127
transformations 14–18; classification
15; distributional purpose and 20;
generalized and singularly 17–18,
122; Generative and Interpretive
Semantics and 21, 101; grammatical
65, 128; lexical and non–lexical 34;
meaning and 35, 45;
nominalization 30, 122; obligatory
15, 98, 123; root 46–7, 102; syntax
and 81
truth, conditions 32, 66; necessary
137; value 24, 31

unacceptability of sentences 26
unaccusatives 126
unbounded movement rules 105
unergatives 126
Universal Grammar 36
University of Chicago 82–3;
Department of Linguistics 84–6
University of Wisconsin-Milwaukee,
conference (1979) 91

van Riemsdijk, Henk 2
verbs, ability to govern rules 132;
causative 139; of communication
56–7; Negative Transportation and
50; performative 79; in
prepositional structures 55;
universal characteristics of *kill* 40
Vietnam War 125, 141
voicing assimilation 61, 70
VSO hypothesis, order in English
157n. 1

Wasow, Thomas 80
Weinreich, Uriel 17
Weiss, Albert Paul 21
Whimperatives 40
Williams, Edwin 2
Wilson, Deirdre 80, 88, 102

X-bar theory 101

Yngve, Vic 107

Zwicky, Arnold M. 20, 63, 80